# Faking It

# FAKING IT

**William Ian Miller**
*University of Michigan Law School*

**CAMBRIDGE**
UNIVERSITY PRESS

CAMBRIDGE UNIVERSITY PRESS
Cambridge, New York, Melbourne, Madrid, Cape Town, Singapore, São Paulo

Cambridge University Press
40 West 20th Street, New York, NY 10011–4211, USA

www.cambridge.org
Information on this title: www.cambridge.org/9780521830188

First published 2003
First paperback edition 2005

Printed in the United States of America

*A catalog record for this book is available from the British Library.*

*Library of Congress Cataloging in Publication Data*
Miller, William Ian, 1946–
Faking it / William Ian Miller.
p.   cm.
Includes bibliographical references and index.
ISBN 0-521-83018-4
1. Identity (Psychology)   2. Social role.   3. Authenticity (Philosophy)
4. Self-doubt.   I. Title.
BF697.M525 2003
179'.8–dc21          2003043750

ISBN-13   978-0-521-83018-8 hardback
ISBN-10   0-521-83018-4 hardback

ISBN-13   978-0-521-61370-5 paperback
ISBN-10   0-521-61370-1 paperback

*For my mother, Shirlyn Miller, and my wife, Kathy Koehler*

Should he by chance a knave or fool expose,
That hurts none here, sure here are none of those.

Congreve (*Way of the World*, Prol. vv. 35–36)


N'as-tu pas honte de vouloir être philosophe plus que tu ne peux?

Chamfort (*Maximes* xliii)

# Contents

# Acknowledgments

The acknowledgments vie with the bibliography for falseness and fakery. I have thus undertaken, in a spirit of authenticity and re-form, to limit my public proclamation of gratitude to people who actually deserve it. (Excuse my gruffness; it is a pose meant to sell the genuineness of my gratitude. Thus does fakery assist the cause of truth by making truth *look* truthful as well as merely *be* truthful.) Annalise Acorn, Don Herzog, and Larry Kramer read the whole manuscript in various stages with great care and to my great benefit. It seemed that at times they were more inside my head than I was. I cannot thank them enough for friendship and colleagueship beyond the call of duty. So too Daniel Halberstam and Kyle Logue. Others who provided more than a few helpful inputs are Anne Coughlin, Dedi Felman, Ellen Katz, and Ed Parsons; three student assistants: Bill Korner, Lena Salaymeh, and Susannah Tobin; and several anonymous reviewers who generously got into the spirit of the book.

My mother and my wife are the dedicatees. One has so much charm that she manages, to the dismay of those around her, to get away with never suppressing the unvarnished truth. The other's grace and equally great charm lie in her genius for making people feel that she really means it when she says she wants them to stay. One takes no prisoners, the other invites them in. Both are indomitable and have squared off only two or three times in the past twenty years.

Parts of chapter 13 appeared as "Of Optimal Views and Other Anxieties of Attending to the Beautiful and Sublime," *Journal of Visual Culture* 1 (2002), 71–85, which is reproduced by permission of Sage Publications, Thousand Oaks, London, and New Delhi.

# ONE

# Introduction: Split in Two

IT HAPPENED AGAIN TODAY: I was bluffing my way through some material in my Property class about which I knew no more than what the teaching manual told me, it being the extent of my researches on the topic. On such occasions I present the subject in the pompous style in which professorial banalities are often uttered, meaning thereby to prevent student questions by elevating myself to the regions of the unquestionable. God forbid one of them should start thinking deeply about the stuff and expose the limits of my knowledge.

Then it hits: all of a sudden my voice transforms itself into a parody of my father's voice, an imitation of the voice he used when he was doing his best to assert pompous authority. How does this happen? My voice seems to have acquired a will of its own as it seeks to lower itself into the resonant ranges his had as a gift of nature. My sisters and I would often burst into giggles when our father assumed this style of dominion. The students at least won't giggle, having been beaten down by myriad professors into resigned acceptance of – nay, into slavish respect for – pompous authority. And even if I were to revert to my natural voice I wouldn't succeed in getting it back to normal. Compared with the phony version of my father's it would sound like a whine, and I would find myself correcting it into something utterly alien. Better stick with Dad's until the class ends.

Twenty minutes left to fill, and I have said everything I have to say. Still there is this me standing outside me watching me talk in someone else's voice. Do not look at the beautiful babe sitting over on the right; you will lose all authority if you do that; meet only the eyes of the guys. Is she really that much of a bombshell, or is it that at my age I have lost all discernment, mistaking youth for beauty? Kill

I

that kid over there who is nodding off again. Don't turn to write on the blackboard because Ms. Simmons, the bombshell, will observe the thinning of your hair in back, the beginnings of your tonsure.

While all these thoughts are going on, the me standing outside the me going through the motions of lecturing gets a metathought of wonderment: how remarkable human consciousness is that it can have all these distracting thoughts while split in two and still let me speak coherently on easements. How do I know the lecture is coherent? Because as soon as I split in two the students dive for their pens and the keyboard clacks increase to frenetic rates. They inevitably think I am delivering the goods when they hear my father's voice.[1] When I actually know what I am talking about they occupy themselves playing solitaire on their laptops, or they ostentatiously look back at the clock on the wall behind them (spiting their wristwatches) to make sure I know how impatient they are for me to have done with it.

Funny how easy it is to do *mental* tasks with all the voices inside your head critiquing you while you continue the performance, but how hard it is to act convincingly when you become self-conscious of your *physical* movements, such as whether you are walking naturally, or blinking too much, or looking like a law-abiding driver when the cop pulls up next to you at the stoplight. So though I feel that I am faking it and fear the roof might come caving in on me at any moment, since the physical demands are minimal and there is a barricade-like lectern to provide cover for most of my body, the roof (almost always) stays put. Within seconds the me standing outside me remerges with the me putting on the show, and time is up and I am safe for another day, unless, that is, I should overhear a student grumble to another about what an awful class it was. But you never hear complaints after a day of bluffing. You know you get your highest approval ratings from the students when you keep it easy and falsely authoritative; as long as they can take good notes, most of them feel they got their money's worth.

Is it the case that my experience of seeing myself as if outside myself was generated by guilt over faking it? Is that me outside me, in other words, my conscience? Or is it the form my conscience takes when it really means business? That hardly seems right. For often that me outside me simply looks on in contemptuous bemusement. Unlike the conscience, it seems to take the performing me less seriously than a truly moral policeman would. It cares less that I am a moral failure than that I may be a social failure. It will suffer my being a knave but will not suffer my being a fool. It shares much with Adam Smith's impartial spectator, whom we shall meet again, except the me outside me is not really impartial; he is too hard on me most of the time, determined to unnerve me. In truth, sometimes that me outside me appears when I teach Bloodfeuds, where I know my stuff, and there it is elicited not by anxieties of fakery but rather by my being so much into the subject, so excited by the material, that the students, I fear, must think I am a total nerd. That me outside me wants to make sure I am maintaining a certain level of dignity, and it doesn't seem to matter whether I am about to lose respect by being exposed as a fraud or simply by not having properly modulated my sincerest enthusiasm. Besides, why think that that me on the outside isn't faking also, or playing a false role by playing me as an ever so self-tortured being?

As I am sure you know, the anxious feeling of faking it can arise in almost any setting. It can harass you in routine polite conversations; it can disrupt what you thought had been an authentic emotional moment in matters of mourning or love. You see yourself suddenly as a phony, a hypocrite, when until that intrusive moment you were blithely at one with your role, with words, deeds, and thoughts all united in service to the cause at hand.

I have often felt myself to be a hypocrite for paying lip service to pious views I do not quite believe, some of which I downright don't hold at all. I have feigned sorrow at the departure of guests, faked joy at their arrival, simulated delight at a colleague winning a MacArthur so-called genius award, shammed grief at the passing of the neighborhood self-appointed policer of leash laws, assumed a façade of concern for a student's bad grade or interest in stories of other people's children. And I fear others will repay my shamming by exposing me as a fake, a fraud in the roles life has assigned me: as dad, son, spouse, friend, law professor, writer, Old Norse scholar, Jew, citizen, decent human being. Why is it that I cannot help feeling foolish at times going through the motions of playing the roles I have to play to pass for a properly socialized and sane person? And why, when I happen to immerse myself joyously into a role, do I later – not always, mind you, but often enough – wonder if I haven't made a fool of myself by overdoing it? And how do I manage to escape being exposed as a fake as often as I do, unless it is all a setup?

To be a proper person behaving properly we must engage in a certain amount of self-monitoring. Most of such monitoring is routine and hardly the stuff to generate great anxiety. I thus automatically modulate the volume of my voice to the level appropriate to the occasion (though my teenage girls are constantly shushing me in restaurants); without an anxious thought, I engage in minor gestures of grooming to make sure my nose isn't about to humiliate me, my nails are clean, my zippers zipped and buttons buttoned. More anxiety-provoking are the demands to display proper emotions at the right time and place. Tears are a problem, often failing to appear when they should and showing up when they shouldn't. Just trying to display interest when it is polite to do so, or to suppress signs of it when it is impolite to show it, can make us uneasy about how poorly we are playing it. It does not help, for instance, to let the fact that I cannot take my eyes off the big zit on the chin of my interlocutor serve as a substitute for my not being able to maintain the faintest modicum of interest in his conversation.

But I must confess, and I would bet you could confess it too, that I have found myself feeling quite pleased or relieved in the midst of some emotional turmoil – a lover's quarrel, a funeral, a moving moment – that tears actually showed up. I cannot quite repress the "Thank God" of relief, or the "Way to go, Miller" of self-congratulation. And who is saying that "Way to go"? Me? Or a fake "me" that I pretend to be when I am trying to please? Or is it the voice of a stranger, a father, a conscience, an intruder? Or all of the above? Those internal conversations that make up much of what we think of as thinking – are they monologues, dialogues, or sessions of the Israeli Knesset?

This book is unified by the intrusive fear that we may not be what we appear to be or, worse, that we may be only what we appear to be and nothing more. It is about the worry of being exposed as frauds in our profession, as cads in our loves, as less than virtuously motivated actors when we are being agreeable, charitable, or decent. Why do we so often mistrust the motives of our own good deeds, thinking them fake good deeds, even when the beneficiary of them gives us full credit? And why do we feel that even our bad deeds might be fake? Remember how as a teenager you tried pathetically to show how tough and fearless you were by shoplifting, drinking yourself senseless, and other things still unconfessable?

And related to all this is the question, who is this you that is being so hard on you? Is it just plain you? Or is it you in a specific role and, if so, what role? You as a fairly hostile observer of guys like you, you the hanging judge? Or is it nothing more than you the ironist with regard to roles you must play? We know that many roles are supposed to be nothing more than fakery of a sort, playable with one hand tied behind one's back; we know that virtue itself cuts all kinds of deals with a benign form of hypocrisy that keeps us polite, kind, and acting properly. Yet we still feel a bit tainted by what we think are our own half-hearted commitments and our uncertain or unverifiable motives, about our less than full-hearted performances in the various roles we must play. Or perhaps it is not so much a unified self that feels thus tainted; maybe it is something foisted on the part of us that remains behind by the part of us that stands outside ourselves.

Much of the book deals with self-consciousness – not self-consciousness in the sedate sense of being aware of ourselves as think-ing beings with a past, present, or future but rather self-consciousness in the sense of that unpleasant emotion that interrupts our blithe and unself-conscious "naturalness," which, however, may be no more than "*acting* naturally" and not knowing we are. It deals with being watched and judged by ourselves and by others as we posture and pose. It treats of praise and flattery, of vanity, esteem, and self-esteem, false modesty, seeming virtue and virtuous seeming, deception, and self-deception. It is about roles and identity and our engagement in the roles we play, our doubts about our identities amidst the flux of roles, and thus about anxieties of authenticity.

These topics are as old as the hills, having been treated many times by poets, novelists, moralists, philosophers, and theologians. God

Himself seems to worry about these kinds of disorienting moments, long before He ever felt it necessary to split into Father and Son and watch Himself perform. When Moses asks God what name he (Moses) should give the people as his warrant for a claim to lead them, God tells him to say to them that "I am who I am" sent him (Exod. 3.14). God is playing games with His name, giving it as a kind of riddle, a riddle that suggests that He, not He mind you, has absolutely no anxieties about His unity of being, of being fully immersed in Who He Is. No anxieties of faking it for Him. He, by fiat, is One unified self. But the fiat shows Him protesting too much, for the refusal to fix His name may be because He cannot get a fix on it either. He is posturing when He answers Moses, playing it up, for He is deeply embattled in an only middlingly successful struggle for the hearts and souls of a stiff-necked people who frequently disobey His commandments and who prefer statues of calves to Him when the going gets rough.

Though most English translations of the Bible prefer the present tense, the Hebrew of God's answer supports equally the future tense – "I will be who I will be" – which results in a dramatic shift in meaning as to the kind of character God is claiming to be. "I will be who I will be" presents us with a God who takes His mightiness to be manifested most in arbitrariness, and moreover in a particular type of arbitrariness about His own identity and continuity of character, claiming for Himself an infinite right and power to be a shape-shifter, that He Is Never What He Appears To Be, all signs and wonders, masks and veils. The future tense seems better to accord also with the riddling way of naming Himself.

Shape-shifting and name changes: deeply anxious about his identity and role, Saul becomes Paul; and Augustine claims for himself a wholesale change from false to true, but he is so vain of his anxiety as not to be anxious at all. For recognizable proto-modern anxiety – I skip over many a fearful epic warrior who covered his fear with bravado and, for the moment, ignore Jesus, wondering about his own full immersion into his role in Gethsemane – there is Hamlet, the grandest of poster boys for feeling that he is faking it. I am drawn to Hamlet too because his worries about roles and feelings of falsity or inadequacy take place in the context of revenge, my scholarly fixation.[2] It might be the case that the avenger is the most dramatic of all roles,[3] the lead role, a role God is eager to reserve to Himself – vengeance is mine – and what is drama but Faking It, putting on shows, enacting reality, so that the word for the doer of a deed and the word for a theatrical performer mimicking a deed merge and are the same: actor.

This book is possibly best seen as a quasi-novel, "quasi" because it has no conventional plot other than the one every book has of "how many more pages to go" and only the vaguest sense of characterization except for the narrator's voice with its stream of self-consciousness. Don't think me paranoid either; most of my life is spent in sluglike unity of soul, pleased to be drinking a beer, lost in a hockey game on TV (liquid bread and virtual circuses). I honestly believe myself to be a fairly reasonable example of *l'homme moyen sensual*, forgetting for the moment that no American l'homme moyen would use that phrase to claim he is Joe Average or the man on the street.[4]

This is a book about moments that spike out of the much-to-be-admired ho-humness of daily life. These moments invite Comedy to attend, though Tragedy sometimes crashes the party. Fakery and comedy go hand in hand, says Emerson: "The essence... of all comedy, seems to be... a non-performance of what is pretended to be performed, at the same time that one is giving loud pledges of performance."[5] Sounds good, but it is not true of all comedy. The comic does just fine with brute miserable unadorned reality, with stripping veils and masks as well as donning them; in fact, if we substituted the word "tragedy," or *Hamlet*, for "comedy" in Emerson's quote it would work about as well. No genre escapes posing, masking and veiling, and anxieties about authenticity. Ask Hamlet, Othello, or Odysseus. In short, the risk of my faking it is considerably less likely in the lighter moments that follow than in heavier discussions maintaining the dignities and forms of academic disputation.

THE TERRAIN OF FAKING IT is vast. Virtually all social interaction and much psychic life lie within its bounds. The path I follow is not linear, for the goal is not a particular end point of an argument or a thesis but a descriptive travelogue that intends to give the traveler a feel for, an expansive familiarity with, the custom of the country. Some of the views are scenic, others will make us lament the lot of the natives, but the pictures are all identifiably about some aspect borne by the notion of "faking it," as we employ that term colloquially.

At the beginning of William Langland's *Piers Plowman*, Will, the narrator, has a vision of a fair field full of folk going about their chicanery and hypocritical fourteenth-century existences; the William who narrates *Faking It* offers a twenty-first-century revisitation of that vision: a world of posing and shams, anxieties of exposure, and a fear that the genuine may be just another sham whose cover is too tough to be blown. The first stop is a logical one: the vice of hypocrisy. The next three chapters show how falseness and fakery lie at the heart of many of the nice things we say and do, and how inextricably vice and virtue are bound together in their eternal pas de deux and not necessarily in a bad way.

# TWO

# Hypocrisy and Jesus

FAKING IT IS A DOMAIN not completely congruent with the vice of hypocrisy, though there is so much overlap that we must face hypocrisy at the outset. Not all hypocrites experience the anxieties at the core of the faking it syndrome. And not all types of faking it raise a serious issue of hypocrisy. I am not a hypocrite, unless most teachers are, for pretending to find interesting what is dull, or for engaging in the various falsenesses that constitute cajolery. Nor am I a hypocrite for putting on a somber face at the news of the untimely death of a person I didn't especially care for. Says Trollope: "Will anyone dare to call this hypocrisy? If it be so called, who in the world is not a hypocrite? Where is the man or woman who has not a special face for sorrow before company? The man or woman who has no such face would at once be accused of heartless impropriety."[1] Were we to blame the mere donning of a role that our hearts weren't totally into as hypocrisy, we would be hypocrites all the time, except perhaps when asleep.

Even in sleep there is a trace of role-playing, of self-monitoring so as to maintain certain proprieties and a sense of responsibility, though not enough to give rise to hypocrisies.[2] Thus I do not wet the bed, nor roll over and smother the toddlers who are sleeping there too, nor fall out of it, nor face toward the door, where I still expect to see those dead twin girls from *The Shining* come waltzing in. Contrast the care that you take to sleep inoffensively with that of the man (they are always men) next to you on the airplane whose head lolls over onto your shoulder as he snores, snorts, drools, who awakens as the plane lands with no awareness of offenses given nor received, as when you finally overcame reticence and delivered jabs and shoves in desperate disgust to no avail. I never cease to be amazed that people are either so cavalier about their dignity, or else wrongly confident of their ability to self-monitor while sleeping, that they could be so daring as to let themselves fall asleep in public spaces.

The feeling of faking it forces upon us a recognition of a split between something that we flatter ourselves is our "true" self and the role we are playing. More modestly, it is the feeling of our incomplete immersion in the role, with impious thoughts intruding about the role. Sometimes, it is merely a vague sense of dislocation that takes the form of worrying where we are amidst all the roles we must play: I worry about who I am; therefore, I guess, I am. Anxieties about faking it seem a necessary and mostly unpleasant byproduct of the fact that we must play roles, some of which come easier than others and do not necessarily involve us in any kind of moral failure; yet even these manage to give rise to social and psychological discomfort and disorientation.

In contrast, hypocrisy, at least by one account, though often infecting certain roles, is less about role than the propriety of motives you bring to the role. The fear that you may be a hypocrite may not even mean that your motive is bad, only that it is not the perfect one; or that you are unsure of your motives and fear they are a mix of good and not so good; or that you simply cannot get at what your motives are but suspect the worst. And when are you to make your most informed judgment about what your motives are, anyway? In the heat of the moment? Upon reflection that night? By observing what others think your motives to have been and then adopting their views as your own? Or by reexaminations and reconstructions done years later via memory?

We can be hypocrites and know that we are. Judith Shklar describes such a one as a "naïve hypocrite" who "hides acts and beliefs he knows to be wrong" and may even suffer a guilty conscience.[3] Or we can be what she calls the "new hypocrite," who thinks himself a paragon of virtue. The new hypocrite does not feel himself to be faking anything; he may be blithely or smugly delighted with the role he has assumed, experiencing himself as sincerely what he is purporting to be, but be culpably deluded as to the sincerity of his sincerity.[4]

In Shklar's view he "simply adjusts his conscience by ascribing noble, disinterested, and altruistic intentions to all his behavior." The naïve hypocrite is a conscious deceiver; the new hypocrite a seamless self-deceiver.

## Ostentatious Alms

Hypocrisy comes in all sizes and shapes, and I am not about to spell them all out.[5] I will organize the discussion around Jesus' use of the term. First:

> Beware of practicing your piety before men in order to be seen by them; for then you will have no reward from your Father who is in heaven. Thus, when you give alms, sound no trumpet before you, as the hypocrites do in the synagogues and in the streets, that they may be praised by men. Truly, I say to you, they have received their reward. But when you give alms, do not let your left hand know what your right hand is doing, so that your alms may be in secret; and your Father who sees in secret will reward you. And when you pray, you must not be like the hypocrites; for they love to stand and pray in the synagogues and at the street corners, that they may be seen by men."
>
> (Matt. 6.1–5)

In this theory of hypocrisy, it is not the hypocrite's deed but his less than virtuous intention that is faulted.[6] The paupers still get their alms either way. The hypocrite's show of virtue does not come cheap; the less than pious motive of desiring public glory for his pious giving may even prompt him to give more than if he gave secretly. I doubt paupers want to see this kind of hypocrisy driven from the face of the earth. From the paupers' point of view, it may be less psychologically demanding to be an insignificant prop in the giver's pageant designed to impress his social equals. Shows of gratitude may not even be required in the paupers' script; their job is to crowd close and then scramble and fall to fighting amongst themselves for the scattered coins. But to receive from a nonhypocritical almsgiver secretly will exact a more stringent recompense in the form of a convincing show of gratefulness.[7]

Each of the two examples Jesus gives – ostentatious alms and pub-lic prayers – presents a different issue. The alms do not, it seems, help the soul of the giver, yet they are of considerable use to the bodies of the recipients. But the prayers said for the purpose of impressing people with piety, unlike the alms that help the poor, are apparently useful to no one. Jesus elsewhere is explicit about it: "You hypocrites! Well did Isaiah prophesy of you, when he said: 'This people honors me with their lips, but their heart is far from me; *in vain do they worship me...*'" (Matt. 15.7–9; Mark 7.6–7). I wonder, however, whether God doesn't credit these hypocritical prayers to a certain degree. From His perspective they are better than no prayers at all. Hypocrisy is not apostasy; the hypocrite may not be honoring God with his prayers, but he is honoring those who believe that honoring God with prayer is a good thing. He is paying some kind of homage to a social and religious order that believes in the virtue of prayer.

Jesus is well aware that it is no easy matter to keep your mind free of the reputational and other advantages gained by doing good deeds. He thus counsels self-deception: keep the left hand ignorant of what the right is doing. But how do you blind yourself to the honor that comes from good deeds or from a reputation for piety? How can giving in secret, as Jesus urges, keep you from feeling the pride of eschewing public recognition? If you insist that the pauper keep quiet, might you not mistrust your motives for so insisting? It will be considerably easier on your purse if he keeps his counsel about where he is getting his goodies. And if the pauper keeps your secret, does that mean you have chosen to give to an unworthy beggar who himself lacks sufficient generosity to share his secret with other needy folk? Is your generosity thus working to decrease rather than increase the amount of generosity in the world? Yet if you think it a good idea that word about your generosity gets out in a discreet fashion so that other paupers can benefit, can you trust that you will not delight in the fact that you now have a reputation for genuine unhypocritical generosity? Or do you fear you still may be letting Jesus down, that your left hand was peeking?[8]

Jesus knows he is not asking for something easy to achieve if the right motive does not come naturally in the first place. He gives no guidance as to how to make the left hand blind to the actions of the right. One can give a conscious command to certain thoughts to descend into the unconscious, but then the very command that orders the descent will also have to descend and erase itself in the process of carrying out its orders. OK, left hand, do not dare look at what right hand is doing, and forget I ever told you not to look so that you will not suspect the right hand is up to anything suspicious.[9] And forget I told you to forget, and so on ad infinitum. Later in the same chapter Jesus backs off the command to self-deceive, preferring small pious deceptions of others. Do not, he says, fast like the hypocrites who disfigure their faces and put on a good show. Fast in secret and in public look as if you are not fasting, be clean and neat, anointed and washed (Matt. 6.16–18).

## Motes and Beams

Jesus' second kind of hypocrisy involves blaming others when you yourself are blameworthy:

> How can you say to your brother, 'Let me take the speck out of your eye,' when there is the log in your own eye? You hypocrite, first take the log out of your own eye, and then you will see clearly to take the speck out of your brother's eye.
>
> (Matt. 7.4–5)

Pardon the Revised Standard Version with its logs and specks, rather than the King James with its motes and beams. The latter is unfortunately more likely to befuddle the modern reader as to why Jesus would be so uncharitable to a twinkle in your eye, to say nothing of a whole fortification system in the eye of the other.

In the first type of hypocrisy Jesus counseled self-deception: compartmentalize your knowledge so that half of you does not know what the other half is doing. In the case of specks and logs he is arguing against self-deception, albeit of a different sort. We deceive ourselves incessantly, flattering ourselves as to our virtues and blinding ourselves to our faults, while at the same time fancying ourselves to be ever so astute about the faults of others.[10] Jesus is not addressing here the hypocrisy of blaming others for sins we know we ourselves are guilty of but will not confess to; this is not the case of casting stones at the adulteress when we too are adulterers.[11] The log/speck image focuses more narrowly on how our partiality to ourselves fouls up our judgments about the moral merit of others. The hypocrisy here is unconscious and does not give rise to anxieties about faking it; your motives may not be bad, it is just that cognitive bias prevents you from getting a disinterested view of the truth. You fall victim to a false but sincere belief that you are seeing the world objectively and seeing it whole.[12]

There is another aspect to the blindness – its mutuality: the other person whose specks you are magnifying is doing the same to you, but there is good reason to believe he is not magnifying your faults to the same extent that you are understating them. La Rochefoucauld pinpoints the phenomenon with the observation that somewhere not quite in the middle lies the truth: "Our enemies get closer to the truth in their judgments of us than we get ourselves" (M 458).[13] We are not inventing faults in our enemies; they really are there. True, our self-love and self-interest lead us to exaggerate them, but we are considerably more trustworthy in our negative judgments of others than we are in our positive judgments of ourselves. The entire psychotherapeutic industry is built on the supposition that other people are often in a much better position to read our inner states than we are, the belief being that even the obscuration wrought on the therapist's vision by his desire for lucre and by his not being inside our heads is not as distorting as the mayhem self-love wreaks on our ability to see ourselves very clearly.[14]

## Stoning Adulterers

In contrast to the mote/beam problem, the hypocrisy of casting stones at the adulteress when you yourself are an undiscovered adulterer is conscious hypocrisy. (Jesus does not call this person a hypocrite, but we do.) You are engaging in a knowingly false pretense regarding your true legal and moral condition, and you are especially culpable because one suspects that your concern to conceal your own

sin may be driving you to be not very particular as to the guilt or innocence of the person you are stoning. But be careful not to be too
zealous a stoner, for the type who would seek to deflect suspicion from
his own guilt by aggressively hunting down similar sinners is himself
suspicious. Be somewhat reserved when you stone adulteresses.

It is not even clear that such conscious hypocrisy is morally worse
than the mote/beam situation of merely being blind to one's own
faults. Take the ever-present anxiety regarding racism and accusations of it. Is the person who fears that deep down she might be a
racist, and aggressively blames others for their racism, worse than the
person who does not know he is one and blames others for theirs? The
academy is filled with the latter (I could a tale unfold...that would
harrow up thy soul), who sport giant I-beams protruding from their
eyes. The former, the person who fears her own racism, comes almost as a breath of fresh air. We can reasonably believe that her
blaming the speck in others' eyes is, in part, a way of chastising herself. She is faking nothing. She hates racism in herself and in others,
and she knows that she is no less guilty than they; that she prefers
not to blame herself in the presence of others may only be because
the chances of such self-blame being read as sincere rather than as
a form of self-serving fakery are not very high. One would mistrust
such self-castigation as so much ingratiating herself with the victim
group, and also as trying to give herself a better warrant to blame
others.[15] The truth is that there is almost no tasteful way to proceed
in this domain that does not subject one to doubts about posturing,
favor currying, and camp following.

To the cases of the person who is unaware of the beam in his own
eye and the adulterer who is painfully aware but casts stones anyway,
add this: suppose we have bad desires, but through force of will we
do not act on them. Do we then have a warrant to blame the lecher
for his lechery, or the glutton for his gluttony, without being called
a hypocrite when we are dying to do the same but use all the self-
command at our disposal to refrain? Perhaps our own bad desires
should incline us to be charitable to the person who gives way to his
bad desires. Yet all too frequently we are inclined to blame him with
special energy because of his having cashed in:

Why dost thou lash that whore?
Strip thy own back; Thou hotly lusts to use her in that kind
For which thou whip'st her.

                                        *Lear* 4.6.161–163

Don't we wonder whether our self-control is two parts cowardice – the fear of getting caught and rendered ridiculous – and one small part virtue? And what of those who have weak bad desires, or strong ones but are physically impotent, or who are so unattractive that opportunities for unchasteness are few and far between, captured nicely thus in the fourteenth century by William Langland:

Ye have no more merit in mass ne in houres (prayers)
Than Malkyn (Maude) of hire maydenhood (virginity) that no
    man desireth"?[16]

It is not unusual to find such people hinting, hypocritically, of their own triumphs over temptation, faking the virtue of self-command when they never had any seriously disobedient desires or were without means of cashing in on the ones they might have had.

We tend not to be all that charitable to reprovers or rebukers of others' vices. We excuse parents because it is their job; so too teachers and clergymen – though to a lesser extent – because rebuking also comes with their role. But volunteer rebukers are not cut much slack. They are so many tattletales or fun spoilers; we think of them as officious meddlers motivated meanly by envy, or vainly by showing off their virtue, hypocritical in the manner of the noisy almsgiver. This may be why Jesus, after rebuking the glory-seeking almsgiver and not quite unaware of the ironies of his own position, is soon moved to rebuke rebukers by warning them to make sure they do not have telephone poles stuck in their eyes, for the rebuker is asking to be blamed as a hypocrite in both ways we have seen Jesus employ the term.[17]

## Hypocrisy and Formalism

Jesus also uses "hypocrite" as a hostile epithet to hurl at adherents of certain formalistic practices, who are not as willing as he is to adopt his more expansive readings of the Law. Thus when Jesus heals a crippled woman,

> the ruler of the synagogue, indignant because Jesus had healed on the Sabbath, said to the people, 'There are six days on which work ought to be done; come on those days and be healed, and not on the Sabbath day.' Then the Lord answered him, 'You hypocrites! Does not each of you on the Sabbath untie his ox or his ass from the manger, and lead it away to water it? And ought not this woman, a daughter of Abraham whom Satan bound for eighteen years, be loosed from this bond on the Sabbath day?' As he said this, all his adversaries were put to shame; and all the people rejoiced at all the glorious things that were done by him.
>
> (Luke 13.14–17)[18]

The ruler of the synagogue may have given up too easily, or Jesus was better at making sure he argued the case before a friendly audience. The woman had been crippled for eighteen years; she could have waited until Sunday. Or if I am being too cavalier about her suffering, then the ruler of the synagogue might have emphasized that Jesus do his healing a day *earlier*, on Friday; otherwise Sunday would be fine. There is some suspicion as to Jesus' motives; he wants to make a point not about healing, but about healing on the Sabbath. The woman's sufferings are not his chief interest; they take a back seat to his desire to test the Law. He cannot really complain that those who adhere to the customary understandings of Sabbath observance should object; that is precisely what he wanted them to do. Nor is the animal analogy apt, for there is no glory in feeding and watering animals on the Sabbath, but plenty in healing the sick.[19] And Sabbath work prohibitions were never understood to include not eating or not feeding those who could not feed themselves. You can't make the animals *work* on the Sabbath, but you can *feed* them within the rules of Sabbath observance no less than you can set food out for humans.

There may be crazed amounts of fussiness and persnicketyness in the rabbinic rules as to what is work and what not, but there is no hypocrisy. If anything, the vice in the rules is the obsessive concern to get it exactly right. The problem is one of having to draw the line somewhere when you make a rule, and the rule that distinguishes between feeding animals and healing non–life-threatening disorders is hardly irrational. This is not a case, which Jesus seems to want to make it, of saying one thing and doing another that exposes the Sabbath work rules as so much hypocrisy. If there is any hypocrisy it may indeed be that of Jesus, who cannot see the beam in his own eye and who is doing pious deeds (healing) for less than pious motives (political advantage and glory). *His* left hand may be peeking.

It is not as if Jesus would not have an answer to such a charge of hypocrisy. He is a teacher, a moral and religious teacher, and the techniques teachers use involve them in testing appearances, putting on shows, shocking their students, forcing them out of complacencies, playing devil's advocate, teasing, conning, insinuating, pleading, feeding, entertaining, faking, and, surely, testing. To test Jesus' good faith one would have to suppose that he would equally support anyone else healing on the Sabbath: that would get any suspicions of his own self-promotion out of the picture and would focus the argument on the proper interpretation of the Law and the status of ritual observance.[20]

The terrain of religious observance is the ground upon which hypocrisy first grows. Well into the early modern period, hypocrisy is understood to be a vice of false piety, and accusations of it played a major role in battles between letter and spirit, form and substance, inner and outer forms of devotion. Hypocrites were those who preferred letter to spirit but could equally be those who feigned spirit to avoid the harsh compliance with the letter of ritual forms. In other words, a charismatic Protestant could be as much a hypocrite as a Catholic, though in Jesus' view hypocrites were more likely to be sticklers for form.

Ritual is especially problematic, because in much ritual the form is the substance, as in eating fish on Friday or, among Jews, of obeying Sabbath and purity rules. It is about obedience and conformance. Just do it, in other words. But that knowledge is never quite sufficient to assuage anxieties about the mental state that is properly to accompany the observance of the rules. What motives are safe from hypocrisy? Does Jesus mean to suggest that rote, automatic observance of such ritual acts and prohibitions is hypocrisy, merely because they have become habit and custom?[21] Or that because not doing them would bring blame? Or that the doing of them would bring approbation?

Subject to some major anxieties I mean to expose in a later chapter, one might argue that the function, if not the purpose, of successful ritual is to finesse the issue of motives. The point of ritual is to have as an acceptable motive nothing more elaborate than "that's what we do." And that is satisfying in itself.

# THREE

# Antihypocrisy: Looking Bad in Order
## to Be Good

"HYPOCRISY IS THE HOMAGE vice pays to virtue," says La Rochefoucauld (M 218). Hypocrisy is a parasite, operating by mimicking the attractiveness of virtue, appropriating its rewards. Most other vices are more particularly associated with specific traits and feed and sustain themselves. Vices such as avarice and fractiousness are not parasitical on their opposing virtues: generosity and amiability. Other vices exist in a kind of symbiosis with their opposing virtue, but parasitism is not at its essence, as it is with hypocrisy. Thus lust and gluttony charge their batteries by occasional regimens of temperance and abstinence. The glutton and the lecher may self-servingly think their abstinence is virtuous; they may sincerely believe themselves to be turning over new leaves, but by the time they are turning over the hundredth new leaf surely they must know that their attempts at virtue are only so much foreplay to their vice, an enhancing of its deliciousness.

### Of Hairshirts

Once people suspect hypocrisy, many start to mistrust all appearances of virtue as so much glory seeking and shamming. Montaigne goes so far as to claim that virtuous deeds done openly are ever more compromised the grander they are: "The more glittering the deed the more I subtract from its moral worth, because of the suspicion aroused in me that it was exposed more for glitter than for goodness."[1] Because virtue looks good, it looks bad. What are the virtuous to do? Pretend to vice? In fact this antihypocrisy strategy is often tried – recall that Jesus counsels it with regard to fasting: pretend that you are not fasting when you are (Matt. 6.16–18) – and it immediately gives rise to its own styles of hypocrisy, vanity, and playing at virtue.

In one of Mark Twain's burlesques of Heaven we find Sir Richard Duffer, a butcher from Hoboken who died with a carefully cultivated reputation for meanness; he was awarded a baronetcy in Heaven for having *secretly* furnished the homes of "honest square people out of work" with meat.[2] Take the more famous cases of St. Thomas à Becket and St. Thomas More, who secretly wore itchy hairshirts underneath their sumptuous robes to punish themselves for the vanity of their rich clothing and high office. Better to appear completely given over to unapologetic luxury than to appear virtuously dressed in unostentatious habit and be suspected of ostentatious piety. Yet it is hard not to suspect Becket and More of smirking to themselves, vain of their hairshirt secret, or congratulating themselves on the brilliance of a move that turns their showy sumptuousness into fake showy sumptuousness, all to get around the stricture against trumpeting one's virtue.[3]

Similarly, it is hard not to imagine the simpler Richard Duffer undertaking considerable extra labor to keep his generosity secret. We can see him delighting in his reputation for meanness, precisely because it is false, taking no small pleasure in a smug contempt for those fools who fall for his perfectly engineered deception, who are so wrong in their opinion of him. The townspeople's false blame purifies his virtue and shoots him straight to Heaven, at least according to this theory of obsessive hypocrisy avoidance.

There are certain false fronts that are not part of the niceties of politeness and decorum but instead turn the people who are their objects into fools: this is the sin of Frank Churchill in *Emma*, who by keeping his engagement to Jane Fairfax secret is assumed by others, namely Emma, to be available for flirtation. The unknowing are thus entrapped into humiliating themselves by fancying they are being attended to by Frank in ways they are not. When the sham is revealed people resent it, and with good reason. It is not likely that the denizens of Hoboken who disliked the falsely mean butcher will feel much more charitable toward him once his secret is revealed. No one likes being made a fool of, even (or especially?) in the interests of someone else's trip to Heaven. It is not as if Duffer's strategy doesn't impose costs on the unwitting others; they have had the vice of censoriousness thrust upon them against their will.

With Becket and More, two very sophisticated actors, the suspicion of hypocritical antihypocrisy is stronger. They are not being vain of their virtue in the vulgar sense of parading holiness about, literally trumpeting it, but instead are being vain of their virtue for their internal audience, for the benefits accruing to their self-esteem.[4] Their secret self-mortification, however, eventually gets noticed. That is why I can write about it. When Becket died it was apparent when they stripped him, and we know of More's too. They, I suppose, knew we would know, for by playing to their internal audience they were also, just maybe, playing to a future earthly audience in addition to the one in Heaven.[5]

Wearing a hairshirt, even in secret, is ostentatious in a way that other, less lurid kinds of devotion are not, especially back then, when the competition in matters of holiness was a political as well as a social and religious issue.[6] Even if the motives for wearing hairshirts for mortifiers of the flesh such as Becket and More were untainted by competitiveness or glorying, they would know that others might suspect that their motives were tinged with saintly ambition. They surely struggled with incessant temptation and could not always keep the pride of finery and high office at bay. The hairshirt is a testimony to that. But did they not also indulge in some self-satisfaction in knowing they were enduring itching silently, ever so patiently, while suffering the additional punishment of being blamed for their pride of office?

Unless, that is, hairshirts had already become a fad and you could not trust that the people you encountered were not also wearing one. Various ways of mortifying the flesh followed the rules of fashionability; in the early centuries of Christianity, stylites – pole sitters – were in vogue; in the fourteenth to sixteenth centuries pus drinking had its day.[7] One can imagine a group of wags, all with hairshirts under their brocaded doublets, querying in their cups: tell me Philip, where do you go for your hairshirts? Do you order the lice separately?

It might be that the real cross to bear was not the hairshirt but the suspicion, your own as well as that of others, that you were thought vain no matter how hard you tried not to be. And for all your pride in your self-mortification, in the end you fear that the actual suffering too is a sham. If the hairshirt was hard to bear at first, it gets easier with time, and eventually you may even come to find it pleasurable. As Trollope says of Mrs. Prime: "Nice things aggravated her spirits and made her fretful...She liked the bread to be stale...She was approaching that stage of discipline at which ashes become pleasant eating, and sackcloth is grateful to the skin. The self-indulgences of the saints in this respect often exceed anything that is done by the sinners."[8]

In such a moral regime anxieties regarding the purity of motive behind otherwise virtuous-looking deeds arise with aggressive insistence. You become anxious about doing good; you start to question your motives. Even when you satisfy yourself on that score you are not sure that others will not see you as motivated by vanity. Should you employ Duffer's or Becket's strategy of playing the part of a sinner so as to avoid the imputation of being vain of your virtue, you hardly feel yourself more authentically and purely virtuous. Instead you worry that the very charade of hiding your virtue has become entirely too self-conscious to be authentic; your last hope is that all your self-torturing and labor will themselves serve as sufficient atonement for whatever imperfections may stain your motives. Or, as in the case of Benjamin Franklin, you throw in the towel on matters of humility: "For even if I could conceive that I had compleatly overcome [pride], I should probably be proud of my Humility."[9]

That you find yourself canonized doesn't settle the matter either, for it will be suspected that you were angling for that honor, especially if, as in Becket's and More's cases, you made sure you were martyred. There is as much earthly (though posthumous) as heavenly glory in sainthood, rivaling in every way the glory of conventional military heroes who die in battle. The old Vikings made no bones about it: posthumous earthly glory was the best we could hope for, a kind of Heaven on Earth:

Cattle die, kinsmen die;
You yourself shall die just like them;
But words of praise for him
Who does great deeds never die.[10]

## Non–Self-Tormenting Virtue? Et in Arcadia Ego

Not all moralists in the Christian world were so hard on vanity. Some began to celebrate it for all the good consequences that flow from it. What's wrong with wanting to look good, especially if it means you have to cultivate virtues to do so?[11] People still, thank God, went on being vain of their virtue; others tricked themselves in the way Jesus suggested they do, and still others in a slightly different style saw virtue as their duty and were virtuous because duty demanded it. Yet others were simply virtuous, good because they were good, and, yes, they knew they might be praised for being good. But they, except perhaps when challenged by some misanthropic moralist, did not torture themselves about it. They were confident that they were *primarily* motivated to do good because they were disposed to do so, and not for the approbation of others, though they might not mind that they got it.[12]

But is our belief that such simply virtuous souls exist motivated in some small way by wishful thinking? We want to believe in the fantasy of innocent simplicity in which we do not suffer from what Dostoyevsky's Prince Myshkin called "double thoughts,"[13] his term for that self-torturing and rather unfair questioning of our own good motives. Did I really help that person out of generosity of spirit, or because I would feel guilty if I didn't, or because some good-looking person was watching and would think me something special and fall in love with me, or because I could finally show Miss Hoeffs, my junior English teacher – who said I would never amount to anything and gave me a D to help her prophecy come true – that she had been wrong about me? How do I keep the thoughts of a nice inheritance and life insurance proceeds from intruding on what I thought was my sincere, gut-wrenching grief? Can I convince myself that the reason I don't carry much life insurance is that I want to make sure my family doesn't feel guilt for reveling in the proceeds and can really sincerely miss me when I am dead and gone?

How to escape such miserable thoughts! Thus the fashion of the pastoral, with its central theme that in Arcadia the shepherds were uncomplicatedly innocent and authentic in their desires and deeds; or the cult of children; or the belief in the patient, humble peasant pure in virtue, a belief that was quickly discounted because that virtuous peasant never seemed to reside on your manor but in the next village, or in literature as Chaucer's plowman or poor parish priest.[14] Why weren't those poor as meek and blessed as advertised?

The occasional vogue of the pastoral – Marie Antoinette dressing up as a shepherdess at Versailles or suburban rich kids joining hippie communes – speaks to the desperate need for the possibility of unself-conscious virtue. The shepherd is conceived to be too simple to entertain the ironies of appearances and reality. But maybe the shepherd has his own doubts: "Damn, I can't seem to feel as authentic as I'm supposed to. Am I just going through the motions because some jaded aristocrat expects me to sport innocently with so many Daphnes and Amaryllises in the shade? Am I motivated in part by putting on a show for these rich guys who come around during the spring and paint me? These people don't understand the moral paradoxes of shepherding and the complexity of maintaining a life of simplicity and authenticity. Being authentic is hard work. It takes so much effort I have dropped into last place among my comrades in sheep-stealing."[15]

We know that when the sophisticated try their hand at shepherding they make a mess of it, as the failures of Brook Farm attest.[16] The rustics with whom they hobnobbed thought them phonies or merely comical; and the sophisticated came to suspect each other of hypocritical posturing. Truth be told, actually living with those crude and constantly bickering soulful shepherds had even fewer charms than tea and crumpets in Concord. Adding drugs or gurus from India, as in twentieth-century versions of Brook Farm, doesn't seem to work either. And when someone insists his new brand of the authentic life really is working, we often mistrust his intelligence or sanity, as with adherents of new age spirituality.

If not shepherds, surely children must be full of innocent, uncomplex virtue: Dad, I missed you so much, did you bring me a present? A Victorian girl, rather than call into question whether virtue could survive the benefits of the publicity of it, wondered whether goodness itself could survive actually *wanting* to do good deeds. Part of her problem flows from her definition of goodness; good deeds, in her view, must be unpleasant. But as inadequate as we know that definition to be, it is hardly an unrecognizable view of what children and a more than a few adults take it to be:

> If you wanted to do it, then it wasn't goodness. Thus being kind to a person you liked didn't count at all, because you wanted to do it; and being kind to a person you didn't like (like poor Old Betsy at Down) was no use either; because – as I thought then – the person always knew perfectly well that you disliked them, and so of course the kindness could not please them... Goodness never made me feel nice afterwards.... [It] simply made me feel mean, hypocritical and servile.[17]

Children are no more likely than shepherds to find virtue a simple matter; what could be worse than being labeled a Goody Two-shoes? It is not that their virtue is innocent, but that their vice is. Even that is false, for they are the most charming and skillful of operators.

### Putting Vanity to Good Use

By no means, as just noted, was everyone a rigorist, nor were all rigorists crabbed, joyless souls. Even St. Thomas Aquinas cuts hypocrisy some slack. He rightly distinguishes between the lack of goodness and the pretense of goodness. The person who intends bad things puts his soul in much greater jeopardy than the person who merely wants to look better than he is.[18] There also arose a satirical aphoristic tradition that took mischievous delight in exposing human virtue as so much vanity. According to this tradition, virtue was nothing more than the end result of our desire to look good to others and to ourselves; it was an attractive and useful byproduct of our quest for esteem and self-esteem. To this end we engage in all kinds of deceptions, donning masks of virtue and using veils to cover our honest feelings, and then disguising from ourselves our less than honorable deception of others by various tricks of self-duping; thus in the end we honor virtue, not by being errant hypocrites, but by coming to believe that our hypocrisies are virtuous. And as long as our hypocrisy is of the first type Jesus exposed – of being moved by the desire for being known as virtuous for the sake of self-advancement, for honor's sake – the poor get their alms.

This kind of hypocrisy is very sociable. It cares greatly what people think, and, for the most part, to be well thought of one must do good deeds. It means having to be reasonably respectful of others, engaging in small acts of civility, cultivating tact, sparing others the pain of too much truth whose only virtue would be to hurt them needlessly and feed your own vanity for being a tough truth teller. Though at times you may actually feel like a hypocrite, that confers larger moral stakes on most of these routine matters than they deserve.

Some took the argument about the benefits of our vanity one step further; if the vanity of wanting to be thought good could produce good, then, it was both seriously and satirically argued – most famously by Mandeville in the early eighteenth century, but quite frequently in the century before him – that our plain old vices themselves produced good even if we took no care to gloss them over. Forget about working to appear virtuous. Vices created demand in the economy that prompted virtues (in others) of hard work and enterprise to meet them. The vanity of wanting sumptuous clothing and a fancy equipage did an inadvertent good. Never mind giving alms for suspect motives. Why, lordy-be, spending it on yourself was a form of almsgiving; it was the virtue of trickle-down economics.[19] No need to waste energy being a hypocrite: vice is one kind of virtue, though surely Mandeville's argument about the virtue of vice is its own form of hypocrisy; it provides shameless spendthrifts and gluttons a convenient rationalization for why it is good to be as disgusting as they are.

The usual hypocrisy of false good appearances thus gives way to a new hypocrisy of shameless redescriptions of undisguised vice as generators of virtue, prompting in these new, complacent sinners what the sixteenth century called the sin of *security*: namely, a culpable sense of self-satisfaction, of invulnerability, of spiritual and moral obtuseness. As Thomas Nashe, writing in the late sixteenth century, beautifully puts it: security is "forgetting mortalitie; it is a kind of Alchymical quintessensing of a heaven out of earth."[20]

That however removes us from faking it to the in-your-face pursuit of one's own desires and interest: errant, undisguised egoism. But as Jon Elster and others have pointed out, and Mandeville notwithstanding, people were ashamed to avow bad or selfish motives openly. In Adam Smith's words, "Though it may be true...that every individual, in his own breast, naturally prefers himself to all mankind, yet he dares not look mankind in the face, and avow that he acts according to this principle."[21] People would claim fake virtuous motives, and then, by mechanisms Elster seeks to disentangle, magically generate self-deceptions that succeeded in transmuting their initial selfishness into more virtuous motives.[22] If you want to appear virtuous to others (and to yourself, too) you might actually have to do more than entertain a few pious thoughts and paste a perpetual look of pitying concern on your face. You might actually have to do some deeds that qualify as good. And lo, by hook or crook, with the very help of that pasted look, you end up doing good deeds with a proper motive, having fooled yourself into goodness.

It was a simpler matter for the people sounding trumpets while giving alms who so annoyed Jesus; they were not trying to pretend their almsgiving was not also glory seeking. They had no anxiety about imperfect motives because to them there was nothing wrong with glorying. Faking different motives than the ones you have becomes necessary only once glorying gets a bad name. The Greeks held the desire for honor to be a noble motive, as did many an honor-driven culture. Obviously the Jews trumpeting their almsgiving felt there was nothing to be ashamed of in openly professing a desire to win praise for displays of generosity. Of course you were in it for honor; what better motive could there be worth owning up to that doesn't sound presumptuous or self-satisfied or hypocritical to allege? Perhaps the motive could be simply obeying the Law, though that would be susceptible to a charge of being falsely modest. But Jesus offers the motive of salvation, heavenly glory for an eternity. How isn't that the ne plus ultra of glory seeking?

I cannot help suspecting that the claim Jesus is making is as much an aesthetic one as a moral one. He dislikes the aggressive posturing: too noisy, too much trumpeting and chest thumping. Jesus prefers the *look* of modesty, the decorousness of private almsgiving rather than public spectacle. To obtain a more tasteful form of almsgiving he is willing to offer a bribe: a reward from the Father, much better, because less evanescent, he claims, than vain earthly glory. Such an open offer of a quid pro quo is itself, however, rather vulgar. Could Jesus possibly believe the reward, the payoff of heavenly bliss, should be the motive for giving alms?[23] If so, almsgiving becomes no less selfish than it was when it was being trumpeted about. This must be why Jesus counseled keeping the left hand ignorant of the right hand's activities. The thing to be hidden from yourself is not just the knowledge that your virtue will get you praised in the here and now but the reward the Father is holding in escrow for you. I hope that that is what Jesus means, for I cannot shake the belief that the truly virtuous soul, one I would want to gain a Heaven worthy of housing him, would be moved primarily by an honest desire to help a person in need. He saw something that needed to be done and he did it.[24]

Neither did Calvinism's doctrine of predestined salvation and damnation resolve the problem of double thoughts, those worries about the quality of one's motives. In Calvin's view you had already been paid off in either gold or lead long before you did your good deed – long before you were born, in fact – but that did not prevent you from worrying about the moral status of your motives for doing good. Wouldn't a person predestined for salvation do good deeds with the purest of motives? Could a soul predestined for Heaven be so corrupt as to want praise for his virtue or for wanting to have the reputation as one predestined for salvation?[25] Mightn't your less than perfect motive be, God forbid, a sign of your predestined damnation?

We are conflicted, but not always. Sometimes we just do good and don't worry that it may be good business to do so. Yet at other times, in a plague of self-conscious scrupulosity, we doubt our motives and desperately want to have our doubts assuaged. We may find some solace before the next inevitable attack of scruples in amiable winks at our endless vanity, especially when they come from a soul as perfectly good as David Hume's:[26]

> It has been found, that the virtuous are far from being indifferent to praise; and therefore they have been represented as a set of vainglorious men, who had nothing in view but the applauses of others. But this also is a fallacy. It is very unjust in the world, when they find any tincture of vanity in a laudable action, to depreciate it upon that account, or ascribe it entirely to that motive... Vanity is so closely allied to virtue, and to love the fame of laudable actions approaches so near the love of laudable actions for their own sake, that these passions are more capable of mixture, than any other kinds of affection; and it is almost impossible to have the latter without some degree of the former... To love the glory of virtuous deeds is a sure proof of the love of virtue.[27]

Next, consider that hypocrisy has an easier time suborning some virtues than others. It unrelentingly harasses virtues such as piety and sincerity, but some virtues develop pretty strong immunities to hypocrisy. These immunities are of different kinds, and it is the job of the next chapter to set the matter forth.

# FOUR

# Virtues Naturally Immune to Hypocrisy

HYPOCRISY, AS HAS BEEN NOTED, started its career in the area of assumed piety. It was a matter of feigning holiness before it was anything else. In the secular sphere everyone expected an endless cycle of cons and deceptions, lies and cheats. Look at the world of Chaucer or Langland or Ben Jonson, in which everyone is an operator, everyone has a scam. That wasn't hypocrisy by their understanding except to the extent that assumed religiosity was part of the scam. But once we extend hypocrisy to be a risk of all virtue we find that it is drawn to some virtues more than others. I examine next the intersection of hypocrisy, in the sense of the divorce between virtuous intention and the virtuous appearance of our deeds, and three virtues: courage, politeness, and self-command.

## Courage and Faking It

Here is the bald statement: courage is not susceptible to Jesus' first kind of hypocrisy, the hypocrisy of the trumpeting almsgiver and the ostentatiously pious. Consider this vignette, which represents a rough amalgam of many accounts that appear in soldiers' memoirs: you have been ordered to charge the enemy position. You are scared out of your wits, scared of dying, of being mutilated; but you are just as scared of being seen as a coward, that you will curl up sobbing, cringing, and sniveling, that you will befoul your pants. You also fear that everyone can see your cowardly soul written on your face. You want to get a nice safe wound and get carried to the rear. You swallow your ration of rum; the order is given to charge, and, incredibly, you charge, motivated partly by sheer conformity – everyone else is doing it – partly out of terror of shame, partly out of fear of being left behind alone, partly out of bewilderment, partly to get a reputation for courage so that people will cut you some slack, and most of all so that you will cut yourself some for being so damn scared. You charge ahead, too scared, too confused by the noise and mayhem, to have any real insight into your motives. Later you are written up for a Military Cross or a Bronze Star.

Among all the motives that pushed you forward, not one of them is prompted by the perfect prompting to virtue in Aristotle's sense: being courageous because you are disposed to do courageous deeds by cultivating a disposition that seeks to do virtue for its own sake. Yet you charged ahead. But you feel yourself a fake. What business did you have getting a medal? Had they read your thoughts or felt your fears they would have court-martialed you for your cowardly mind and bowels. It can't be true, you think, that a hero and a coward have the same overpowering feeling of fear and confusion. You feel a fraud; you mistrust your motives.

But you are not a fraud: courage, perhaps more than any other virtue, has to be more accommodating to the inner states that motivate it. Most of us think of courage, even more than of temperance and continence, as the virtue par excellence of self-command, of overcoming contrary desires – not of not having bad desires. The stakes are so much higher and important in facing death and danger or in avoiding mutilation and pain than in saying no to another orgasm or piece of cheesecake. Yet no matter how reasonable the desire to escape pain and death may be, that does not mean we blame the coward less than the lecher or glutton for giving in to the desire to scratch his itch. The sins of these seekers of pleasure are comical, but the sins of the coward might get him lined up before a firing squad and shot, or forever treated as an object of contempt.

Courage is also a virtue that is properly motivated by the desire to have a reputation for it. Are we going to call Hector, Achilles, Beowulf, and others like them hypocrites for wanting to be known for their courage, for being infinitely vain of their courage? Not to have such a desire was to refuse to take the steps necessary for cultivating the capacity to deliver when the crunch came. Honor societies knew that. In them, modesty was suspect. Keeping modestly in the background looked more like excessive prudence, which was mistrusted as so much cover for fearfulness.

So hard is it to be courageous that we are willing to let people engage in all kinds of precommitment strategies to raise the costs to themselves of failure if they fink out. We wink at most all the tricks of self-deception they might employ to fool themselves into fearlessness, and we still deem them courageous if they come through. We thus understand why they make boasts and vows, why they drink themselves into confidence, why they work themselves into rages, why they shame the coward. True, some people did have the option of not boasting and vowing: those who had already proved unambiguously their mettle or who were so big and strong that no one doubted they could win any fight they got into. But most needed to buck themselves up by whatever means necessary to feel they might actually have a chance of delivering when the time came.

Courage is thus courage even if the doer of brave deeds trumpets them about, or does them so that others will trumpet them about. Courage is not like almsgiving and praying.[1] We may prefer that courage be motivated for the pure sake of the virtue, as it sometimes is, but if we hold out for that we will get very little courage. We cannot be so persnickety about motives when a person is knowingly risking life and limb. Though courage is not immune to being faked, it is often the case that faking legitimately qualifies as the real thing.[2] Of course, not everything goes. A person too stupid to perceive the risk, or too insane to have any awareness of danger, is not courageous. One must recognize the risk, even if that level of risk does not make one fear.

A common sentiment expressed in war memoirs of combat soldiers, manifestly brave men, is that they felt themselves cowards despite being cited for courage, felt they had faked it.[3] They knew they had done deeds that are commonly thought to take courage, but these moral rigorists were hard, too hard, on themselves; they felt more like cowards who were lucky that they had not been exposed for their false seeming. They were not just being modest, though they were that too. They really were puzzled by the praiseworthiness of what moved them to deliver.

Even in the case of bluffing, when you are trying to get out of a violent confrontation by feigning aggressiveness or fearlessness, when you intend no courageous deeds whatsoever, fakery and courage converge. You must make the other believe you will deliver, and that raises the level of risk in your own world: the risk that you will further provoke the other to run you down when you turn and run or, worse, the risk that you will have to deliver if your threat fails to work.[4] Thus to increase your risks is itself a kind of courage. It takes guts to fake it in a rough world.

Jesus asked that the right hand and left hand turn a blind eye to each other; he counseled faking yourself out. How this was to be accomplished he did not say. Over the centuries, fighting men and armies have developed techniques designed to do just that. So much of training is instilling techniques of tricking the mind into not fearing. Drill, rum rations, shaming, exhortation speeches, boasting, vowing, good luck talismans – all these are meant to distract you, to delude you into optimism or into not thinking about the risk you are running, or into separating your body from your fears if you cannot get rid of your fears. A large part of military science might be reduced to this: deceive both the enemy and yourself regarding your courage.[5]

How are you supposed to forget that you intentionally hoodwinked yourself, so that you will be able to believe that you have conquered your fear and not that you are just pretending? It is the same old issue: how can you fake yourself out intentionally? How does the dupe not see through the con, given that the dupe and the con man are the same person or at least occupying the same body?[6] Not all the techniques are of the bootstrapping type: some – drill, training – work by turning you into an automaton so that no matter what your inner state your body will do what it has been ordered to do by rote. Others replace one kind of fear with another: boasts and vows increase your fear of the shame of not fulfilling them to balance against the fear of death. Still others use chemicals that aid the mind in its bootstrapping efforts. The optimistic energy provided by alcohol, for instance, has its own eraser built in to help you forget that

you drank it in order to forget *why* you drank it, and also of not caring very much even if you don't forget where your newfound courage
has come from; you will take it any way you can get it. Much bootstrapping makes great use of the emotions to obscure rationality: the
exhortation speech, the rebel yell, the "Battle Hymn of the Republic."
Except for congenital optimists, who need no rum to delude themselves into believing this is not their day to die, most of us need all
these techniques and more to find our courage, to fake ourselves out.
And, though imperfect, such courage is not, by reason of its imperfect
motivation, hypocritical.

## Politeness

If courage is largely immune from hypocrisy, if because of the sheer
difficulty of being courageous we allow the courageous act to compensate for or obviate its less than perfect motivation, that cannot be
our excuse for politeness. Politeness doesn't need an excuse; fakery is
openly admitted to lie at the structural core of the virtue. Politeness is
immune to many forms of hypocrisy because a certain benign form of
hypocrisy is precisely its virtue. Thus politeness gets one of the very
few of Ambrose Bierce's definitions that could almost be called sweet:
"the most acceptable form of hypocrisy." An evocative eighteenth-
century definition – "Politeness may be defined a dextrous management of our Words and Actions whereby we make other people have
better Opinion of us and themselves" – could serve equally well for
the vice of flattery as for the virtue of politeness.[7] Dextrous management indeed.

Politeness need not be so cynically construed. We could give it a
nicer spin by noting how, at relatively little cost, it saves people from
unnecessary pain in social encounters. It is a certain willingness to
disguise our true beliefs and engage in small flatteries, small pleas-
antries, and white lies. It is to pardon or ignore small annoyances
and inconveniences. It means having the tact to cover for the faux
pas of others or to state your own claims in ways that will not make
for discomfort. It means responding to the cues people give you to
reaffirm their self-esteem as regards variously their appearance, taste,

general competence, and importance, despite your diverging opinion. It means making a show of attention, veiling boredom, wearing a mask that manifests amiability or routine concern for their concerns. It means making the interaction safe for others, with the expectation that they will return the favor.

By describing politeness in this manner I am loading it with a little too much niceness and demanding more from it than it need deliver. I have moved it in the direction of the more seriously grounded virtue of graciousness. Graciousness makes its object believe it emanates from a truly generous spirit, not from a merely polite one, from a spirit gifted in making one feel welcome and at ease, especially in situations in which you have reason to feel you are incurring a debt that may not be completely dischargeable. Politeness always has something of a ritualized predictability about it. That is why it works; it is not rare, and it is usually not very difficult to manage. Politeness can be "mere" politeness, and it can be cold, whereas graciousness cannot be cold or "mere" without ceasing to be gracious. We count on politeness as by right, whereas graciousness is by grace; it is more than we have a right to. Not that graciousness can't be faked, but that faking it is such a demanding chore that only the truly gracious would have the wherewithal to pass off a fake as the real thing.

Politeness keeps small-stakes events small stakes, nondescript encounters nondescript. A polite person does not pull an Icelandic saga stunt and kill another guest who gets assigned the seat he wants. He is committed to forgo revenge or to postpone it in the interests of sparing those present an embarrassing scene. The redressive moves that are allowed must preserve their deniability and must still employ the forms of politeness. We know the ways: by being "perfectly polite," namely, by calling attention to the unfeltness of the politeness by exaggerating its formality; or by "begging to differ," though this takes careful management to make sure the aggression remains passive and hence deniable. A third, raillery – pointed jesting that entertains the company more than it unnerves them – actually works against the grain of politeness. It is in fact a safety valve and a socially acceptable revolt against the constraints of politeness. Raillery allows for aggressiveness that is meant to be laughed off and provides a marked contrast to those perfectly polite jabs that are no laughing matter; these latter send impulses that clench the jaw and thin the lips.[8]

So much of politeness is by rote. You can be polite without great expenditures of spirit, except in those scrambling emergencies in which demands are made on your resources for tact and poise.[9] But it isn't always easy to play it by rote. Why is it at times such a chore to tell those white lies? Why is it not an uncommon experience to find that the amount of effort it takes to be polite does not seem trivial, but a true imposition, leading us to wish desperately that we could, as Jane Austen would have it, draw back from "the toils of civility"?[10] In those moments in which our politeness is being produced laboriously, it is hardly surprising that we are inclined to feel as if we are faking it. In fact we want, subtly, to let the other person suspect we are faking it. We want him to sense the pawing of our truthfulness at the door of its cage.

Perhaps even more painful are the unwelcome appearances of the feeling of faking it when we would much prefer to be lost in the role of making polite conversation. Instead we experience a vague dissociation of the kind I noted in the introduction. We see ourselves in a critical way; our utterances sound especially inane, our facial expressions feel unnatural. We fear that our very self-consciousness about the superficiality of the polite performance will interfere with the role we already worry we are botching; we struggle against the urge to apologize for how badly we are playing it, the urge to beg forgiveness for our especially inane polite inanities, for our general awkwardness in merely being polite – you have to pardon me, I got only three hours of sleep last night.

Our shows of politeness are not directed merely to the specific person who is the object of them, nor to our inner self, nor to the wider audience, but also to others who are not quite separated from our identity, what Goffman calls members of our "team." Team members collude; they also pay for one another's failures. Collusion among friends and spouses is common fare, as when you show engagement in a story you have heard your spouse tell a hundred times before but that you also know is a pretty good story for those who have not yet heard it. The engagement may not even be feigned, for the interest of the audience energizes you to reexperience your pleasure in the tale.

Suffering for the faults and failures of team members is sometimes a simple matter of corporate liability or guilt by association, but it can be more complex. I offer this homely example of my wife playing – to borrow from Jane Austen again – Elinor to my Marianne, for whom it was impossible "to say what she did not feel, however trivial the occasion; and upon Elinor therefore the whole task of telling lies, when politeness required it, always fell."[11] My wife feels that part of her role in being associated with me requires her to engage in what I feel are excessive gestures of politeness to compensate for what she feels are my failures to meet the minimum standards of inoffensiveness, whereas I view my "failures" in this regard as efforts to compensate for what I feel are her excesses of politeness. The more penetrating of our guests must suspect that her displays of excited interest in their tedious tales or her sympathy for their petty disappointments are partly to compensate for my having wandered out to do the dishes in the midst of the conversation. Most are not so penetrating, but those who are give her credit for caring to make atonement for my failures.

It's disgusting, she says to me later, that we fall into such predictable gender roles: politeness feminine, failures of it – certain scripted failures to be sure – masculine. How can you write about this stuff, she says, pick it apart in such tedious detail, and then get it all wrong in the flesh, and not see how rude you were to Mrs. Z? That is more domestic revelation than it is permissible here to indulge, except to say that when I get the vacuum cleaner out while a guest is still seated and tell her not to mind me but to please pick up her feet for just a second so that I can get the inordinate number of crumbs she has dropped, it is really only a function of my compulsive disorder. It has nothing, I assure her, absolutely nothing, to do with my wanting her to decamp.

If the demands of politeness can cause occasional anxiety among homogeneous suburbanites, imagine what adding class, race, and ethnic difference to the mix does. Big-time faking is on the menu. How do we get our attempts at politeness understood as polite rather than as an offense? Should I use a lot of cuss words talking to this working-class guy? Does it make any difference if I am pretty naturally foul-mouthed anyway? If he is cussing, is that a sign of his refusal to make any concessions to my class and education, or is he too dim to know the rules, or is it his way of outmachoing me? Or is it that he is engaging in that heavy male refusal to engage in the niceties of feminized politeness, a refusal that is itself a form of manly politeness? No, no, try not to talk about basketball with the black guy, but then what if he brings it up? Is he doing that because he is graciously conceding that that is all we might have in common? Or is he parodying some role he expects I will expect him to play, thus making a fool out of me? How is one to avoid self-consciousness in this setting, when not faking it can itself be so easily construed as fake?

Every time I talk to people with southern accents, I notice my vowels moving in their direction, without willing them in that direction (as I notice my consonants moving in the direction of working-class guys). I am not aware of consciously trying to mimic their accent; but I am aware that trying or not, it just seems to happen by some overpowering urge, perhaps fear, to show myself to be a real regular guy, to indicate a willingness to meet halfway between my way of talking and theirs. It is thus a bit cowardly. They may think it is mockery of them, and it may contain some small element of that. Yet I do not feel I am mocking them – rather the contrary. I am honoring them, deferring to their way of talking. But will they read it as such? Is it merely the infectious musicality of their way of talking? I sure don't hear them imitating my northern Wisconsin vowels. Even in the phonological domain I am being outmuscled.

I struggle, out of a minimum of self-respect, to get back to my own vowels, but they seem to elude me. I try to mimic the vowels of a factory worker from Green Bay, which is pretty close to how the real me talks, but they end up distorted by the Southern vowels still wanting to form themselves. I seem to be unable to recover the way I talk normally. Not only do I lose my vowels, but I also lose the thread of the conversation as I begin to worry more and more whether I will ever recover my accent, whatever my accent is. How the hell do I talk naturally, anyway? If I know, then why am I always shocked to hear what it is when I am forced to listen to myself on tape? Nevertheless, I keep that silly grin of conversational engagement on my face and forge ahead. No matter how fake it is and how cowardly it feels, it is harder to prevent that grin from appearing than it is to paste it on and keep it there.

Goffman quotes Santayana, who claims that the polite role played in these small interactions presents an authentic us, at least a truer us than would be revealed if we acted on urges to blurt out the "truth," whatever that may be. But implicit in his tone is the force of the contrary sentiment he wishes to deny – that we experience much of our politeness as hypocrisy:

> Under our published principles and plighted language we must assiduously hide all the inequalities of our moods and conduct, and this without hypocrisy, since our deliberate character is more truly ourself than is the flux of our involuntary dreams.[12]

Truth, it is admitted, is a relative matter here. Our deliberate character is not completely the true self either; yet it is truer than any momentary desire to blurt out some hostile statement, truer than an evanescent anxiety that it is cowardly or hypocritical not to blurt out the hostile sentiment. Why think the real you is suffering from Tourette's syndrome if only you had the nerve to display the symptoms? Part of being a truly polite person means carrying on politely when one feels like a fraud for carrying on politely. La Rochefoucauld exposed the same bias in our thinking: "Most young people think they are being natural when really they are just ill-mannered and crude" (M 372). We hold a biased view that somehow vulgarity is natural and authentic, but those who have witnessed frat guys engaging in yahoo behavior see that it is forced and contrived, needing the assistance of Bud and buddies. One must train no less to be a yahoo frat guy than to be a person of politeness.

Though La Rochefoucauld has other intentions, Santayana's mission is to assuage us, to tell us that we should not feel false for being polite. He rightly asks why we should think that a whirl of hates and peeves is to be credited with more truth than putting on a pleasant front. Those hates and peeves are true only in the sense that we have them at this precise moment. But why give those passing vexations, annoyances, irks, and frustrations so much moral and social force by giving blustery vent to them, thereby letting them create a state of affairs that will endure long after the impulses have subsided?

Backed now by Santayana's assurances, I should feel less anxious about faking my politeness. But he helps only a little. His tone does not quite disguise his own inability to banish his feeling hypocritical for suppressing some of these urges. Part of him, it seems, like part of me, still feels that politeness, like prudence – both surely praiseworthy in their proper place – are to be suspected as a way of giving a virtuous name to our cowardice.

WHEN OUR POLITENESS FAILS in conversational settings, it seldom fails because we blurt out a hostile truth or because of meddlesome anxieties of being exposed as not meaning our hollow niceties. It fails because unless the other is unusually interesting or talking about us, we find it hard to pay attention. Thus La Rochefoucauld:

> One of the reasons why so few people are to be found who seem sensible and pleasant in conversation is that almost everybody is thinking about what he wants to say himself rather than about answering clearly what is being said to him. The clever and polite think it enough simply to put on an attentive expression, while all the time you can see in their eyes and train of thought that they are far removed from what you are saying and anxious to get back to what they want to say.
>
> (M 139)

La Rochefoucauld, in general, and my account part ways only on emphasis. My actor is motivated to play his part, to play it well. He may feel he is faking it, but he still wants to fake it well, not to be praised but to escape without making a fool of himself. In La Rochefoucauld's world, people are moved more to seek approbation than to avoid shame.[13]

I should be a little more relaxed given that my rational self knows that the other person has no strong motive to expose my shamming; his self-esteem intervenes to make him believe that for him the show is sincere. In typically mordant fashion La Rochefoucauld, as usual, has two appropriate maxims: "Social life would not last long if men were not taken in by each other"; a more particular application of the same idea yields this: "However skeptical we may be of the sincerity of people who speak to us, we always believe they are more truthful with us than with anyone else" (M 87, 366). The second is truer than the first, for it is not clear how much we are taken in by the other. We don't believe the other so much as "believe" him with a belief of convenience, a belief for the occasion; it is still a belief, but not a deep belief. The second maxim, wonderfully insightful, captures the feeling of disbelief in the sheer effrontery it would take someone we pretty much know to be a liar to lie to such as the likes of *us*, not because he should be able to see that we are on to him, but because we are more deserving of the truth than anyone else. We flatter ourselves that he wishes to flatter us with truthfulness, so much more flattering because we see he rarely treats anyone else with this distinction.[14]

If we are mistrustful of him it is nonetheless polite to take his show of sincerity at face value. Our cowardice has an interest in sustaining our politeness, for without it we might feel obliged to call him on it and make a scene. In low-stakes matters, it is safer and lazier and more polite to trust his sincerity. Besides, the nastiest of soul-destroying conversations, the most vicious displays of contempt, and some of the most delicious revenges, take place not in spite of politeness, but in using its forms to a precise T.

### Self-Command: Sense, Sensibility, and Shallowness

Politeness must often employ the virtue of self-command or, as we would now say, self-control. Routine politeness needs little if any self-command, but when we need to suppress rather overpowering transient urges to nuke or "love" (dive on) our interlocutor, we make demands less on our capacity for politeness than on our capacity for self-command. Unlike politeness, which is hypocrisy gone good, self-command is not blamed as being hypocritical, though it is about donning veils. Paradigmatically, self-command is understood to be more about omission than commission, about not revealing or acting on feelings and motives rather than overtly misrepresenting them. Unlike politeness, self-command seems to mobilize itself more on one's own behalf than on behalf of others. Those who praise it, such as Jane Austen, Adam Smith, and many others, are not unaware that people who show great self-command leave themselves open to being suspected of deception, of playing their cards too close to their vest, of always taking care to be one up, of being too well defended; or simply of being cold fish – affectless and insensible.

Certain cultures put demands on a capacity for self-command we now would find nearly impossible to maintain. Thus Lord Chesterfield, in the mid-eighteenth century, claims never to have laughed in public: "I must particularly warn you against [laughing]," he writes to his son, "and I could heartily wish that you may often be seen to smile, but never heard to laugh while you live . . . it is the manner in which the mob express their silly joy at silly things" as when everyone guffaws because someone pulled a chair out from under a man about to sit down. (The example of the chair is Chesterfield's and is a useful reminder of how enduring certain forms of broad humor are across time and space.) "I am sure that since I have had the full use of my reason, nobody has ever heard me laugh." And again, "A man of parts and fashion is therefore only seen to smile, but never heard to laugh."[15] A most extraordinary self-command this is, mobilized not to spare others' feelings, to suppress anger, or to muster courage, but to maintain an air of being above it all, an air of hauteur, an air of putting on an air.

To serve virtue, the veils (and the masks) employed by self-command are not to be used to set up a betrayal; the deceit must always be in the service of propriety. You must still make others believe that you are not operating nefariously, or that you are not a cold fish or becalmed on the soft surges of your daily dose of antidepressants. If self-command is not presented just right, it can by degrees shade into what Jane Austen coolly blames as "cold insipidity,"[16] a mere quiet decorum brought about by having nothing to say and being lost in posing as self-possessed to cover up one's utter vacuity.

Smith says that the virtue in self-command is in controlling and subduing our strong passions to the point where an impartial spectator can sympathize with them. It is not about ridding ourselves of our passions in either the Stoic or the Buddhist style. Let the passions roil inside as long as your actions and expressions are consistent with the demands of propriety. In fact by not expressing your emotions you will at times actually be able to dampen them, not because, as in our folk wisdom, feigning calmness calms you in the end, but because by acting properly calm when vexed, you will win the approval of impartial spectators; and that approval will firm up your resolve to keep yourself under control (TMS VI.concl.3-4).

Self-command raises different moral issues depending on which passion needs to be controlled. Not showing your fear, according to Smith, is always praiseworthy. The refusal to display your anger also calls for praise unless, he says, you control your anger out of fear (VI.iii.10). Controlling your fear is primarily about maintaining your honor; controlling your anger, on the other hand, is primarily about conferring the benefits of peace on those around you. And where do controlling and suppressing the expression of love fit?

In *Sense and Sensibility*, Jane Austen puts the issues of propriety, authenticity, and posing with regard to emotion display, especially as regards love but also of peeves and annoyances, at the core of the drama. Elinor, the woman of self-command, of prudence and sense, is contrasted with her emotional and impolitic younger sister Marianne, the woman of sensibility. Each (with the narrator weighing in mostly on Elinor's side) thinks the dominant trait of the other – self-command and spontaneous emotionalism – is a sign of shallowness, whereas neither can quite suppress the vanity of thinking her own style to be the one most in accord with true inner depth. Marianne suspects that Elinor doesn't feel things very deeply, for if she did, she would be no better at disguising her loves and hates than Marianne herself is: "The business of self-command [Marianne] settled very easily; – with strong affections it was impossible, with calm ones it could have no merit" (ch. 19).

Marianne divides the emotions into two classes: those we can control and those we cannot. In her view, if you can control them, then you are not feeling them with the same force as is the person who cannot control them. In her psychology the faculty of self-command is constant across people; what is variable is the intensity of their passions.

If Marianne suspects Elinor of having little or no feeling, then Elinor thinks Marianne's emotionalism to be playing at emotion, to be shallowness itself. Emotionalism is not about having and then expressing deep feelings, as Marianne would flatter herself into believing, but about bad manners. Why should there be any necessary connection between the display of emotions and their authenticity or depth? Emotions come and go in a moment; their very lability, their mercurialness are signs of the fundamental shallowness of most of our emotional experience. Marianne is simply overdramatizing these passing feelings in the name of a phony theory of authenticity – pilloried, as we just saw, by Santayana – which seems to hold that whatever hasty view we form as to the state of our feelings of the moment is some kind of truth that must be outed. Elinor and Austen join in suspecting Marianne's emotionalism to be a pose, the pose being only partly that it poses as the authentic unmediated expression of her emotional nature. The other part of the pose is that she is a fashion follower, caught up in the trendiness of the romantic movement, all the vogue among the young in the early nineteenth century.

If self-command is a pose, a putting up of false fronts in the interests of propriety, it at least owns up to this kind of posing as precisely its virtue. It openly approves of not revealing certain inner states that it would be best not to impose on others or, for prudence's sake, would be best for oneself to keep in reserve. Marianne's position, in contrast, though it ostensibly rejects veils, still must be packaged to sell. Marianne cares to *appear* authentic, not just to be so. Her feelings must be displayed, and that gives her all kinds of choices as to how best to present them. Besides, many of her feelings are had in solitude as when wandering lonely as a cloud, and to get credit for these, she must confess them after the fact, thereby making much of her emotionalism a report of her emotionalism.

One comes to mistrust displays of feeling that attempt to get one credit for feeling oh-so-deeply. Who strikes us as the bigger phony – the free-spirited flower child dancing barefoot to music only she can hear, or the quiet person, very conventional, who locks her thoughts and feelings inside? Back in 1968 it took a very stoned and unself-critical hippie to forget that he was acting, posing, and living life as theatre. What was being a hippie except self-consciously putting on costumes that one was not entitled to wear: the army surplus clothing, the pea coats, the Indian – both North American and Indian subcontinent – outfits. It was not, as I recall someone once saying, about being against the war or getting back to the earth, but about having Halloween 365 days a year. Only a few were aware that it was not authenticity that was being sought, but an inauthenticity so overdone as to play up the falseness of all poses. Any real feeling of authenticity tended to be chemically induced.

Not all phoniness, of course, is on the side of emotion display and letting it all hang out. When the style of sober gravity was in vogue among Puritans in the sixteenth and seventeenth centuries, merry old souls lampooned it mercilessly as phony and fashion following, as errant hypocrisy and humbuggery.

Marianne's style is also criticized as parasitical. It can be indulged in only because Elinor is there to smooth things over after Marianne gives offense, as my wife is there to let me behave less than graciously to guests who are overstaying the limited duration of my welcome. But Austen also hints that the parasitism is mutual. Elinor shines because Marianne is there to make the scenes that put Elinor's extraordinary poise and tact on exquisite display. Each provides a foil for and relief from the style of the other. They even encourage each other to play out their allegory of sense and sensibility by taking such clear delight in each other's mastery of her particular defining trait.[17] They know that they make a good team.

Marianne's impetuosity and imprudence turn out to be not that imprudent (she marries better than Elinor), whereas Elinor's prudent reserve almost costs her her dear Edward, whom she gets only by an improbable marring of the plot. As properly as she has behaved, there seems to be a lesson here. Her self-command needed more leakage so that sufficient glimpses of the passions being hidden were still discreetly discernible.[18] Sometimes you need to let on that your disguises are disguises. One needs to keep reminding people, too, for they forever fall right back into believing the disguise. Your four-year-old can watch you put on a monster mask and then be terrorized when you say boo to him immediately after putting it on.

In sum: don't think that because hypocrisy is a disgusting vice that dissimulation, imperfect motive, and the feigning of views and opinions are not necessary to the cause of virtue. But because virtue must cavort with such suspect company, can we be blamed for mistrusting the moral state of our soul when we are being little more than polite company? And suppose you decide that you will damn all dissimulation and pretense in the interest of unvarnished truth. I give you next the ugly sight of naked truth. And when I have finished I suspect we will all admit the virtue of those small hypocrisies – call them reticences if you will – that make us civil.

# FIVE

# Naked Truth: Hey, Wanna F***?

SO YOU THINK there are times when the demands of politeness, the burdens of restraint are more than you can handle? You think it is easy to shed the trappings of civility? Then why does it take alcohol, exhaustion, or a dare to get you to let the truth about your desires and feelings all hang out (for the daws to peck at)? Norbert Elias would have us believe that it was the work of centuries to make us think politeness was easier than directness. It took a lot of time, a shifting of political and social arrangements, he argues, to make our self-restraint feel more natural than our lack of restraint. But I doubt there was ever a time when it was easier to be truthful than to put on masks and veils, even if the kinds of masks and veils in other times strike us as crude and vulgar now.

Yet there are some who chuck all veneers of civility, claiming (though this is often a pose) to be under the sway of a strong emotion, such as anger, or a strong desire, such as a sexual one. Others do not offer the excuse of a strong desire as long as they have pals, drugs, or booze urging them on to be more vulgar than mere "nature" would ever let them be.

Suppose two people take one look at each other and immediately desire to do the deed. Though it has been known to succeed in certain cultural settings and though it types me as a middle-aged hetero white male of puritanical, uncool, and conventional propensities to be revolted that it does, it usually is not (or at least was not) the case that one says to the other by way of introduction or within minutes of being introduced, "Hey, wanna f***?" I know it is phonily prissy of me not to write "fuck," but it strikes me as even phonier to assume fake boldness or a fake flip casualness and write it. That

*The New Republic, The Nation,* and other respectable organs use "fuck" hardly indicates that it does not involve its user in pretense: the pretense of the weenie feigning coolness. No way to avoid pretense either way. God knows, "Hey, wanna f***?" gets said more than I want to believe, and I would guess the lumpenproletarian biker or bathhouse visitor no guiltier on this score than upper-middle-class affected hip types or any average – I cannot, father of teenage girls, bear the thought – high school junior. If as an empirical matter such directness has become common fare, then let what follows stand for a piece of history rather than a discussion of contemporary mores.

Few (I hope) have the nerve to cut to the chase like that even on a dare. You may have misread the other's desire; nor do you want to think of yourself as that vulgar, even if you have the excuse of doing it on a drunken dare. So problematic is the allure, and the corresponding contaminating power of sex, so holy in a bizarre way, that one must assume all kinds of lengthy ritualized behaviors that avoid directly avowing the desire. So what do we do? We talk, we perform, we engage in elaborate rituals. In short, we rewrite the three-word question into pages and pages, reconstructing it as one elaborate periphrasis.

Nor is the word "f***" to take all the blame. Were you to say, "Would you like to fornicate with me?" you would do no better. In fact you would instead decrease substantially your already low chance of scoring by revealing yourself a vulgar priss rather than just a vulgar yahoo. Clinical language would do what it did in junior high health class: prompt guffaws and giggles. Trying a more romantic tone might be worse, for it suggests that the person asking really thinks he stands a chance, and shows him oblivious to the fact that the constraints imposed by *when* he is asking leave him with "Hey, wanna..." as pretty much his only option: A "Pardon me, you wouldn't by any chance like to make love?" should get him laughed at by the yahoo as well as by the stickler for decorum.

Decorum, respect for others and oneself, and politeness almost always involve saying things in more words than the most direct and most efficient statement of the desire would accommodate. We teach our children not to grunt "ice cream"; we discourage the use of the imperative mood except in the most exigent of circumstances. Politeness requires the indirect expression of reasonable desire, not the complete suppression of it. So it is "May I have some ice cream, please, if it wouldn't be any trouble?" The child adds even more words, mostly in justification, about having had no sweets that day and having eaten a very good dinner, which is a lie, but no matter. The more indirect, the more polite, the more likely it is that the child will get the ice cream as soon as the modestly elongated request is concluded.

Be indirect, and ye shall be served – not too indirect, though. Cultural rules vary greatly on this. Excessive indirectness in the democratic West smacks of Eastern slavish groveling, yes-sahib kind of stuff. People who are ever so hesitant about making even modest requests provoke bursts of frustrated annoyance: damn it, out with it already, OK? And ye shall also not be served all the time. This is the lesson that hits the two-year-old hard when the magic word "please" doesn't work to get her candy anytime she says it. The power of the "please" not to please as advertised may well be a child's first sense that the world is not as enchanted as claimed. Parents, not science and technology, disenchant the world.

Eventually we hope to make such politeness second nature, so one would never think of it as fakery to express the desire as "may I have" rather than grunt "ice cream." But our direct vulgar desirer answers: "I don't grunt 'ice cream'; I ask nice like my mother taught. I say, 'Hey, can I have some ice cream if you got any?' I even add a please. I still get my ice cream when I want it, not much more than a second later. But I don't want to take three weeks of boring talk to get what I want now from that babe; besides, in three weeks I may not want to do it anyway." Given his unwillingness to take risks on the duration of his desires, and his desire to live very much in the present, I suppose he makes sense.

Contrast this with the shy guy who is more than willing to take the days, weeks, months (I leave "years" to those much more persevering than I can imagine) to fulfill his dreams, but who feels ever so acutely that his periphrases are transparent. He thus dies a thousand deaths before asking a woman out for a first date even though he has no thought of doing anything except talking. He is sure that "Would you like to go see *Twelfth Night* with me next Saturday?" will be heard by her as a little hum in the background not quite covering the "Hey, wanna f\*\*\*?" she will impute to him – and that at some level, not far beneath the surface, he imputes to himself.

Sex, quite often not as satisfying as ice cream, can be craved as much at certain times in the presence of certain others. Yet people go through elaborate performances in which they purport to be interested in what the other person does, what books she likes, what food, what movies. They act interested in aspects of the other's soul as well as body; they, mostly the men, fight a desperate battle against the powerful gravitational forces that pull their eyes down to check out body parts beneath the eyes. Even fixing the lips with a look that endures more than a nanosecond is taken as not much different from blurting out the most vulgar declaration of desire.

What is especially interesting in this ritual of faking is that it inevitably becomes more than *mere* fakery. It can lead to disgust for one's initial desire or to a total extinguishing of it, as when the soul of the other turns out to be unignorably dim, shallow, mean, defective, or boring. You find you don't wanna do it with this person anymore. A nicer consequence of faking interest in other things beside *the* thing is that faking in this domain becomes, if not quite an end in itself, then surely a process with considerable charm. Deferring gratification has its own rewards, small pleasures that are sufficient – well, not quite – unto themselves.

Beware of making the easy assumption that it is a sign of how deep the desire is that one is willing to invest so much time in talk, talk, talk, and more talk. The amount of time you put in can support exactly opposite meanings; it can mean you really really want to do it so much that you are willing to invest considerably in getting there, or it can equally mean you really want to find a colorable excuse for postponing the dark deed.[1] Delay is more than just a rational means to get where you thought at the start you wanted to go. It also reveals to you and to the other that you are discounting somewhat your belief in your own desire. You think you wanna do the deed, but in fact you are scared of it, too – so much risk of humiliation or of befuddlement. Part of you is willing to run away without actually doing it as long as you get some assurance that the other desired you or at least did not find you repulsive.

The faking of interest in other things besides the *big* desire lets your ambivalence about sex and your doubts about your desire have their say, giving you the chance to escape if you wish. The part of you that wants to do it is, you fear or at least wonder, not you, or not all of you, or not the real you. You have the feeling sometimes that your desire exists independently of you, that it is an invader from the outside. Or you experience it as your genitals engaging in a coup d'etat that will not bring a stable regime into power. The new regime will collapse about fifteen minutes after the takeover, if, that is, it has not already failed attempting to storm the breach.

But also beware of thinking that blurting out an unadorned vulgar desire is any indication of its strength or clarity. If avoiding sex is vaguely a part of your complex set of desires, there is probably no better way to accomplish it than by coming on with a "Hey, wanna f***?" Even if you truly want to do it, coming on like that is a way to defend yourself against the pain of rejection because you have to go in expecting to be refused; you in fact are inviting refusal. If you ask like that and do mean it, your question is dealt with as not having been meant and, if you are lucky, is laughed off as a bad joke. (Treating egregious violations of norms of propriety as merely failed attempts at humor is one of the classic strategies of tact to salvage a bad situation.)

Who possibly can expect such an offer to be accepted, assuming it is a male making it to a female? Not so dumb, those vulgar yahoos; their very vulgarity proves to be the perfect defense against the pain of rejection, which, I am sure, these touchingly sensitive souls would rather avoid. Their vulgarity, to be sure, is more than a defense against rejection; the indecency of the come-on provides its own form of very cheap erotic thrill. Bizarrely enough, though, the eminent refusability of such an offer is politeness itself compared with offers made in such a way that all avenues of polite refusal are closed off, the kind of offers mere acquaintances and relatives make: you wouldn't by any chance be free sometime this year to come over for dinner, would you? Let's pick a date right now.[2]

And those souls who in fact have an unambivalent desire and express it with vulgar directness seldom do so outside a cultural or social setting where it stands some chance of success. The yahoo male will be drawn to yahoo females in a place where yahoos congregate. And once he is there, alcohol, drugs, and raucous conviviality will provide an excusing plea should he misjudge. Even such direct expressers of desire as then-Governor Bill Clinton did not abandon all decorum when seeking the services of Ms. Jones. With pants down, he asked if she would "kiss it." Kiss it?! In the midst of the most vulgar of come-ons delicacy pokes (sorry) its head up through the harsh soil of raw desire. Could we expel euphemism from this domain even if we wanted to? This may be the realm of the unnamable, where euphemism must intrude.[3]

Direct vulgarity is a strategy more available to men than to women. Should a woman come on like that to a man and be turned down, it would leave her nearly defenseless, because the yes is assumed, though, truth be told, the male "yes" really means, if not "no," then "Well, I guess I will if I have to." We must distinguish, however, between those males who actually stand a better chance coming on like that – people whose best moment is the first no matter how vulgar the first moment may be – and those for whom time works small miracles. Charm needs time, and not all that much depending on how much physical unattractiveness it needs to compensate for. Funny thing about charm: it can be openly seen to be so much roguish fakery by the object of it. That is often part of charm's charm, but the charming person need not feel as if he is faking it for being charming; he may be fully immersed in wanting to be admired and liked for his charm. And when he sees that his charm is working, why then, he just may pop the question, "Hey...": or better, the object of his attention will spare him that burden and ask first.

One of central themes – if not the central theme – of a good portion of nineteenth-century English novels of manners is how to get the truth across despite the veils with which we clothe it, or equally how to repair the damage when we let truth show a little too much skin.

No one does better than Anthony Trollope, especially in his delicious treatment of this theme in *Framley Parsonage*.[4]

Miss Dunstable is a rich heiress set upon by impecunious aristocratic fortune seekers. She is too smart to believe that their declarations of love are sincere, and she is something of a plain speaker herself, possessing "a thorough love of ridiculing all the world's humbugs." She has a friend, a Mrs. Harold Smith, who has an insolvent brother about to lose his landed estate unless he can come into funds fairly soon. Mrs. Smith urges her brother, Mr. Sowerby, to woo Miss Dunstable, not as others have done with declarations of love, but with the truth: that he is in financial straits and he wants her money. "Needy peers have tried . . . and have failed because they have pretended that they were in love with her. It may be difficult but your only chance is to tell her the truth." But Mr. Sowerby is of insufficient courage to ask so directly for her money in exchange for his bloodlines, and he commissions his sister to make the proposal for him.

Even she, a cynical pragmatist, quails. When Mrs. Smith tries to set forth the terms of the conversation to be "that the truth should be told scrupulously on all sides; the truth, the whole truth, and nothing but the truth," Miss Dunstable, discerning immediately what is coming, concurs. But Mrs. Smith can't get herself to speak the truth without varnishing and veneering her shameless proposal to make it a little less unseemly, a little more palatable. Miss Dunstable, however, will have no comb-overs on the bald truth, and with almost sadistic delight she calls Mrs. Smith back to the task and to the rules that Mrs. Smith herself proposed about getting to the naked truth. " '*Magna est veritas*, as the dear bishop said,' exclaimed Miss Dunstable. 'Let us have the truth, the whole truth, and nothing but the truth, as we agreed just now.' "

Miss Dunstable begins to cross-examine her friend and keeps forcing her back to the unvarnished truth. And Mrs. Smith is offended! It is Miss Dunstable, to Mrs. Smith's mind, who is the one not minding her manners by not letting herself be fleeced without making a scene about it. And so Mrs. Smith admonishes Miss Dunstable for not making her tasteless task easier:

"But you are so hard on one, my dear, with your running after honesty, that one is not able to tell the real facts as they are. You make one speak in such a bald, naked way."

"Ah, you think that anything naked must be indecent; even truth."

"I think it is more proper-looking, and better suited, too, for the world's work, when it goes about with some sort of garment on it. We are so used to a leaven of falsehood in all we hear and say, nowadays, that nothing is more likely to deceive us than the absolute truth."

The chapter goes on more mischievously as to how little truth we can tolerate, and how even the most straight-talking person needs respite from it, some softening, some fakery. Several points are dramatized here that were made more crudely earlier in the discussion. Truth telling is hard to do, even when it has been resolved upon, even when it has been laid down to all parties as a challenge, even when we are drunk. And here it is the cynical would-be truth teller, Mrs. Smith, who cannot bear not to pull a sheet up over the naked truth she vowed to adopt as her best strategy to obtain the hand and fortune of Miss Dunstable for her brother.

Especially astute psychologically is the depiction of how hard it is to *keep* telling the naked truth once we have embarked upon it. We can blurt out a line of unvarnished truth or steel ourselves to make one quick statement of it, but to have to keep it up for a whole conversation without easing up, without backtracking to take the sting out of parts, without restating it in ever softer ways, is nearly impossible for anyone but a sadist, a persnickety literalist, or someone in the throes of a fairly enduring fury. That is why Miss Dunstable must keep calling Mrs. Smith back to the ground rules and why Mrs. Smith starts to blame Miss Dunstable for not making it easier for her to make her crudely self-interested proposal a little less crudely.

The social psychological and philosophical literature focuses on the ways in which we see the world through rose-colored glasses and hear what we want to hear, or how the beams in our eyes blind us to the truth about ourselves. It may be harder, though, to speak hard truth to others than to speak it to ourselves. The deception of others is prior to the deception of ourselves, evolutionarily to be sure, but even psychologically. Many of the cognitive biases that lead us to sugar the truth to our own advantage may be hard-wired, but they are surely reinforced, maybe even generated in part, by our inability to *tell* unkind truth, not to hear it told.[5] Our sympathetic mechanisms put barriers in the way.

There are other, more self-interested reasons we keep the truth to ourselves. We don't trust what it would mean for the entire conversational and moral order if we were to speak truth except euphemistically. We fear the chaos, and the revenge that would recoil upon us. There is also a connection between the primitive taboo against saying the name of God and the still thriving taboo against saying the naked truth. We clothe His name in aliases, as we clothe our bodies, and as we clothe harsh truth in conventional social fakeries and poses.

Not all truth needs to be treated so charily. It is only certain kinds of truth that are taboo, those that can be thought of as naked and thus as ugly. We cannot avow openly, as Adam Smith says, our naked self-interest or the desires of our body, except perhaps when it needs to sleep and eat, and even these needs must be mentioned with some delicacy (TMS I.ii.1). This means, rightly, that sexual desire, no matter how beautiful the desirer and the desired may be, is ugly truth that needs proper clothing. But should I with exuberant sincerity praise the beauty of your singing voice or the grace of your prose, all due directness is not only tolerated but also welcomed.

The tag "the truth, the whole truth and nothing but the truth" becomes its own joke in this Trollope passage and elsewhere, for it is ever more difficult to fulfill the more it is demanded. It is a tag whose association with perjury is much more insistent than its association with truth. It sets up conflicting demands: the *whole* truth must be limited by rules of relevance; we never get *the* whole, but *a* whole. The "nothing but" requirement lets in too little, for very little can meet a "nothing but" truth standard. Varnish there must be. Though it is trite to say so, it might be that the ugly truth is one of those things that are best gotten at indirectly or as byproducts than when it is demanded nakedly; something in us reaches to pull up the sheet to cover the shame of its nakedness.

The core irony of the passage, it turns out, is that once truth enters the social domain as a strategy to advance self-interest it is magically transformed into a fake, a pose, an act, and it becomes more deceiving than the standard deceptions and poses of politeness and civility: "We are so used to a leaven of falsehood in all we hear and say, nowadays, that nothing is more likely to deceive us than the absolute truth." The choice facing Mrs. Smith, in other words, is not between truth and hypocritical niceties but between different social posturings: one of small lies and indirection, which we can pretty much play by rote and still get the message across, and the other, naked truth, which requires dares, drink, or drugs to steel ourselves to perform.

The next two chapters examine certain ritual practices – prayer and apology, itself a form of prayer – and explore how these are variously infected with hypocrisy and the anxieties of faking it. These are followed by a chapter – chapter 8 – devoted to more homely matters of praise and flattery, both of which are also intimately involved with prayer, if not so much with apology.

# SIX

# In Divine Services and Other Ritualized Performances

MANY SITUATIONS DEMANDING POLITENESS – routine greetings and inquiries about health and welfare – are ritualized, but ritualized without our sensing that it is ritual with a capital *R*. The big *R* attaches to formal events that mark major life-cycle changes – as in Bar and Bat Mitzvahs and other initiation rites, communions, weddings, funerals, graduations – or to occasions of paying public homage that often require singing or reciting in unison, as in the national anthem or prayer services. Big *R* ritual seems to involve something that we can call, if we do not fear being struck down by some offended power, hocus-pocus; it is distinguished from the small rituals of daily life by a sacred separation.

The expression "hocus-pocus," being mock Latin, also raises another aspect of Ritual. It is often carried out in a language we don't quite understand, as when I pray in Hebrew or Catholics used to pray in Latin, or when Protestants recently used the King James Bible, or when kids have not a clue as to what the words are or mean, though in English, when they sing Christmas carols or the national anthem or say the pledge of allegiance. What of the "forgive us our trespasses" of the Lord's prayer, where it was understood that cutting across Mrs. Keappock's lawn ranked right up there with murder in what got God really mad. What eight-year-old knew what "plejallegiance" was or why one nation was "invisible"?

Reform movements in religion often make the inaccessibility of sacred language to the laity the rallying point of their program. But that seems to miss the point of what defines sacredness: its inaccessibility. So much of the uncanniness of successful Ritual depends precisely on our not understanding what is said, probably because we think Ritual should be dealing with the mysterious, the incomprehensible, the ineffable. Thus certain branches of Protestantism managed inevitably to find newer forms of obfuscation to make up for the gap in Ritual Dignity that was undone by each new modernization of the Bible translation, even those sects, it seems, that at their official core are hostile to all Ritual. Some of these sects go for speaking in tongues; others have hymns do the work of separating Ritual out from the too familiar, hymns whose forceful musical phrases make the lyrics become bearers more of transporting melody than of literal meaning. Or, to put it another way, the words bear the meaning of the melody, not the melody the meaning of the words.

The worry that we are faking it – whether in fact we are or aren't – has a special flavor in these contexts, especially in formal prayer services but also in other big Rituals. Why, for instance, do we feel more urges to get the giggles in them than in nonritualized settings? The giggles are not brought on by the mere demand to play a role we are not up to playing, for then we would get the giggles every time we feigned interest in a conversation. Something else is at work here that has to do with the special status of Ritual, Decorum, Seriousness, Prohibition, and faking it in highly contrived settings in which we might be a little spooked, a bit unsettled by what we feel are the costs of not convincingly faking it. For one, the powerful demand for solemnity and grave behavior is almost felt as a dare not to get the giggles. More than the willful disobedience in the Garden of Eden, getting the giggles is the profoundest revolt against authority that we have at our disposal, perhaps because it is really not at our disposal but comes unbidden, the very image of unvarnished truth. For another, Ritual seems to invite us to suffer breaks with total immersion and see the whole pageant as the highly contrived performance it is. The actors for a mere moment are seen as puppets, mechanical, as ciphers, and this vision is loaded with comic possibility.[1] The urge to get the giggles bears testimony to the fact that the demand Ritual makes on us to suspend disbelief is at times no easy task.

Part of the way Ritual achieves a feeling of sacred separation from the commonplace is by not letting you forget that the whole thing is staged and then asking you simultaneously to forget you know that it is staged so that you can be transported by it. There is much comic possibility in the contrasting visions. When we see people with their "game faces" on in a moment when we are less than fully immersed, they can look ridiculous. I know the "we" here is not universal, but it is common enough, especially at certain ages, younger rather than older. Only rarely do I feel the urge now to get the giggles at funerals or weddings, or during graduation speeches and religious services. I was plagued by such urges when younger. But the truth is that as we grow older the threat of the giggles becomes quite remote. Moreover, with advancing age ancient rituals are more likely to move us, to fill us with mystical moments of connection with people long dead. When I was young, such rituals, if ever moving, were moving, not because of their ancient links of past to present but because of the music. Also, the duty to set a decorous example for my kids puts a damper on things, though this in itself can trigger the giggles, especially when one of the kids has already succumbed to them. Then too, I fear, I am tired now, and less likely to find mirth in, or rage against, absurdity.

I have no intention of ridiculing the religious, being mostly respectfully so myself in the sense that, though only moderately observant, I "believe" that if someone speaks serious ill of his parents the heavens will open up and strike him dead; or should the blasphemer blithely continue unharmed it is more because the gods are asleep than that they did not care to kill him. I also believe in an absolute obligation to pass on my Judaism, such as it is, to my children. I should be rightly cursed and feel in fact that I will be damned, if I, out of laziness, should break a chain 3,000 years long. Far be it from me to pretend to great virtue. I do not do nearly as much as I should for however concerned I sound. I do just enough to pass it on to avoid the curse. If my kids wrestle with the same fear of the curse then I will have done my minimal duty.

In other words, I have a very primitive sense of belief in some force that might play havoc in my life if I don't shape up. Occasionally I ask this force, whom I do think of as God, to refrain from focusing hostile intention on me, and whom I ask also, on occasion, rather to do so on my enemies or bad people in general unless they are my friends. I used quotation marks around "believe" in the previous paragraph to indicate that I am half-joking, but only *half*-joking. The belief basically boils down to the experience of something that can aptly be described as getting the heebie-jeebies in settings where a pure rationalist or secularist should not have them and who then finds himself anxiously explaining them away as silly and irrational. It is belief, but belief that is subject to a moderately high discount rate.

My sincere feeling of engagement in religious ritual enlivens itself mostly in a rather small domain in which the ritual has a primitive feel to it. The circumcision ceremony and the blowing of the shofar, or ram's horn, have that power, as do the reading of the sacrifice of Isaac on the second day of Rosh Hashannah[2] and the celebration of the Passover seder, which was also Jesus' Last Supper. There is a danger, though, in a fascination with the primitive. One does not want to get too carried away with it: circumcision OK, but no killing animals or humans. The Nazis, I guiltily remind myself, loved the cheap thrills of primitivism, and they manufactured stagy primitive rituals, which got them to feel visceral connections to imagined fake pasts.

So much of the so-called primitive is invented for the purpose of looking primitive. Phony or real – much in the way that the forms of sentimentality are irresistible – the primitive can move us even when we suspect it is part of a quest for false authenticity. But the shivers from the shofar don't come cheap – to say nothing of those sympathetic agonies that convulse those witnessing a circumcision; there is nothing false about them. The shofar follows hours of prayer, and the ritual has been performed every year, not for mere centuries but for millennia. The continuity is everything; it legitimates the feeling of connectedness and gives substance to the heebie-jeebies it elicits. A resurrected ritual of ancient pedigree long dead strikes us as no less phony than a wholly invented new one. But an unbroken chain of title two and half thousand years long immunizes chills and thrills against any fear that you might feel embarrassed or fake for feeling them.

## Staying Focused during Prayer

Being bored during prayer services has a long tradition. Bishops complained of congregants laughing at martyrologies in the seventh century.[3] Monks suffered from *acedia*, or despair, a disease whose chief symptom was paralyzing boredom from having to pray all the time.[4] Rabbis post advice on the Internet as to how to overcome boredom while praying.[5] Memoirists, when describing the horrors of childhood, invariably devote attention to the miseries of church attendance.

Must we never be bored while praying? Do all species of boredom in church undermine the sincerity and authenticity of our service to the service? Maybe we are being too hard on ourselves? One of the chief thoughts that makes us doubt the authenticity of our prayer is that we feel we have to mean it; we are not often sure we can meet that standard when the prayer is a formal one, composed by another. Just what does it mean to mean a prayer when you are praying in a language you don't understand? Are no Jews except those who understand Hebrew sincerely praying during services? It can't mean that. But this does not mean that a person mouthing syllables that make no linguistic sense to him will not suffer an occasional sense of wondering whether he is not engaging in a charade. That very feeling is much of the impetus behind reform movements that argue for making scripture and liturgy accessible.

Meaning the words is one thing, praying as a ritual performance is another. You may not be attending to the words, but you mean the act of reverence, which need not mean you are actually experiencing feelings of reverence, only that you are carrying on your commitment to attend services and take part. Some days your thoughts will be properly pious, and other days you will be distracted; still you pay lip service on those days – doing it when you don't feel like it and aren't into it – and that is what demonstrates your commitment. Those who say a standard prayer before meals are seldom thanking God with a feeling of gratitude or thankfulness. Nonetheless, they are paying their respects.

Catholics make a useful distinction between mental and vocal prayer. The former requires a high degree of attention, or else why do it? No one, after all, is checking to see whether or not you are. Mental prayer is meditative and usually takes place in private settings. By definition, it ceases the moment it is not centrally occupying consciousness. Vocal prayer, in contrast, tends to be communal and part of a service, office, or Mass. Here a more accommodating attitude is taken: respectful attention, conforming your outside behavior, and saying the words; and as long as your thoughts don't turn to images inconsistent with the prayer you are OK. No levity, no fantasizing about sex, but you do not have to be thinking about the precise words you are saying beyond the mere saying of them. This view would wisely deem you to be properly praying when you are beset with anxieties that go to whether you are appropriately focused – even when, that is, you feel you are faking it. That feeling, after all, can be construed as evidence of a respectful concern about proper conformity to the demands of the occasion.[6]

The claim I just made – that the feeling of faking is a kind of homage – is perhaps too generous. It depends on why you feel you are faking it. You must evince *respectful* concern about whether you are meeting the demands of the occasion, but respect is precisely what you feel you are faking with your lips and posture. Your thoughts are variously roaming from anxiety about faking it (which is arguably respectful) to erotic thoughts about someone a few rows up to the right or left (a complaint frequently registered in medieval popular moral literature) to wondering why there are only three people taller than six feet in my synagogue service and one of them is a recently converted Dutch woman. Surely, wondering why the beauty sitting there last week is absent today means that you are completely faking it. What about thoughts devoted to praying but that are impious? You, for instance, loathe the tune of the prayer you are singing, worried that because you hate it you will be humming it for days. And indeed three days later your worst fears have been confirmed, making you wonder whether the malevolent DJ is your punishing conscience or just one of God's mischievous messengers.

You start wondering whether it is the obligation of every Jew to go through the motions of service attendance to spite Hitler, or because you feel guilty if you don't, or because you have to set an example of proper faking it for your kids, who are also complaining about the interminability of the service.[7] Though each of these distracting thoughts and events detracts from full immersion in prayer and thus can give rise to the anxiety of faking it, only some of them convict you of serious faking. Others come close to the line, but one suspects that these kinds of doubts have been widely experienced. How could they not, given that everyone since you were a small child has been lecturing you on the assumption that that is what was going on in your head?

Some prayers more than others are likely to be faked or to engender doubts about whether they are being faked. We can, for our purposes, divide prayers into two main kinds that have considerable overlap with the mental/vocal categories the Catholics employ: prayers that are likely to generate the anxiety that we are faking them and those that do not. Certain kinds of prayers grab us more readily than others – those, for instance, not said in divine services as part of a scripted pageant but that we compose ourselves. These are the prayers we find ourselves saying when we wish to mobilize the deity quickly or thank him profusely, often when we are in the embrace of some strong emotion such as fear or relief. To be sure, such prayers follow predictable forms and arise in predictable settings, but they have the authenticity of spontaneity.[8] Not that spontaneous prayers cannot be faked; I would imagine that in certain charismatic religions one must fake them all the time.[9]

Prayers of petition, particularly for immediate delivery from enemies, prayers in which in the biblical sense we "cry out" to or "cry unto" God, are much less likely to be beset with anxieties of fakery than prayers of thanksgiving, unless the gratitude is an expression of the "phew" of relief, as when narrowly escaping death, shame, or a visit from a Jehovah's Witness. Thus prayers uttered in foxholes are completely sincere, although some soldier memoirs take note of the self-conscious form these prayers take when a nonbeliever finds himself praying for the first time since his childhood.[10] One soldier began, "God, if you get me out of this scrape, I promise to believe in you." But a prayer taking that form is not faked – quite the contrary. It is as sincere a form of asking God to reveal Himself as can be made. The person praying may indeed sense the irony, if his fear allows any room for irony, but he feels no anxiety on account of not being into his prayer; he rightly does not feel that he is faking it.

64

Routinized prayers of confession, on the other hand, involve layers of shamming, lies mixed with feelings of fakery. How many Catholics did not invent sins to confess as kids? To have none was to convict yourself of the sin of pride or of having a log in your eye, or, worse, it was to tip the priest off that you were hiding something really big. No way you were going to confess the sins of your sexual awakening. Got to go to confession: what bad things did I do this week? I am sure I lied to my mother three times and fought with my sisters. That will do yet again this week, but can't I be more imaginative? Faking it and feeling that you are faking it, already from mere babes.

Prayers in which we humble ourselves before God by proclaiming how unworthy we are of His grace or of His beneficent attention have a certain amount of playacting and shamming built in. There are people who manage to convince themselves of the truth of their abnegation; some may indeed be sincere, but they must avoid the snares of the hairshirt problem – feeling proud or quite pleased with how good they are at humility and abnegation. "Who am I to beseech thee, O Lord; I who am but a disgusting worm, nay, the wormiest of all, the lowest of the low – first place, in fact, among the low." Prayers of confessional abnegation are usually combined with a petition for grace or forgiveness; surely the petitionary part is not being faked, but the same cannot be said for the abnegatory parts.

This kind of prayer is at its core in grave tension with itself, a tension captured nicely by the ever-nasty sensibility of Ambrose Bierce, who consistently makes La Rochefoucauld look like a sentimental softy: "*pray*, v. To ask that the laws of the universe be annulled in behalf of a single petitioner confessedly unworthy." It takes chutzpah to make a demand on God, to presume on His attention and time. Despite your care to engage in rituals of humiliation, to don sackcloth, to cover yourself with ashes, to flagellate yourself, there is a presumptuousness in your demand for attention. These abnegatory rituals themselves are attention-getting. You may very well mean the prayer, but you may also sense your showmanship in the abnegation, especially because such shows are themselves highly scripted. If you really feel your special vileness, not just in a vaguely philosophical way that makes you indistinguishable from the rest of sinful and corrupt humanity, how could you dare approach the font of purity?

Some, though, felt their wormhood so sincerely that they despaired of God's grace and did not pray. No faking there at all. The theologians intervened to proclaim them guilty of the sin of despair, the sin against the Holy Ghost. You must not abandon prayer. Your self-esteem is not to be so low that you are ever to doubt God's powers regarding your salvation; if you are in your own sight as a grasshopper and think others see you the same way, you get hit with forty more years in the desert (Num. 13.33). But there is reason to think that petitionary prayer, surely the foxhole variety, is the surest sign of despair there is, a giving up of all hope except the last very long-odds gamble that God will pay heed to your cry for help. The Victorian schoolgirl quoted earlier saw it that way; her routine prayers for chocolate pudding or for illness to befall her teachers were never answered "so that on the whole I thought Him incorruptible..." When she realized that any God she could believe in would have to be impartial, prayers of petition ceased to make sense to her: "It was as if you were trying to bribe the judge." "After that, prayer became synonymous for me with giving up hope; if ever I prayed again, it was only in a final frenzy of despair."[11] In that frenzy one is too distracted to indulge in anxieties of fakery.

When the stakes were high and sincerity was of the utmost importance, as in a communal fast decreed to beg God to relieve a drought, the Jewish oral law (the Mishnah) sought to reduce the risk that the person chosen to lead the prayers would not be properly motivated. He was thus to be a man "who has children and whose house is empty (i.e., he is destitute) *so that his heart will be perfect in the prayer.*"[12] Now there was a man who would mean his prayers; his humiliation was not a ritual show put on for the occasion but instead was his true lot in life, imposed upon him by his poverty and the desperate need of his children. I must confess to taking some small pleasure in seeing that my anxieties on this score are not postmodern nor even modern but have been troubling people for millennia.

We don't feel we are faking when we bark out those daily prayers beseeching God to damn people and things. These precations are almost always exaggerated. Indeed they are ritualized exaggerations; they are meant, but not literally. You don't really want to consign someone to hell for an eternity for cutting you off in traffic; you do not even wish to apply a hammer to his kneecap; you would settle for someone keying his car or for him to gesture apologetically. The curse of "Goddamn it," by being overstated, helps dissipate our momentary desires for violent revenge and is itself cathartic. Curses are prayers that thus partly answer themselves by giving relief. No matter how many times you use them, they have a certain inexhaustible potency and charm. Chaucer's perfectly told *Friar's Tale* makes the point nicely about the difference between actually meaning our exaggerated curses on the one hand, and meaning only to exaggerate and blow off steam on the other. The person who really means those curses goes to hell along with what he asked to be damned should he not relent.[13]

Formal prayers are the problem. Of these, some have more immediacy than others – the psalms, for instance. Many are curse poems directed at enemies or are grim solicitations for help in taking revenge. Some even berate God Himself for abandoning His faithful worshiper, the narrator of the poem.[14] These are passionate themes that prompt our sympathetic identification with the psalmist. Those few that are hymns of general adoration and glorification make that identification harder. I surely can mean a prayer that asks for a good harvest, but not with the fervor I ask for vengeance upon my enemies. Back when calories were scarce for all except the rich, prayers for a good harvest engaged a petitioner more fully than now, in America at least, where calories are not scarce enough. Hymns of thanksgiving, when coupled with glorying over the mayhem God has inflicted on our enemies, also have a good chance of being, in the words of Adam Smith, the subtlest theorist of sympathetic identification, "enter[ed] into."[15]

Like the simple melodic beauty of the best Protestant hymns, in which the music simply lifts you up by the shirt collar into meaning whatever it is you are singing, the poetic power of the Psalms gives one chills that can be mistaken for reverence for God or can be fused with it. They induce, almost involuntarily, a sense of respectfulness as a tribute to the sheer force of the imagery and emotional intensity of the verse. The infectious power of calls to revenge focus attention, especially in perhaps the grandest *cri du coeur* in world literature: "By the rivers of Babylon, there we sat down, yea we wept..."; or some command our notice because of their stunning lyricism, gaining the added push of its being mobilized in moments of genuine danger from real enemies: "The Lord is my shepherd, I shall not want...."

It has hardly been Judaism or Protestantism that has benefited most from the easy confusion between aesthetic awe and feelings of religiosity. That laurel belongs to the Catholic Church. The spate of conversions to Catholicism among the cultured, among aesthetes, from the mid-nineteenth century well into the twentieth, must surely have led some of those converts to wonder whether they were not faking it, getting their religion all nice and pretty, and confusing awe for human productions in painting, song, architecture, sculpture, stained glass, and verse, for divinely inspired chills. But why not welcome whatever works? We piggyback on the religiously inspired productions of others, letting their inspiration lead us to our God.

## The Amidah

Once we get away from cursing, thank-yous for escapes from close calls, cryings out to deliver us from enemies, pleas to God not to expose us as fakes to our friends and enemies – once, that is, we are beyond the immediately personal into the prayer service itself – the anxiety of faking it is much more intrusive. Let me give one example that comes from the Jewish liturgy, but that I would imagine is not dissimilar to the experience of many Catholics during lengthy litanies, and Protestants in charismatic sects when too many people start speaking in tongues and it is time to go home for lunch.[16]

The standard Jewish liturgy contains a prayer called the Amidah, quite possibly the most ancient prayer in the formal liturgy, nearly 2,500 years old.[17] It is long and is to be read silently in Hebrew while standing (the word "Amidah" comes from the root for "to stand"). Depending on the holiday, it can run to some ten pages or more. Given the limited facility many in the congregation have for reading the Hebrew script (even fewer understand the Hebrew they are saying), it could easily take the scrupulous person fifteen minutes to read. When finished, you can sit down. Once the congregants have completed their silent devotion, the entire lengthy prayer – this is the truth – is repeated out loud from the altar.

Ritual always involves repetition but not of this magnitude and duration (the cantor at my synagogue last Rosh Hashanah managed to burden each syllable with so many notes that the repetition of the Amidah lasted eighty, yes, eighty excruciating minutes). One senses a whiff of rabbinic cunning: the ancient sages suspected that many would not resist the temptation to cheat at their silent devotion and so decided to visit the sins of the fakers upon faker and nonfaker alike. Maimonides, in the twelfth century, admits as much. The Amidah is repeated, he says, "in order that anyone who has not recited the prayer [silently] shall be regarded as having discharged his obligation." Thus those who do not know the prayer, he says, finding a pious reason, get the benefit of the presiding reader reading it for them.[18] But he is ruthless, for if you recite it without proper devotion you are to recite it again, he says, this time devoutly.[19] The Sages meant it when they said you were to mean this prayer when you said (or did not say) it.

In contemporary conservative congregations, most people, I would guess, are faking, skimming at best, but mostly skipping whole big sections. One can hear the buzz of fake Hebrew. People surreptitiously look to see what page others are pretending to be on and then decorously turn a page ahead of that. Finally a few people start to sit down. I strategize as to when I, who could barely muddle through my Bar Mitzvah portion, can plausibly sit down and not expose myself as a cheat. I read a few sentences, then switch over to the English translation on the opposite page for a few, then back to the Hebrew. Then I skim a bit, then pretend two pages are stuck together, then just gaze around. I sit down after about a third of the congregation has already given up, mostly to set a good example for my kids. Within a minute or two all but five or six people are seated. No more than six minutes have passed since the congregation launched forth on its silent prayer, not enough time for more than the gifted few to have read it even in English.

A complete convergence of communal faking with no one owning up to it! It's one of those secrets that everyone knows, and everyone expects that everyone knows, but no one is quite willing to confess. The secret is as well kept as the one men so carefully guarded from one another for centuries (obviously not from women), recently exposed when Viagra came out; every guy thought only he had the problem. A recent convert with whom I was discussing faking the Amidah told me that she would stand there, reading at her pathetically slow pace, making sure to say every word to herself, painfully self-conscious about holding up the service and feeling she did not belong. She blamed her lack of practice with Hebrew script, even her non-Jewish genes. She began to fake, she said, to avoid feeling so exposed, and then she suffered feeling like a complete fake Jew for faking the prayer, believing herself to be the only one faking. I told her to relax, that by faking the Amidah she had proved herself at least as much a Jew as I was. But I warned her that she would feel that somehow her fakery was worse than everyone else's and that she would still not quite believe they really were faking it to the same extent she was.

What of those five or six left standing? There was the one convert, but the rest were zealous young religious types, who unlike the old religious types did not have the grace to know that they should not be keeping everyone waiting because we were going to have to repeat it anyway. Says Maimonides: "One who recites his prayers with a congregation should not unduly protract its recital."[20] Devotion to God must give way to mannerliness and consideration of others' limited capacity for by-the-letter devotion. Eventually, even the rabbi would get impatient with the zealots and begin the repetition from the pulpit while they continued their silent devotion.

I WAS YOUNG when I first cheated at the Amidah. It was at a Jewish religious camp I was shipped off to for the summer when I was eleven. My being sent to this camp was, I suspect, my parents' way of exorcizing their guilt about the secularism of our home while at the same time getting the benefit of the peace and quiet my absence would yield them. Here I was first introduced to a group of boys who competed more zealously for who could daven the fastest than for who could run fastest or catch the best.

*Davening* is praying, rocking back and forth as you half mumble, half-hum the Hebrew you are pretending to read. Needless to say, this too led to all kinds of anxieties, and I for one could never rock back and forth during prayers without feeling a complete fool and fraud. I always did so rather embarrassedly, botching the performance horrendously. How did anyone overcome embarrassment to fake this adequately? (Conservative Jews still engage in a modest rock, reform Jews have gone completely, WASPishly still.) It was simply beyond me, of an ilk with cheering with abandon at high school pep rallies, with doing karate yells, or with saying "groovy" in 1968. To my mind there was no way a self-respecting, self-monitoring person could do or say these things without feeling like an idiot. I could never do full-Megillah davening, even when I was the only one not doing it, as was the case at this camp. I would be only too happy to claim this willingness to stand thus apart as a kind of moral courage, but it was no such thing: I was too self-conscious, more embarrassed in my own eyes for doing it than I would be in their eyes for not.

Was my self-consciousness a pathetic form of incipient self-hatred, seeing the world a little too much through Christian eyes, or did young Jews growing up in the shtetl have the same anxiety about davening, in their case experienced as faking being a pious adult? Or was it only fearing that I would look so obviously hypocritical, trumpeting self-evidently fake piety? I settled for a very mild sway, a mere shifting of my weight from foot to foot. Given the long time a Jew is asked to stand during prayer my small movements were thus explicable as purely natural and thus, I fancied, not too hypocritical nor so indecorous that I would be embarrassed if a Christian saw me. Thus did I join the fray in a kind of lame fashion, starting light years behind, being about the only kid in the camp not to come from a kosher home. Keeping kosher in Green Bay would have meant vegetarianism because there were too few Jews to support a butcher; and in those days most intelligent people felt vegetarianism would lead to death by malnutrition, if not by pretension. Pretentious vegetarianism still lay a few decades in the future.

For half the summer I braved the looks of the faster readers waiting for me to sit down, for in this camp the rabbi waited until all had finished before beginning the repetition. I wish I could say I had coldly calculated that, by standing and facing everyone's hostility, I was winning points in the piety game. Truth be told I had been skipping paragraphs right from the start, and I was still the last kid standing; I had been cheating too modestly. I was completely snookered by the other kids, who I believed were not faking it in the least. I could not believe that religious Jews would do such a thing or would need to do such a thing.

Maybe these guys could really read their Hebrew at the speed of sound, some apparently at the speed of light (a colleague remonstrates that I should not seek to attribute to others my ineptitude at reading Hebrew script). There was for me only one solution: give up on my nickel and dime faking and fake wholesale. I developed the technique of mumbling out a real Hebrew phrase here and there so that those around me would hear the place on each page I was staking my false claim to. Each day I sat down a little earlier, until I had risen to be in the top third, now a really adept speed-reader myself.

Formal secular rituals generate similar anxieties, even a routine "Star Spangled Banner" before a ballgame. Everyone knows that you can start cheering during the last line of the anthem without being sacrilegious, though it would be bad form, no matter how big the game, to start yelling before "oh say does that star spangled banner yet wave." Knowing when to cheer does not present much of a problem; it's how to stand and whether to sing. Should I take off my hat, do I put my hand over my heart, do I stop chewing my gum? Do I sing robustly with all the signs of patriotic fervor, or do I kind of hum along? Do I purposely sing an octave lower to outmacho the guy next to me? While all this is going on, how are the feelings of patriotic reverence supposed to be attended to? Unless there is a flyover. Then I am moved to tears by the beauty of those jet fighters, by the precision of the flight, by their sudden appearance and equally sudden departure, by the noise. I have thoughts like, "Oh Lord, I will accept a raise in taxes if it goes to making things that beautiful; yes, increase defense spending as a form of subsidy to the arts." Complete and total reverence. And then it is time for the kickoff.

That digression into football prompts other memories in which hard spiritual choices were to be made: whether Rosh Hashanah was compatible with getting to the Packer game on time; the game trumped the second-day observances, but what about the first day? As for Yom Kippur, my father insisted Yom Kippur won. That did not stop the president of the congregation from hiding, though not from my discerning eye, a radio earpiece under his prayer shawl and covering his head with the shawl in an act of extreme piety better to hide the sacrilege. One can bet that he was sincerely praying, he being a gambler, that the Packers might cover the spread.

## Cynical Ceremony

The Amidah, despite being widely faked, is part of ritual that people take seriously. Consider, however, a culture of complete cynicism with regard to its Rituals. That is how Stephen Greenblatt describes Thomas More's world, one "in which everyone is profoundly committed to upholding conventions in which no one believes."[21] What do we make, for instance, of Richard III's cynical farce, which fooled absolutely no one, of rejecting the offer of the crown and then "reluctantly" accepting its re-offer? What of the consecration of a bishop that is a charade because everyone knows he bought his office? "The point," Greenblatt says, "is not that anyone is deceived by the charade, but that everyone is forced either to participate in it or watch it silently." The more you can make people swallow, the "more outrageous the fiction, the more impressive the manifestation of power." The claim apparently is that these rituals are so fake that they constitute an in-your-face challenge to hoot them down. When those in attendance fail to do so, they then have to accept themselves as cowards or, if not quite broken in spirit, at least safely docile in the face of the usurping authority.

If we concede that such breaking of the spirit may be one of the effects of the performance, it hardly should be conceded that its purpose is to cow those present by forcing them to endure an obvious fraud. Do Greenblatt's examples show that the conventions are dead and that no one believes in them? It rather shows the contrary. The coronation ritual still has the power to make a king even though the ritual has been hijacked; the same with the consecration. The only way the king so crowned or the bishop so invested can begin his usurpation is to employ the machinery of the inaugural rituals. After the lapse of time, when the rules of prescription solidify theft into right, few remember – or if they remember they no longer care – that the ceremony was infected when it was performed. They care only that it was performed; the earlier ceremony is cured of its falsity by the passage of time.

The validity of rituals whose chief actors were impure or unholy was oft debated, but practical and realistic considerations favored one outcome over the other. What of the sinful or the atheistical priest who ministers sacraments to the faithful, or the faithful priest who had a nocturnal emission the night before?[22] Are the faithful damned because the priest is unworthy of his position or ritually impure? A prayer the cantor sings on the high holidays asks that God not punish the congregants for whom the cantor is praying because of his sinful condition.[23] The Catholic Church, surely, could not have functioned if it did not defend the position that the sacraments are efficacious independently of the virtue of the priest administering them. The sacraments must be understood to have their force independently of the moral condition of the clergy.

The faking going on, especially the faking of Richard or the simoniac bishop, pays homage to the power of the ritual, not just to the power of the usurper forcing attendance and huzzahs. The claim of universal cynicism underestimates the power of paying lip service. Out of pious impulse we refuse to credit lip service with the importance it deserves. It is all we usually ask from others and all we are inclined to give ourselves. The church forcing people to say the credo, totalitarian regimes making people swear allegiance, even liberal regimes demanding loyalty oaths, might do so as a sign of their power to constrain people's wills, but mostly they do it because they know it works. You say it, we got you. You say you believe long enough and you will believe, if only after a fashion. Maybe such beliefs are only "beliefs," but they are not disbelief or rejections.

Belief comes in all degrees of intensity; very few in the West believe so firmly in Heaven that they will seek martyrdom to achieve it. Most have some small discount built into their beliefs without making their belief no belief or reducing it to a mere "belief." The appalling displays of dignity-destruction that were a frequent occurrence during Stalin's purges – in which people were made to profess belief in a new orthodox position they did not understand and then had to deny that belief weeks later and then reaffirm it weeks after that – are especially horrifying because even these people came to believe, or ceased disbelieving, the crazy and nonsensical claims being forced upon them. *Animal Farm* and *1984* are not exaggerations, but understatements, as the unnerving Gulag memoirs demonstrate.[24]

A strong-minded recusant could profess allegiance to an entity he loathed and make his mental reservations while professing. As long as the authorities did not ask him too frequently to profess allegiance he could, with luck, maintain his initial commitments. But should the authorities become more insistent and keep him under surveillance and force him to speak against his beliefs again and again, then it would take an extraordinary commitment and continuous mental effort to keep up his faith. Eventually the mental reservation itself might become a vehicle of self-deception in which you convince yourself that a real you exists independently of all your words and deeds, that you really are still a Catholic living a secret life in a hostile Protestant regime, or a rational human being trying to muddle through in the mass lunacy that characterized the totalitarian regimes of the twentieth century.[25]

The converso Jews in fifteenth-century Spain were subjected to surveillance and had to live outwardly as Christians, attend Mass, pray to what they believed was a false Messiah. Those who actually succeeded in secretly maintaining their Judaism must have devoted incessant labor to it and must have given each other much mutual support not eventually to become what they feigned to be, as no doubt most did.[26] But Kurt Vonnegut's "We are what we pretend to be, so we must be careful what we pretend to be" makes no allowance for the predicament of those poor souls who must pretend to a belief to save their lives, desperately hoping, against long odds, that they can summon the psychological and moral force to defend a "true" self against the insidious intrusions of their forced pretending.[27]

WITH PRAYER SERVICES CONTRAST APOLOGY, our next topic. In apology we seldom worry about whether we mean it because we so clearly don't and often don't care that we don't. Apologies are riven with suspect motives. And if an apology has all the appearances of sincerity, it is suspect for that reason alone. In a nutshell, the problem is that remorse is easy to fake.

# SEVEN

# Say It Like You Mean It: Mandatory Faking and Apology

SOME EMOTIONS ARE EASIER TO FAKE than others, and some are easier to hide than others. La Rochefoucauld says that as a general matter it is harder to disguise emotions we have than to pretend to have those we do not.[1] The truth of this matter seems to require a big qualifying "it depends." It depends on which feelings we are trying to cover up and which we are trying to feign. It is much easier to disguise what Hume called the calm passions than to disguise the violent ones. I can cover up benevolence more easily than my sense of disgust, my sense of satisfaction in a beautiful object more easily than my grief.[2] And though it is not hard to feign interest, concern, amusement, and other emotions that are commonly feigned in routine conversation, one can almost choke at times trying to feign delight in the unexpected arrival of a visitor or in a colleague's big raise.

Some emotions are characterized by postures and facial expressions that are easy to fake: joy, surprise, female sexual pleasure, anger, disgust. Very few are impossible to fake in some way, and that is a very good thing. If we had to rely on really feeling an emotion to display it, most of us would have been murdered long ago by people we offended.[3] Imagine, as an evolutionary fantasy, that the signs of our emotions and other inner states were unfakeable or unveilable. How different human society, if even conceivable under such circumstances, would have to be. It is the susceptibility of our emotions to being disguised or faked that diffuses the violence latent in so many of our social interactions. We can thank the synergism of our own acting ability and capacity for mimicry coupled with the ease with which the bulk of humanity can be conned and duped.

Blushes are unfakeable, and some researchers insist a really joyful smile is too, but most of us aren't all that discerning.[4] If a culture insists on a blush to indicate shame or embarrassment you have to plan your faking well ahead, and that is one of the reasons women employed rouge or pinched their cheeks.[5] But if all that is demanded is a sign of fluster for embarrassment, or gestures of shamefacedness for shame, we can fake it without cosmetics. Most of our fakery gets by with an acceptable facial expression, plus words to the effect that we are feeling the right thing. "Oh, I am so happy" – grateful, sorry, sad, mad, disappointed, interested, amused, and so on. People are usually willing to accept the emotion words we employ about ourselves without too much cavil, even in the most staggeringly insipid conversations involving phrases such as "getting in touch with your feelings."

It is easier to fake emotions that have short duration, but it is very hard to fake consistently and seamlessly emotions, such as love, that have slow decay rates or are meant to inform an entire state of relations. Of the big-time moral sentiments, arguably none is easier to fake than remorse, the emotion at the core of apology. Neither remorse nor guilt, with which it bears considerable overlap and is often spoken of interchangeably,[6] has a characteristic facial expression. If we think of people as having a guilty look, the cat that swallowed the canary, it is not that such a look is a necessary accompaniment of true guilt or remorse or that it cannot be faked if the occasion demands it. Remorse takes place mostly on the inside, the biting and biting again of conscience, as is captured in the root sense of Latin *remorsus* or the Middle English calque: *agenbyte* (*of inwit*). There is nothing much to see; we therefore develop rituals that garishly dramatize displays of guilt or shows of remorse, from breast-beating to donning sackcloth to handing over cash to offering our heads for decapitation to saying magic words such as "I'm sorry." Thus the apology.

## Accidents versus Intentional Wrongs

In most of the cases I have dealt with so far, the social actor suffers from feelings that he is faking it, fears exposure as a fraud, feels he is a hypocrite, when he may in fact not be; or he wishes to be rid of an anxiety that makes him feel something less than all there, not totally engaged, always feeling that part of him is standing outside himself about to get the giggles or turn away in disgust, or provoke that part of himself still performing to crumble in shame or flee in panic. The case of apology is rather different. The anxiety belongs less to the apologizer for faking it, which he often knowingly is doing, than to the person apologized to – for being taken in or for having to accept an apology he knows is false.

Let's divide the acts or omissions that provide occasions for apologies into two broad categories: those in which we did not mean to harm the other, and those in which we did. Our sincerest apologies come for the harms that we did not mean to inflict. We not only feel remorse but, depending on the gravity or kind of harm, we can also feel specially hated by the gods as well as greatly mortified and embarrassed. That our unintended wrongs should lead to the self-blame of remorse defies standard philosophical and legal understandings that insist it is right to hold someone to strict accountability only for intentional wrongs.

We know that is hooey. Just as we curse the doorsill that we trip over or the lintel we smash our heads on, we blame ourselves or suspect we will be roundly blamed and cursed for being the mere instrument of another's harm, intentional or not.[7] The stupidity and carelessness of others can provoke us to vengefulness as readily as pointed assaults can. In the latter case we may have to express some admiration for the other's courage or enterprise, or even grant that he has a reason to want to harm us. And the fool who does not apologize for his inadvertent harm becomes like the lintel we smash our heads against. We animate him with hostile intention, with *willful* stupidity, and we hold him to blame not merely for not apologizing but also because his failure to apologize makes us suspect him of evil intent or of trying to get away with something for nothing.

As an example of the sincerity of apologies for accidents, take the case of a man, call him Larry,[8] who in complete carelessness runs out from between two parked cars and gets hit by a motorist, flipped head over heels, but miraculously pops up in haste to assure the driver he is all right and to beg the driver's forgiveness, claiming correctly that it was 100 percent his fault for darting out. The driver, white as a sheet, is in turn falling over himself, shaking, apologizing, begging forgiveness from Larry. Both are sincere and profuse in their apologies; one for causing the accident though he in the end is the one who got hurt, the other for being a prop in an accident he did not cause, but in which another got hurt. Larry knows that the driver will blame himself for merely having been in the wrong place at the wrong time. Larry is thus apologizing for the harm of making the driver think he needs to apologize to Larry. The only faking going on is Larry's. He is pretending not to be hurt. In fact, he is so embarrassed and apologetic that he has not yet processed how hurt he is. His very adrenalin-motivated urge to apologize has intercepted the pain he will begin to feel as soon as he limps away. It is hard to find mutual apologies so sincere.

I add two qualifications. There are times when the impulse to apologize for accidental harms is muted or intercepted. What if the person we inadvertently smash into is someone whom we already do not like? We will apologize readily, perhaps more readily, because the other person, knowing our distaste for him, has special reason to think it was no accident. Or if he does accept that the harm was not intended he may doubt that we are really sorry. He suspects we will be taking a small delight in the happenstance. He is probably right too. "You know, this was a complete accident, I am so sorry." Then comes our mental reservation: "But as long as it happened, I hope it really hurt."

The second qualification requires that we make note of the kind of insupportable person who never thinks anything he does is wrong and who thus never feels he has reason to apologize. The harms he inflicts are, to his mind, the fault of the other: "It is your fault for getting in the way of my fist." "You should've started out thirty seconds earlier for work; it is your fault for being in the intersection when I went through the light."

Some cases mix intentional with accidental aspects. In these, it is precisely the lesser amount of presumed intentionality that makes the apology stand a better chance of being sincere. Take these two instances: (1) when the harm we meant to inflict leads to a more serious or to a different harm than we intended. In these cases the apology that goes to the excess is often sincere. "I am so sorry you broke your arm. I only meant to push you away." (2) heat of passion cases. These are often followed by a quick change of heart because the heart that did the wrong was out of control at the time. We meant to do what we did but with insufficient thought to the consequences, and so we are eager to disown the action. We really do feel remorse when we see the damage we did.

But why should the other believe we are sincere when we apologize? Apologies for heat of passion cases tend to engage in a sleight of hand. They are tricky: "I am so sorry, I don't know what got into me. You see, I mixed drinks with my antidepressants, and it made me go bonkers; that isn't like me at all." Sounds pretty good, until you realize that it is as much an excuse as an apology, a sidestepping of responsibility by way of blaming some fictive self who just happened to be occupying your body at the time, but who has now left town without so much as a promise not to return.[9] One should be wary of apologies that take this form, even if the excuse gets the wrongdoer "only out of the fire and into the frying pan" in J. L. Austin's homely reminder that "few excuses get us out of it *completely*" (emphasis in original).[10] Although it is true that I can both be contrite and wish to give an account of how I came to harm you, it is a delicate matter to keep such an account from taking away with one hand at least some of what the apology gave with the other.

### Regret versus Remorse

Accept then, though it may still sound impious, that it is rarer to be really remorseful when we meant to harm someone than when we didn't. Let me emphasize that of course people can and do feel genuine remorse for the wrongs they have intentionally done. Minds can change. The problem nevertheless remains: how does the wronged person know that the wrongdoer is not feigning his remorse, faking his change of mind? Or that his sorriness is not of a less noble kind than true remorse? Thus we are indeed sorry we got caught and are paying a price we didn't anticipate paying. In these cases we suffer the amoral emotion regret, not remorse or guilt. It is regret, not remorse, that you feel for most gambles you have taken and lost.[11] You feel regret, not remorse, that you sold your stock the day before it went up or bought it the day before it went down. It is regret, not remorse, you feel for things you got caught at but would do again if you thought you could get away with them.[12] Any sorrow for the harm caused to the other is secondary; you regret it only to the extent that you feel it to be causally connected to the punishment you are now suffering. Bierce in his usual style nails the point in his definition of *penitent*, adj.: "undergoing or awaiting punishment." And this penitent person is sincere, sincerely regretful, and thus insincerely remorseful.

The problem is compounded because the notion of being sorry is serviceable not only for remorse and regret but also for disappointment, pity, compassion, and the miseries of envy. Thus an allegorical Envy, in the Confession of the Seven Deadly Sins in *Piers Plowman*, confesses in answer to Repentance's query whether he is sorry for his sins: "I am evere sory; I am but selde oother."[13] Some pirates about to be hanged in the early 1700s whom the authorities urged "to turn their Minds to another World, and sincerely to Repent" are also "sorry": " 'Yes,' answered one, 'I do heartily Repent: I Repent I had not done more Mischief, and that we did not cut the Throats of them that took us, and I am extremely sorry that you an't all hang'd, as well as we.' "[14] The villain Aaron in *Titus Andronicus* goes down with all guns firing in the same way:

> Lucius: Art thou not sorry for these heinous deeds?
> Aaron: Ay, that I had not done a thousand more.
>
> (5.1.123–124)

Why we find such defiance charming is another matter.

But because the dominant sense of "I am sorry" is meant to register remorse and thus signal an apology, we end up thinking of all those nonremorseful uses of "I am sorry" as some kind of perverse or deformed apology. Thus Sinclair Lewis can write that Mrs. Babbitt "apologized" to her husband for *his* hangover headache.[15] These "apologies" are not faked in the same way that the paradigmatic apology for a harm you meant to inflict is faked. They are often sincere gestures of commiseration and pity in a low-stakes routine way. Sometimes they are so rote as only to mark that you acknowledge having heard the complaint and are responding in a polite way that is no less scripted than answering "fine" to a "How are you?" Yet this kind of I'm sorry can on occasion mark remorse. When a mother says she is sorry her child scraped his knee we are still in the realm of low-stakes commiseration, but when she says she is so very sorry the child gashed his forehead and requires fifteen stitches to close it, the apology may reflect the mother's remorse for her failure to protect the child against the injury.

There are also compulsive apologizers, ever anxious about the harms they believe they may have caused others. They sincerely mean their apologies, but they seldom have anything to apologize for except their accidental wrongs. They are truly remorseful.[16] But such people devalue the worth of their apologies by apologizing so readily that their apologies become nervous tics. They find themselves apologizing for harms they did not commit or, in an especially extreme variant, apologizing to the person who harmed them. This latter style can be a form of pathological cravenness, or its own kind of moral heroism – the form it takes, for example, with Dostoyevsky's Prince Myshkin.[17] What does an apology mean coming from someone like this, however sincere it might be, for whom real remorse seems to come too easily or who seems to take a little too much pleasure from apologizing?

## Making Faking Hurt

How do we get around an apology's easy fakeability, its not being meant or its being meant but motivated by the wrong sentiment? How can we come to trust sincere ones as sincere and not just as good renditions of sincerity? We can develop techniques to engineer real changes of heart or hone our detection radar to unmask the false heart. Or we can settle for accepting sincere regret as a reasonable substitute for uncertain remorse by making sure the apology hurts the person giving it. The second approach has much to recommend it and is a big part of the cultural history of apology. The church, for instance, imposed three stages in the sacrament of penance: contrition of the heart, confession of the mouth, and satisfaction. Contrition was at one time held to demand real tears, and confession meant confession to a priest. Both tears and words could be faked, but the effort to put on a good show would tend to conform and transform the inner spirit into genuine remorse, either by some mysterious transformation or by actually instructing and cultivating the moral faculty of the penitent.[18]

No absolution, however, was to be granted until satisfaction had been made. Satisfaction was understood to be a temporal punishment. It might be no more than saying some prayers, but it could also involve lengthy fasting and stiff alms. Depending on how strict the priest prescribing penance chose to be, he could make sure the sinner felt regret for his action, if not remorse for his sin.[19] St. Thomas speaks of satisfaction as "compensation for injury inflicted." It is a species of "vindictive justice," and he is all for it.[20] At the very least it meant the restitution of any illicit gains.

Thus the prayer of Claudius in *Hamlet*, who is racked with guilt and contrition, is without effect because he is not moved to make satisfaction or restitution of his ill-gotten gains. His is a case in which the proper sentiments are not faked – his conscience is paining him – though that does not settle the question of whether his feelings of guilt are not something of a sham nonetheless. He is suffering remorse, but his remorse is not as strong as his love for his queen and the crown he gained by the wrong he committed. What is the status of remorse that simply torments us but does not motivate us to make amends? Is it weak remorse, or merely a fake remorse, a kind of performance of self-castigation we put on for ourselves? Moreover, one suspects that Claudius' remorse may be as much motivated by fear – Hamlet is closing in – as by true self-blame.

Although making satisfaction did not solve the problem of faking contrition of the heart, it surely raised the costs of doing bad deeds. One Jewish tradition imposes an even stricter control on repentance. Maimonides defines a perfect repentance to require the monitoring of one's future behavior to see whether one truly means the I'm sorry now. The test of sincerity is that it will alter future behavior. "If a man had sinful intercourse with a woman, and after a time was alone with her, his passion for her persisting, his physical powers unabated while he continued to live in the same district where he had sinned and yet he refrains and does not transgress, he is a sincere penitent."[21] This is more than monitoring the penitent's future behavior; it is a testing, a courting of temptation – dangling the goodies before his eyes – and thus a tormenting and hence a continued punishment of the penitent. The strictness of the sincerity test is lessened by a corresponding duty in the wronged party to forgive, and evidently to trust the penitent to alter his behavior. This from the tractate on torts: "The injured person, however, is forbidden to be harsh and to withhold forgiveness...But once the offender has asked forgiveness and has entreated him a first and a second time, and he knows that the offender has repented of his sin...he should forgive him."[22]

TAKE THE EXAMPLE of how one bloodfeuding culture dealt with the problem of ascertaining the sincerity of shows of sorrow for inflicting accidental harms. The following is a case from an Icelandic saga dating from the early thirteenth century: X accidentally hits Y with a pole in a game in which poles were used to goad horses to fight each other, not to whack people. X immediately calls timeout and says, "I am sorry, I didn't mean to hit you." Here is the crucial addendum. "I will prove to you that it was an accident. *I will pay you sixty sheep* so that you will not blame me and will understand that I did not mean it."[23] To prove lack of hostile intent you had to pay up.

How much more would you have to pay to show you were really sorry if you had initially meant to harm the other? Among these people apologies weren't acceptable for intentional wrongs without massive cultural machinery brought to bear to buy off the avenger's axe in elaborate ceremonies of reconciliation and peacemaking, usually after, not before, a few people had lost their lives. You might have to lay your head on the knee of the person you wronged and beseech him to give it back to you.[24] Usually no one offered his head without some prior assurance that it would not be severed, so that this highly charged ritual was loaded with playacting and posing, but the dangers of glitches were real and people felt the emotional intensity of the performance. This was Ritual, not *mere* ritual; one smirk from anyone in the audience, and the agreement not to take blood could vanish.[25]

Honor cultures make apology and forgiveness, even for accidents, very dangerous stuff because both look as if they might be motivated by cowardice. When the wrongdoer was a child or an old man or a woman, I'm sorry's could be accepted without much anxiety. But for warrior-aged men the presumption was that harms were intentional unless proven otherwise. The burden was on the harmer to show he did not mean it, but that got him caught up in fearing to look cowardly by looking too fearful to face the consequences of claiming the harm to have been intentional even if he hadn't meant it. The apologizer, it was suspected, harbored a cowardly and abject heart. He was apologizing because he was scared of having the damage he inflicted revisited upon him in revenge.[26]

But the person who readily accepted an apology was also suspected of harboring a cowardly heart, revealing himself too scared to hunt down and kill the person who knocked him down. His fear, it was believed, biased him in favor of interpreting ambiguous harms as unintended. Isn't the connection between ready apology and forgiveness and cowardice still true today? My quick and ever so concerned I'm sorry for inadvertently bumping into someone is more quickly given if the offended person looks angry and big enough to avenge himself on me. And I am cravenly eager to forgive the same big person when he bumps into me. Cowardice makes these apologies and forgivenesses sincere, but not more remorseful than regretful.

Because of its associations with cowardice, only the strong and powerful could risk granting forgiveness (it was one of the prerogatives of power)[27] – but not frequently, and they rarely apologized. Not having to say you're sorry is another prerogative of power. Because it looked like weakness to apologize, some people felt they had to stand by even the stupid things they said or did, posturing stubbornly until they "reluctantly" acceded to the demands of reasonable people to back down and make amends. A trivial accident between two people with no prior enmity could easily explode, becoming the first incident in a formal enmity that could last years. But "reluctantly" still deserves the scare quotes I gave it because the reluctance was no less likely to be faked than the apology it was pretending to refuse to make. The risk was that if you acted your reluctance to make peace too well you would end up stuck nervously awaiting the avenger's axe for having refused to pay up.

The offer of sixty sheep shows that this apology was not cheap. The injured man could accept them because it could be claimed that the compensation set a high value on his honor. Being struck, even accidentally, was a dishonor – not only because the motive behind it always allowed for some ambiguity as to the degree of its intentionality, but also because others might be taking pleasure in the victim's pain, laughing at him in the way bystanders laugh when someone has a pratfall. People often look foolish for being the butt of an accident. We have special demeaning names for such souls if they make a habit of this particular kind of bad luck: sad sacks, schlemiels, losers, people sadly without much honor.

The sincerity of X's apology cannot be divorced from the compensation payment, which plays two roles in the transaction: it is compensation for the dishonor to Y of having been struck, and it is proof that he is willing to pay more than lip service to the issue of intentionality. The apologizer can be trusted at the minimum to feel sorry for the loss of his sheep and thus also to be sorry, though indirectly, for the harm done to the other. That much they could verify. Any true remorse was unverifiable.

Move this into more familiar surroundings, less dramatic but recognizable to any parent with more than one child. You tell one kid to apologize for some harm he did to the other. He refuses. You, in a sterner voice, order the apology. Continued refusal. You threaten him; in Ann Arbor, the threat might include Draconian measures such as a timeout for which the threatened sentence of fifteen minutes in his toy-filled bedroom is inevitably commuted to five minutes. The kid still resists giving the apology until you take a menacing step toward him, upon which he turns to his sibling, not completely frontally, but 45 degrees off center, and sneers an I'm sorry in the most unapologetic tone mutterable. Then back to us sternly: "Say it like you mean it." He then makes a small improvement in tone, still without any sign of contrition, and the matter ends right there.

It ends right there unless, foolish parent that you are, you insist on asking for a better rendition of meaning it. The kid then has you boxed in, for he will always find a way of uttering the apology to show that he doesn't mean it, thereby managing to glory and triumph in the face of you and the offended sibling until you finally concede. A wise parent will accept the spat-out hostile apology that shows the first slight improvement. To whose satisfaction? Well, to the parent's, and to the wronged sibling's.

True, the satisfaction is hardly perfect. Is any satisfaction perfect? Even so-called perfect satisfaction is attended by the disgust or heaviness of satiation, or by desires for more as soon as the all too briefly enduring glow wears off. Q: What is the substance of satisfaction to the wronged person in an unfelt apology? A: The pain it costs the apologizer to give it. His refusal to play the role of true penitent is the specie of the compensation payment. His dissatisfaction with having to apologize is what he pays over to make satisfaction to the injured party. That is clearly not true for all apologies, but it is true of many of them, and many in which the stakes are quite high. In this case the apologizer doesn't mean a word of what he says; and it especially hurts him to say it because he doesn't mean it. His unwillingness to say the I'm sorry he is forced to say is his sixty sheep, designed to make him feel sorry for his own predicament of being under compulsion if nothing else.

It does not matter that in the saga example the apologizer, on his own motion, is paying over his sheep to convince the injured party that he meant no harm and that in the case of the child, the parents force the kid to pay over words everyone knows he does not mean. In both cases, the wronged party is satisfied to the extent it hurt the apologizer to make his apology; in both cases the apologizer must humble himself before the person he injured. Apology is a ritual, pure and simple, of humiliation. The humiliation is the true compensation. The sibling apologized to might even prefer seeing her brother disgraced in this way than spanked, though that too would be a pleasure if she could be satisfied that the spanking hurt, something she knows will not be the case in a professorial household. But if she had to choose between having her brother forced to apologize and getting a ten-minute timeout? Easy case: make him say, "I'm sorry."

The kids who refuse until seriously threatened to spit out their unfelt apologies are truly better destined for the world of honor than the world of therapy to which they had the misfortune to be born. Sometimes they simply will not say it; they will not apologize no matter what. Smash their toys if you want; they won't budge. Got to admire them for it. Thus it is that to force an unfelt apology is not completely unsatisfying, for it is not easy to overcome the nearly infinite will to power of the average five-year-old. If our little tyke has to say uncle, he will still say it defiantly – but he is beaten and he knows it, his very defiance being the proof of his loss. In a strange way this is a win-win outcome. The apologizer, by willfully exposing the fake apology as a fake, gains the dignity of some kind of sullen defiance, and the original victim gets the joy of how much it hurts the apologizer to go through the motions of his fake apology. His very dignity-preserving gesture of defiance is his admission as to how much humiliation he is suffering.

Someone deeply committed to the rhetoric of forgiveness, apology, healing, and restoration of relationships will think my account of apology a travesty. He would say that the story of the unapologetic child is not a story about apology; that I have committed an error of categorization, confusing punishment with apology, merely because the punishment takes the form of a farcical apology. But it matters that the punishment takes the form of forcing an apology rather than, say, imprisonment. The ritual, even if performed badly, pretends to make some sort of amends to the wronged party, which the latter can choose to accept or not.

A more pious message lurks in the parent's orders: in the future, little boy, you should do the groveling and humiliate yourself; your conscience should prompt you to it; that is what remorse is. Right now, because your conscience is treating you too favorably or is to-tally undeveloped, we will do some playacting. We will dress up as your conscience and make you grovel and beat your breast for you. You must be made to lower yourself before the other and be beaten to it if necessary; better if your conscience do the lashing than that we do it. Should your conscience remain undeveloped or fall victim to partiality in your own cause, at least learn to fake it convincingly in accordance with propriety, if not morality, as though it were merely an issue of politeness. When it comes to mending fences, appearance and form are rather more than nine points of the law. Saying it *like* you mean it is usually all that will ever be demanded and all that is verifiable anyway.[28]

Apology ceremonies, indeed many reconciliation ceremonies, don't disguise the fact that they are humiliation rituals; only in America could we think otherwise. In ancient Israel you rent your clothes, and fasted, and lay in sackcloth, and went softly.[29] The Emperor Henry IV at Canossa stood in the snow for three days before an unforgiving Pope Gregory VII finally relented. Lear stripped himself naked and went mad and still couldn't dare to face the Cordelia he had wronged. In Montenegro you crawled and groveled with your rifle slung around your neck until the party you wronged lifted you from the dirt.[30] God humiliates Himself by becoming Man and then gets scourged, mocked, and crowned with thorns, before the Father will deign to accept an apology from mankind for the first disobedience of Adam and Eve. Many a spouse has had to grovel even more before a wronged partner, undertaking all kinds of miserable tasks with compensatory solicitousness to make up for what the wrong-doer suspects are unforgivable wrongs. And to what extent are these submissive gestures "meant"? And do we know that it is remorse and not regret that moves them?

## Forgiveness and Punishment

Suppose that our now well-trained child has learned to say "I'm sorry" when appropriate and to say it nicely. Not only that, but he has come to accord his inner state with his words so that he is now a fully moral being; he genuinely feels remorse when he says his sorries. What about you, the wronged person? Are you going to accept his apologies? Do you not fear that it may have come a bit too easily? Won't you make him stand in the snow for a few days anyway, make him wear some sackcloth, eat some ashes, maybe even want to see him crucified? Why should anyone believe a sincere apology could dispense with punishment?

But our sincere apologizer answers, "I am punished; I have been punishing myself with remorse; my sense of well-being will be destroyed forever if you do not forgive me. Even with your forgiveness I will be scarred by the memory of my transgression." "Fine and dandy," you say, "but I still want sixty sheep." You even believe him; you accept him as being truly remorseful. Moreover, should he be faking, he is faking with such skill that the performance alone merits crediting; it would be tasteless and graceless not to reward such masterful acting. As La Rochefoucauld would have it, "Some disguised deceits counterfeit truth so perfectly that not to be taken in thereby would be an error in judgment" (M 282). The implications of La Rochefoucauld's maxim are not easy. Apparently, the deceit is not so masterful that it passes without being noticed as a deceit, even at the moment it is working as a deceit. Deceits, it seems, can work in more ways than by simply deceiving. They can elicit awe for their chutzpah, or daring; how is it that snake oil salesmen sell their wares though every one knows they are lying? As Trollope rightly notes, "A man may lie in such a way as to deceive, though no one believe him."[31]

Yet do we really believe that people are as hard on themselves as they should be even when they are feeling truly remorseful? Might they not actually be pleasuring in their guilt, vain of their self-punishing capacity, feeling rather self-congratulatory about it, and oh so moral, proud that they have such a sensitive conscience?[32] Whatever humiliation they suffer by apologizing feeds their self-satisfaction. Where is the compensation to you in their pleasure? Might they not, by feeling ever so guilty, come to believe they are allowed, even entitled, to forgive themselves? We can't let them get away with that, can we? In the words of the diarist Victor Klemperer, "If one settles accounts with oneself, forgiveness is self-deception."[33]

Apologies, faked or real, are often accepted and repaid with forgiveness. To forgive, however, is not to forget; it is not letting bygones be bygones. Forgiveness is merciful when compared with the revenge that is being waived, but it is not an everything-is-hunky-dory kind of thing. Says Adam Bede, "[Forgiveness] can never mean as you're t' have your old feelings back again, for that's not possible. He's not the same man to me, and I can't feel the same towards him."[34] In feuding cultures, reconciliation ceremonies are meant to memorialize, not to consign to oblivion. Compare the status of one who is not known to have done a wrong – one, that is, who is still deemed innocent – and one who has been forgiven a wrong. The forgiven person is not innocent; he is on parole.

It is not as if others have not claimed the contrary. George Herbert Mead is one among many: "A person who forgives but does not forget is an unpleasant companion; what goes with forgiving is forgetting, getting rid of the memory of it." It would indeed be nicer for a wrongdoer if his victims had short- and long-term memory loss, but it would hardly do much to discourage him from taking advantage of their bad memory. Without memory of the wrong, forgiveness converges on stupidity. Thus Trollope: "If you pardon all the evil done to you, you encourage others to do you evil! If you give your cloak to him who steals your coat, how long will it be before your shirt and trousers will go also?"[35]

Forgiveness can be faked, as when you forgive someone and then have him assassinated a few minutes later. The *Godfather* movies take delight in this form of trickery. But real forgiveness need not come with a forgiving inner state to the extent we think of such a state as having the feel of lovingkindness. Indeed the victim is as often forced by social pressure to forgive no less than the wrongdoer is forced to apologize. Or he forgives because it is embarrassing not to once the wrongdoer has given a colorable apology.[36] A stubborn and unforgiving victim eventually will see the sympathies of third parties shift in favor of the penitent wrongdoer, as long as the penitent plays his remorsefulness in such a way that it convinces others of its sincerity. Refusing to grant forgiveness in order to nurse your resentment is tricky business for your honor.

Whether forgiveness is willingly granted or sullenly begrudged, no prudent forgiver should be all that trusting of his forgiven, unless the latter proves himself again and again in the way Maimonides would demand, until vigilance once again can be relaxed. Forgiveness that is honorable and isn't merely a veneer for weakness can be understood as embodying this warning: you have already blown it once; don't blow it again. Some more pessimistic souls deny forgiveness, not because they harbor inconsolable desires of revenge but because they believe that the recidivism of the apologetic offender is a certainty. Thus the narrator in V. S. Naipaul's *The Mimic Men* makes a Biercean point – without Bierce's charm – regarding failings in his employees: "I gave no one a second chance: the man who lets you down once will let you down again. This is especially true of the man whose dereliction occurs after a long period of satisfactory service."[37] Or Bierce: "*apologize*, v., to lay the foundation for future offense."[38]

Indulge me for one more paragraph sounding like a throwback to honor culture morality. The wronged person who "forgives" actually might prefer a faked apology, not just because it is a sign that it hurt the wrongdoer to give it but also because it allows him not to forgive completely and still to cherish some hatred. His forgiveness is discounted to match the insincerity of the apology. Not to harbor some hate against the wrongdoer seems to sell your harms and humiliations too cheaply if they are serious ones.

The wrongdoer's remorse has a way of compromising the avenger's moral standing and sometimes also his resolve. The avenger might be softened by pity, and grant forgiveness under the sway of that most transient of sentiments. The Greeks, who never had a high opinion of pity, noted that it has a very short half-life, decaying quickly into disgust, thus transforming its pitiable object into a pitiful one: "Those who place high hopes in . . . pity . . . are ignorant of how quickly tears dry up; no one faithfully loves one who disgusts him."[39] The unremorseful apologizer is doing the avenger a favor. He saves the avenger from his own penchant for pity and allows the justness of his cause to survive the fake apology when he finally gets the nerve to retract his equally sham forgiveness and take his revenge.[40]

To be sure, these concerns are an issue when the situation is one of a certain gravity. A lot of forgiveness, like a lot of apology, is routine and uncomplicated because the stakes are low and no one gives a damn. But such small encounters can escalate if the ritual forms are not given their due. Apologies are also often given and received by people who love each other or who have absolutely no wish to find reasons to establish enmity. Such people, if they are the wronged party, wish to believe in the sincerity of the apology or, if they are the wrongdoer, hope that forgiveness for their sincere apologies can really restore relations to a peaceful state. For petty wrongs, no problem. The little I'm sorry's of day-to-day interaction are freely traded; your screw-ups are not only compensated for by your apologies, but by my screw-ups too. We content ourselves to trade screw-ups back and forth, along with apologies. But for big wrongs? Hand over the sheep, sixty of them.[41]

I HAVE PAINTED a grim picture, perhaps grimmer than need be, out of pure vexation with so much of the pious blather on apology and forgiveness one must endure. I don't mean to make you mistrust every apology that comes your way. I concede that not all apologies need be between people who are in a state of enmity or who live in honor cultures, nor are we quite without the means to discern a sincere apology when we are dealing with a person we know well. But unfaked apology is not my theme. My purpose is to show how much faking it is a part of real apology. It is a big part of how we teach apology to the young. Apology is so highly ritualized a social interaction that it cannot ever be free of attacks of self-consciousness about acting, playacting, masks, make-up, saying the lines right, and getting hooted off the stage. We will never properly understand apology rituals and their requirement of humiliation and compensation if we do not understand that the ritual form is largely necessitated by how easy it is to fake remorse, and by how hard it is to distinguish genuine remorse that arises as a moral response to the harm done to the other from equally genuine amoral regret that arises from the discomfort the whole fiasco is causing the wrongdoer.

IF RITUALS OF APOLOGY must work to solve the problem of remorse's easy fakeability, consider the difficulty that sincere praise has in trying to distinguish itself from flattery. We have no rituals that compensate for the chances that praise may be flattery or a bastard mix. There may seldom in fact be any way we can consistently tell them apart, especially because the object of either praise or flattery is too pleased either way to care all that much. Praise and flattery provide a coda to the preceding two chapters, which began with prayer, a form of praise, and followed with apology, a form of prayer.

# EIGHT

# Flattery and Praise

PRAISE IS A GOOD THING, we are told. We are thus to extol God out of gratitude; we are urged to praise our children to assist their self-esteem and confidence. We praise virtue and excellence, the motive varying, but partly because the very praiseworthiness of the person or deeds elicits the response almost involuntarily, as when we burst into applause at an amazing performance in art or athletics. Flattery, in contrast, has been cursed by moralists from the earliest of times;[1] it is hard to find a vice more excoriated. It is felt to be cheating, getting a step up on the competition by engaging in a form of bribery. The unfairness of it wouldn't quite justify the vehemence with which it is cursed if it were not that flattery had such extraordinary powers. Few are so virtuous as not to be seduced by it, and thus many are tempted to flatter because they almost certainly stand to gain by doing so. Mostly it was the special vice that undid rulers, or people wealthy enough to have followers and entourages: the "monarch's plague," Shakespeare called it.[2] Men who ruled others needed counsel, and it was much pleasanter to hear one's praises sung than one's errors and vices admonished and blamed.

The flatterer was often pictured as a kind of pimp, a purveyor of pleasure to the organs of our vanity. As with the allure of delights of the flesh, the temptation is overpowering. Flattery is narcotic and addicting. It preys on two desperate and inescapable desires: to be thought well of by others and to think well of ourselves. The second desire depends on the first more than the first on the second; in any event, they are complexly intertwined. Nor is either of these desires *mere* vanity: they are much of what makes us socializable; nor is either entirely distinct from what we, flatteringly, call conscience. We desire and need approbation so badly that we seem more than willing to accept counterfeit coinage as real. Even when we suspect the quality of sweet words and attentive looks, we push aside our suspicions, suspend our disbelief, and bask in the false glow.

Flattery was thought to infect friendship too. A friend, according to ancient moralists, was to make his friend better, not to be an abettor of his vices. A friend should blame his friend's faults so as to improve him, not praise them or indulge them. It is not easy, however, to tell a flatterer from a friend. A good flatterer adopts the tone of frankness and even reproves a person if he thinks it will advance his own standing. Plutarch recommends feigning changes in your views to test whether your friend sticks to his prior views.[3] But that would trap only a very dim-witted flatterer. An adept flatterer can almost always foil the most advanced antiflattery security system.

Moralists have often pointed out that we are our own worst flatterers. The conniving flatterer finds his way eased by the fact that we have paved the way for him; we advertise where we are most vulnerable, where we have an itch that we are desperate to have scratched. Given the world of competitive vanity that characterized royal courts and especially given its rococo flourishing at Versailles in the seventeenth century, it should not be any wonder that La Rochefoucauld would be at his most perspicacious (and repetitious) on this vice: "Self-love is the greatest flatterer of all" (M 2; also M 600); and "if we never flattered ourselves the flattery of others could do us no harm" (M 152).

Praise is good, the inevitable fruit of virtuous deeds; flattery bad. But how do we tell the difference between them? Can we tell when we are being praised and not being merely flattered? Is it possible to praise someone without also flattering him or her? Does the difference simply lie in the intent of the praiser? Or is it equally a matter of how the receiver takes the compliment? That is, is flattering one thing, and being flattered another? "It is not he who flattered me," says Mrs. Yepanchin in *The Idiot*. "It is I who am flattered."[4] How is one not to be flattered by sincere praise? Can a person lower in the pecking order ever praise someone higher in the pecking order without its also being flattery?

## Tainted Praise

The common view is that flattery is a fraud, a fake; the dictionary view is that it is false or insincere praise. But what is the basis of its falseness? That it is not meant? That cannot be true; flatterers can sincerely believe what they are saying. That the praise is false? Although much flattery is false, not all is. I can flatter handsome persons by telling them how good-looking they are. A teacher loves to think that students are telling the truth *and* that they are sincere when they shamelessly flatter her by telling her that her course was the best offered in the school. Can't the poor teacher, desperate for approbation, believe in the innocence of the students' intentions if they say so after she has submitted the grades and the ones saying it are not the ones who got the A's? Yes, and that is just how she flatters herself, though the students may not be conniving flatterers for having flattered.

So flattery can be sincere and can be true. Then what could possibly distinguish it from praise, which is also both sincere and true? Might it be that flattery does to praise what hypocrisy does to all virtue: infects it so that the real thing can never be trusted? Let's assume now that we are dealing with praise, both sincere and true, and see whether we can keep it from being infected with flattery's vices. Praise, no less than flattery, raises the problem of how to handle the benefits that will come your way as a byproduct of the praise you give. Are you blameless as long as you do not praise for the reason of getting rewarded for your praise? How naïve do you have to be not to know that praise is often rewarded by the person praised? Isn't that what motivates a good portion of the praise we give our children and our dogs (and God too)? We hope that praise will move them to do what we want them to do in the future, not merely build their self-esteem. Dog-training manuals are richer than self-help books on this theme.

Praise, even more than flattery, *should* prompt rewards. The person flattered might suspect the flattery is false or that it was motivated primarily to be rewarded, and thus dismiss it if he possesses a steely, virtuous soul. Praise, on the other hand, to the extent that it is not flattery, is itself something of a virtue and should be rewarded. It is, after all, a kind of gift. And gifts demand recompense. The praised person who does not reward sincere praise looks like an ingrate and eventually may come to be blamed as one.[5] But balanced against the praised person's desire to reward the praiser is a concern that rewarding praisers will encourage flatterers, and the praised person doesn't trust that he will always be able to discern the difference.

Leave it to La Rochefoucauld to suspect that there is no difference between praise and flattery. For him, praise is merely a sophisticated form of flattery:

> We dislike praising, and never praise anybody except out of self-interest. Praise is a subtle, concealed, and delicate form of flattery which gratifies giver and receiver in different ways: the latter accepts it as the due reward of his merit, the former bestows it so as to draw attention to his own fairness and discrimination.

(M 144)

La Rochefoucauld is not dealing with low-level, on-the-make flatterers. His praisers are no less vain than the people whose vanity they flatter by praising them. They praise to be praised in return for praising astutely, for their penetrating taste and intelligence. This is much subtler than seeing a flatterer as praising because he suspects it will be rewarded by some material advancement. Here the act of praising is itself its own unsavory reward in a world in which vanity, vanity, all is vanity. We expect, however, that praise will elicit more than admiration for praising well. How often have you seen people tell others how nice they look in order to be told the same? Because we cannot ask to be praised, we often fish for compliments, and praise is sovereign bait for catching praise.

Is flattery any different? We indeed flatter to get credit for discernment, as when we pay homage to trendy positions we strongly suspect are vacuous but fear that we will be seen as vacuous if we do not flatteringly pay our respects. It is the emperor's new clothes all over again. And we surely flatter to be flattered in return. We are always told to spurn flattery when we are its object, but in fact we love it, even when we know it is flattery, when we know the person is sucking up (pardon the vulgarity, but the behavior tends to invite disgusting imagery). It all depends on how he does it. If he smarms and grovels, it is disgusting, but if he passes it off with style, we eat it up. La Rochefoucauld again gets it right: "Sometimes we think we dislike flattery, but it is only the way it is done that we dislike" (M 329). Or as a more recent writer put it a little more crudely: "Flattery in general is neither despised nor hated... What is despised and hated, however, is flattery combined with arse-licking."[6] I want to add another reason flattery has its appeal: even if you know it is the purest flattery and recognize that the person is behaving manipulatively, to find yourself the object of flattery is itself a kind of praise or at least independently flattering. It is recognition of your status as someone whom it is appropriate or worthwhile to flatter. Flattery is homage.

Is it ever possible for a low-status person to praise someone of higher status without the praise collapsing into flattery independent of the motives of the praiser? It is the structure of the interaction, the direction of it, that condemns the praise. Praise flatters its object and demands recompense, though it be apt, true, and innocently motivated. Can there be a purely innocent worshiper of a superior? Wouldn't the virtuous subordinate of a praiseworthy superior fear that if he were to be rewarded by the object of his praise he would look no different from a successful flatterer to all those scrupulous persons who, knowing they would benefit, suppressed their innocent desire to praise?

What is a would-be honest low-status praiser to do? There are three possibilities for praise whose motivation might ensure its differentiation from flattery. First, there is that admiration, as I mentioned briefly, that bursts forth by sheer exuberance and awe for the greatness of the performance or for the stupendous majesty of a great personage. This is the kind of praise the faithful on occasion give to God, and it has all the marks of genuineness.

Second, there is the praise you give your enemy. This is an imperfect example because the praiser is still claiming a rough equality with the praised even though he currently may be a notch or two beneath him. The praise might be infected with a desire to be praised in return or might harbor a cowardly hope that your enemy will go easy on you out of "respect" for your opinion of him. Related to this is the reluctant praise received from the bitterly envious, who would do anything, at great cost to themselves, not to praise you. This is really a subset of praise elicited by sheer awe, but it bears none of its signs of exuberance; it is begrudged and rather more genuine for its gracelessness, which betokens that the givers of it think it is against their interest to grant it.[7]

Third, we can praise anonymously or (innocently) to a third party out of earshot of the person praised. Says Etienne to Henri: "I think M. le Prince the wittiest and most virtuous of men." Etienne gets credit from Henri for his views, as La Rochefoucauld suggests, but suppose that Henri tells M. le Prince: "Mon liege, Etienne thinks you the paragon of wit and virtue." In one coup both Etienne and Henri become flatterers – Henri consciously so, by bearing a message that flatters M. le Prince, and Etienne, presumably against his will, as the author of the praise. Etienne, to maintain the innocence of his praise, needs to be reasonably sure that Henri will not be a carrier pigeon and bear the tale.

I dread to think how many students have influenced a teacher, not by telling her how good they thought her class was but merely by relaying the news that student opinion in general was that the class was a real winner. The strong urge to kill the messenger bearing bad tidings exists in near symmetry with the urge to reward the messenger bearing good tidings. Not just the messenger will get rewarded, but the registrar's office will notice that the whole class curve has shifted A-ward.

With the possible exception of the praise that bursts from us in sheer exuberance, might it be that praise is pure in motive only when it comes from someone who has nothing to gain by it? This is Hamlet's view, expressed when he praises Horatio:

> Nay, do not think I flatter,
> For what advancement may I hope from thee
> That no revenue hast but thy good spirits
> To feed and clothe thee? Why should the poor be flatter'd?
> No, let the candied tongue lick absurd pomp,
> And crook the pregnant hinges of the knee
> Where thrift may follow fawning.
>
> (3.2.56–62)

If God or Caesar praises you, that is praise indeed, as the adage would have it; yet we know that their praise is not purged of interest merely because of the vast difference in their power and yours. Kings and rulers prime the pump, fish for compliments, and elicit praise by flattering their subjects. Why should the poor be flattered? When they have a vote. Refusing to flatter under the circumstances can get people in trouble; it did to Coriolanus. But giving the poor the franchise is not being fair to Hamlet's example. There may not be any case that meets Hamlet's criterion. If not advancement to hope for, the high-status praiser will always have the approval to gain of those they praise; the exultant, adoring, and grateful faces are worth their weight in gold to any leader, whether or not he needs their votes. "Blessed are the meek" and "Blessed be ye poor: for yours is the kingdom of God" may be understood as a flattery of the poor to gain their allegiance. Any teacher who praises his students wonders whether his motives are pure, even when he is tenured. We curry favor as actively with them as they do with us.[8] And why? Because flattery from the high often prompts the low to love in return: "I dare say the beggar's daughter loved King Cophetua. When you come to distances such as that, there can be love. The very fact that a man should have descended so far in quest of beauty, – the flattery of it alone, – will produce love. When the angels came after the daughters of men of course the daughters of men loved them."[9]

Praising our children is often infected with flattery. We praise them to reward meritorious deeds and good efforts but also to cajole, to motivate. The words of praise are looking for returns independent of any truth they may contain. We praise the mediocre performance in hopes of motivating an improved version; it is not that we are praising the effort, for that may not have had anything to do with the mediocrity of the performance. Then too there is what Jane Austen calls "the common cant of praise," as when a girl is called beautiful as an empty form of politeness that no one expects really to be true; indeed Austen calls attention to the practice because in the particular instance she was describing "the truth was less violently outraged than usually happens."[10] Cant admiration of that sort is not flattery, but a small gesture that must be made because not to make it strongly suggests you find the person unattractive (haven't you nearly choked telling new parents how beautiful their baby is?). You get no reward for the cant except the avoidance of being ostracized for not having the grace to do so. And of course we praise, not exactly to be praised in return but to be loved, honored, and, when the object is our children, obeyed. It is very hard indeed to extract praise from the system of reciprocities in which it is embedded and by which it is in part compromised.

The high no less than the low are moved to genuine praise by witnessing great and awesome performances: thus the praise of a general to his troops after a hard-fought battle. We allow the praise to pass as praise, because the men deserve it and because the general means it, even though it will prompt their continued obedience and even though his praise is obligatory – for not to give it would mark him as a callous monster. Before the battle, however, that same general also praised his men, for their prior bravery or for what he claims are their inherently courageous souls, but here the praise moves into the genre of exhortation, with the exhortatory intent overwhelming the purity of the praise and sending it into flattery's camp by the dominance of the instrumental motive.

Exhortatory praise moves us toward those manifestly false praisings, sometimes exhortatory in form, as in the "nice try" we say to the kid who let in a soft goal (the "we" here includes my wife and the other parents at the game but does not include, I must confess, me). This is the stuff of cheerleading and thus pardonable despite my unrepressed distaste for the excesses of the style. To praise with the goal of building the self-esteem of the praised persons independently of their actual mastery and virtue is little different from the flattery bad friends give who abet each other's vices. Or perhaps the proper rule for children is captured by a remark I once heard a wise parent make: you spend their first four years doing everything possible to build their self-esteem, and then you have to spend the rest of their lives tearing it back down to reasonable proportions.

## In Small Praise of Flattery

If one is going to flatter, learn to do it well; it is an art. The bad name flattery has, coupled with its frequent indistinguishability from certain aspects of politeness and charm – or complaisance, in the eighteenth-century sense – gives rise to all the anxieties of playing false roles falsely – or, worse, playing them truly – that is one of the chief themes of this book. It is thus flattery to pretend to be distressed at the distress of others, to act, or even be, indignant over the wrongs they think they have suffered; it is flattery to laugh at the boss's lame jokes, to flirt within innocuous limits that passes merely for being good company, to play the role of an attentive daughter or son to an old powerful fart on the job (obviously), but also merely to nod gravely at some vacuous banality he utters with great pomposity, to seek advice, to adopt a frank and open tone; the list is endless. But many of these behaviors are also the marks of amiability.

It is hard to escape being a flatterer. It is a commonplace that being gruff, frank, and direct is readily employed in flattery's service, especially if it is nicely contrasted with a large population of groveling, oily, servile lickspittles:

> This is some fellow
> Who, having been prais'd for bluntness, doth affect
> A saucy roughness, and constrains the garb
> Quite from his nature. He cannot flatter, he,
> An honest mind and plain, he must speak truth!
> And they will take't, so; if not, he's plain.
> These kind of knaves I know, which in this plainness
> Harbor more craft and more corrupter ends
> Than twenty silly-ducking observants
> That stretch their duties nicely.
>
> (*Lear* 2.2.95–104)[11]

Congreve, rather differently, blames the bluntly truthful soul less as a knave than as a fool: "He speaks unseasonable truths sometimes, because he has not wit enough to invent an evasion."[12] Others go further and blame an uncompromisingly nonflattering style as an excuse to exercise one's malice under the pretense of being virtuously honest. Thus Melville describes the viciousness of a woman he names Goneril who "held it flattery to hint praise even of the absent, and even if merited; but honesty, to fling people's imputed faults into their faces."[13] Frankness is not the only virtue that can be indulged in sadistically (chastity and courage are two others), but it may have a harder time than most avoiding the suspicion that the practicer of it is deriving illicit pleasure from the pain he is giving.

Even flattery in the oily style has its defenders. On October 16, O.S. 1747, Lord Chesterfield writes to his son on the "art of pleasing," "a very necessary one to possess." No one can dispute a good portion of the advice, such as to take care telling jokes that worked well in one company without allowing for the difference in audience; above all, do not open your jokes or humorous tales with "this silly preamble: 'I will tell you an excellent thing'; or, 'the best thing in the world.' This raises expectations, which, when absolutely disappointed, make the relator of this excellent thing look, very deservedly, like a fool."

The core of the letter, however, states the case for the wisdom of cultivating that glib and oily art. It is hard to keep images of smarminess, slime, lubriciousness, and insinuation from intruding, though in Chesterfield's favor, it surely would have behooved Cordelia to have cultivated this art more than she was willing to. "Endeavor to find," he advises, people's

> predominant excellency, if they have one, and their prevailing weakness, which everybody has; and do justice to the one, and something more than justice to the other. Men have various objects in which they may excel, or at least would be thought to excel; and, though they love to hear justice done to them, where they know that they excel, yet they are most and best flattered upon those points where they wish to excel, and yet are doubtful whether they do or not.

"Do not mistake me," he continues, after advising flattering ugly women on their beauty, manifestly beautiful ones on their intelligence, and think that I mean to recommend to you abject and criminal flattery: no; flatter nobody's vices or crimes . . . but there is no living in the world without a complaisant indulgence for people's weaknesses, and innocent, though ridiculous vanities. If a man has a mind to be thought wiser, and a woman handsomer, than they really are, their error is a comfortable one to themselves, and an innocent one with regard to other people.[14]

So far, this is all on the side of kindness, of not hectoring others, of being merely polite. Indeed there is no living in the world if we were to let ourselves get furious at every little imbecility and vanity that is the lot of humanity; we would end up with Gulliver in the stable conversing with the horses, which I admit does seem to have its attractions.

Noncriminal flattery of others' vanity is good policy: "And I would rather make them my friends, by indulging them in it, than my enemies, by endeavouring (and that to no purpose) to undeceive them." People who have their foibles exposed take revenge for their humiliations. There is something distasteful in this, if not quite vicious, but in fact it also matches fairly well that definition of politeness, predating Chesterfield's letter by less than fifty years, we saw earlier: "a dextrous management of our Words and Actions whereby we make other people have better Opinion of us and themselves."

Abetting another's small vanities is flattery, but not abject or criminal flattery. It is also politeness, a virtue. As we have already seen, our politeness can raise anxieties in us regarding our virtue; we feel as if we are faking it, being hypocrites, not so much out of kindness, not for virtue's sake, but out of cowardice, for fear that telling the truth will prevent our gaining the next rung on the social ladder or will get us knocked down a couple of pegs instead.

Chesterfield then gets down to particulars:

Observe the little habits, the likings, the antipathies, and the tastes of those whom we would gain; and then take care to provide them with the one, and to secure them from the other; giving them, genteelly, to understand, that you had observed they liked such a dish, or such a room for which reason you had prepared it: or on the contrary that having observed they had an aversion to such a dish, a dislike to such a person, etc., you had taken care to avoid presenting them. Such attention to such trifles flatters self-love much more than greater things, as it makes people think themselves almost the only objects of your thoughts and care.

This passage goes a long way to confirming Samuel Johnson's devastating description of Chesterfield's letters as teaching "the morals of a whore, and the manners of a dancing master."[15] This is an instruction in fawning, sedulousness, officiousness, and conniving, especially when you shamelessly collude against some absent person by mentioning the care you took not to invite him. But Chesterfield's son is a bastard and must please others to advance or even to hold his own; he must learn to crook the pregnant hinges of the knee, as indeed must many an employee in various job hierarchies in our world. Ugly business, and what do we suppose to be the inner state of Mr. Stanhope, the bastard son, as he carries out this advice? It is a role he is being instructed to assume, but can he possibly play it without a bad taste in his mouth, without some bit of distancing himself from the lines he must say? According to Diderot, whom we will encounter more fully later, he need merely learn how to crook the knee without any according of his sentiment to the role: it is about mimicry; he can make mental reservations as he says his oily lines.[16] Yet Johnson's suspicion is that this is what makes the whore a whore, and a dancing master a dancing master, and nothing more. Shakespeare suggested via the bastard Edmund that playing such a role for the sake of advancement may generate all kinds of resentments and vengeful bitterness in the bastard boy. But it is no less likely that people will come to enjoy the safety and advantages of their serviceable roles and live rather happily and productively as slimy insinuators.

Chesterfield, to give him credit, is hardly confusing praise with flattery. He acknowledges that it is flattery he is teaching, and if his boy learns his lesson he will come to get praised for his complaisance, his charm, his manner and manners. If you are loathsome as a flatterer to the object of your flattery it means only that you are no good at it. If you are loathsome to those who resent, envy, or begrudge your advancement, you can dismiss them as losers at a game you beat them at. Your successful flattery prompts vices in them; they entertain mean thoughts, they tattle on you, and gossip. But that only makes them look like enviers of your talent for advancement, and that is praise indeed, though a skillful flatterer would also find a way to assuage the resentments of his competitors even as he triumphed over them. And then they will emulate you.

Chesterfield accepts as a given, and there is little reason to doubt him, that adept flattery will please all but the most stony superior, and even he will not welcome being told the truth. Our desire to be flattered will make flatterers of our friends out of kindness, of our underlings out of fear and desire for getting a leg up on the competition, and of our superiors out of a desire better to get us to do their bidding. There is no getting rid of the vice, and a good thing too, or many more of our days would be ruined than already are.

# NINE

## Hoist with His Own Petard

There's letters seal'd, and my two schoolfellows
Whom I will trust as I will adders fang'd
They bear the mandate, they must sweep my way
And marshal me to knavery. Let it work,
For 'tis the sport to have the enginer
Hoist with his own petar, an't shall go hard
But I will delve one yard below their mines,
And blow them at the moon.
                              (*Hamlet* 3.4.203–210)

EARLIER WE MET THOSE WORDS and phrases that made no sense to us when we were little and not so little, the "plejallegiance" or the "forgive us our trespasses" of the Lord's prayer. Without checking the gloss on the bottom of the page, few of us know, or remember if we did check, what exactly the image of being hoist with a petar(d) is. When we read Shakespeare we are so often faking reading Shakespeare. Many think the image of petards means being run up a flagpole or tossed in the air and impaled on your own spear (and to justify this the line is often misremembered as hoist *on* his own petard). Even misunderstood in that way, the metaphor is properly conceived as having something to do with plots recoiling on the plotter in ways he never foresaw, of having himself become the inadvertent object of his own machinations intended to undo another. To be hoist with your own petard really means to have the mine or shell you intend for the enemy explode in your own face. A petard is an explosive device – thus the relevance of the image of being blown at (to) the moon.

## Talking to Hamlet

The mere mention of *Hamlet* in a book about faking and feeling like a fake is a temptation to dive in and drown. Consider the plight of Ophelia and Gertrude, who must pretend that they are having normal conversations with Hamlet but know they are staging it for eavesdroppers hiding behind arrases and elsewhere. Bad enough, as I have been supposing, to have to attend to the colleague you are talking to and worry about what you are going to say next. But imagine if that colleague were Hamlet. A reptile on a cold day would be a nervous wreck talking with him.[1] How do you converse with Hamlet and not walk away feeling humiliated unless, like Horatio, you have cultivated a stoical disposition? Hamlet is so much smarter than you, and he delights in never letting you forget it. He makes each conversation a contest to see whether you can follow his speed-of-light access to startlingly original images juxtaposed in difficult and fantastic ways. He tests to see whether you can fathom his incessant punning, his playing with words only a tenth of which you grasp at the moment; and while you are figuring out how to respond to them, another hundred whiz right by you, ones that future editors of Hamlet's conversations will spend years parsing. When you finally steel yourself to open your mouth, he plays with your words, turning them against you or making you not only feel stupid but look it too. Now add that Gertrude and Ophelia have to perform not just for Hamlet but for the eavesdropping Polonius or Claudius and know that by so doing they are betraying Hamlet. It is amazing they don't give up immediately under the stress of the duplicitous conditions in which they are being asked to converse and perform as genuine interlocutors.

No wonder Gertrude can continue discussions with Hamlet quite rationally in the presence of Polonius's bloody corpse. For her, the social situation has become infinitely simpler now that she is not being overheard and can attend fully to her son's whirling words. To credit Ophelia's and Gertrude's attempts to act naturally when they know they are being overheard, recall how hard a time Hamlet has conversing with his mother when he discovers the ghost is eavesdropping on him.

Hamlet and *Hamlet* have beaten me to every punch I have tried to throw. He is obsessed with faking, thinking himself to be, and sometimes not quite inaccurately, a fake avenger, a fake son, a fake lover, a real actor – that is, a professional assumer of roles – a director of actors ("Speak the speech, I pray you, as I pronounc'd it to you"), an expert on various acting styles, especially as these treat of rendering the emotions on stage, a master tricker of others and of himself, a wearer of masks the most opaque of which are donned for soliloquies, a dissimulator of his inner states, a piercer of others' veiled inner states. Never was a soul more self-conscious about faking it or about all the multitudes of meanings in his wondrous cascade of words, with meanings undoing meanings, making everything look as if it were a sham, arabesques of seeming by a man who claims he knows not seems.[2]

Any high school junior knows that the play plays with issues of appearance and reality; the ghost, the play within the play, the discussions of acting, the eavesdropping, the antic dispositions, all make that obvious. We should hardly be surprised that the kings in this play are player kings – either as usurpers, ghosts, or actors; only young Fortinbras is the real kingly thing, the wiliest politician in the whole play, though he must play at being as brashly shallow a man of honor as Laertes is in order to take advantage of the turmoil in Denmark. It is Fortinbras who positions himself to "clean up," in every sense of that expression, at the end, but who will not be a real king until after the play ends.

Polonius, the person who utters the most quoted line in English about characterological authenticity, is a sententious fool who distinguishes himself by being especially deluded about his own psychological acuity:

> This above all: to thine own self be true,
> And it must follow, as the night the day,
> Thou canst not then be false to any man.
> (1.3.79–81)

Sounds good, but what on earth does he mean? To be true to yourself, you might reasonably think, you first need a recipe for knowing yourself. And how are we to go about that, or know when we have achieved true knowledge if we chance upon it? No easy matter given the ease with which we delude ourselves. But suppose you do know yourself, or don't but are still true to yourself; why should that prevent you from deceiving others? A truer non-platitudinous sentiment offered by George Eliot introduces a further wrinkle: "Examine your words well, and you will find that even when you have no motive to be false, it is a very hard thing to say the exact truth, even about your own immediate feelings – much harder than to say something fine about them which is *not* the exact truth."[3] That most brilliant of ladies gives us more insight in such off-hand comments than we get from volumes of depth psychology, Oedipus complexes, and Lacanian *petit objet a*'s.

Part of the problem of getting to know oneself is a lack of precision in language to fix feelings and inner states that resist description. And even if we found the words to do the trick, there are still cognitive biases, such as the effects of self-love, that make the project next to impossible. The very feelings we are trying to describe interfere with the ability to describe them. Maybe Polonius is making a more modest point than the Delphic one of "know thyself." He may merely be continuing the rather narrow advice to a young man of how to live within his means and still cut a good figure in the world. Pay your debts when due and don't overspend – that is, know thy financial limits and so thy checks are true and do not bounce.[4]

Go back to Hamlet's image of the mine and countermine: "I will delve one yard below their mines, / And blow them at the moon." Mines are tunnels the besieger digs to gain entry to a fortress either by going under the walls or by breaching the wall by undermining its foundational support and collapsing it. By the late Middle Ages, explosives became available to help the miners chipping away in the dark with their picks and spades. The explosive engines were by extension also called mines, an acknowledgment of their underground paternity. Countermines are tunnels dug to intercept the miners and kill them.[5] You are a miner picking away, removing dirt and rock working toward the enemy fortress, when you start to hear a chink, chink, chink above or below you: counterminers. Imagine your fear;

they may miss you, tunneling five yards to the right or left; it is the fourteenth-century version of the submarine movies I grew up with. As Hamlet, the counterminer, says: "O, 'tis most sweet, When in one line two crafts directly meet." Craft here means stratagem; it is not a shift to nautical imagery. The countermine to gain its end must be dug so as to intercept the mine. The lines must meet. But if they miss? The miner wins, the counterminer loses, for he bears the risk of loss, the loss of his home base, if he fails to stop the miners.

Countermining is a defender's strategy, but unlike the paradigmatic defensive strategy of awaiting the advance of the enemy, it requires the defender to move forward and intercept. The whole imagery of mines and countermines is rich in its suggestiveness about strategizing and identity, how so much of it must be carried out blindly or in very dim light, secretly. How like our own interiors and subsurfaces, where we hatch our plots and orchestrate our roles but also where we often don't see very well through the murk of vanity, stupidity, and smoky passions; the space and place of operations are obscure. The space is also spooky, magical, and it can turn things into their opposite – hate to love, coldness to warmth – and it is often lethal to songbirds. I offer one stunning example of the magic of the mine. By the rules of fourteenth- and fifteenth-century warfare, should two enemies of knightly rank meet and fight in a mine, they became brothers-in-arms and one could no longer take the life of the other; one also had to help pay the ransom of the other should he be captured or set him free without ransom should they meet again on opposite sides above ground.[6] Talk about transformations of identity and role!

This is surely one of my frolics, but not quite a detour, for strategizing under the ground darkly brings me back to the idea of the roles we play and the degree of our immersion in them. Precisely when does faking it work such a transformation upon the faker that he is more faked out than his audience? He is not always hoist with his own petard when this happens. He is indeed if he is a seducer, the "cunning fool"[7] who finds he has fallen in love with his quarry and now suffers all the anguish of a jilted lover when she dumps him. But there are other times when we devoutly wish to be hoist with our petard, to find that the role we are faking takes over and we end up the grown-ups, teachers, parents, perhaps even the decent human beings, we thought we were only faking being.

This transformation takes place sometimes unconsciously, in spite of ourselves, sometimes half-consciously, as when we try hard to lose ourselves in our role but never quite know when we finally have stopped trying and have become one with our role. And sometimes we make a conscious decision to do the work of refashioning ourselves or our beliefs so that we can genuinely, we think, make ourselves feel what we think we ought to feel and miraculously end up being what we feel we ought to be. Pascal's wager works like this, and so do the various character-transforming methods of Buddhism, twelve-step programs, and the American feel-good-about-yourself movement. Indeed, much of the therapy racket depends on the belief that one can actually purchase a different set of beliefs about oneself and the world. There are all kinds of purveyors advocating various methods of how best to hoodwink oneself.

Not all these transformations of the fake into real are for the better. They can be rather a mixed bag, as the Vonnegut maxim noted earlier warns. Be careful what you pretend to be. Toughness, or a certain hardness, is a very useful trait to have, but the person who undertakes a pose of hardness or flippancy to protect what he fears is his core vulnerable sweetness may end with his sweetness shrunk to invisibility or inaccessible behind the ramparts, though he maintains the belief that his toughness is only a pose.

What of the spacey pose so common in the academy of the absent-minded professor? Some actually cultivate spaciness because they and others think it is cute, and it also helps them evade responsibilities. It is not only a matter of being to the manner born. They miss meetings, are excused from burdensome committees, and never get blamed much because, well, you know X, he's just a space cadet. Sure, they lose a few extra pair of eyeglasses a year, but the time saved missing appointments more than makes up for it. In critical matters they flatter themselves that they can put aside the spacey act and be the real, competent souls they think they know they are. But by this time they have been blown at the moon by their own petard. Having no practice at being focused in small matters, they are as unreliable in big ones.

## Ironists

The ironic pose is a common one and more complex than most. Those who adopt it seem to feel that irony gives them some control over feeling foolish about playing the various roles they are self-conscious about playing. It is a style of making one's less than full immersion in various roles the substance, as well as the style, of one's character. The ironic style is made up usually of a few parts self-mockery, more parts mockery, all devoted to constructing a distance, an ironic distance, between role and self, so that whatever gaffes and screw-ups occur will be cushioned by a certain deniability. To play up anxious self-consciousness in this way helps inure the ironist to it or lets him take a second-order delight in it. The ironical posture also helps improve his chances of being the center of attention by altering the game subtly into one in which he can star for not being as good at the real game he thinks everyone else is playing more adeptly than he could. He often is pleased by his irony, flattering himself with the belief that it takes more intelligence to be so painfully aware and self-aware.

At the very least irony keeps him, or so he believes, from being hoist with the petard of uncritical full immersion into the conventional roles he is called on to play. But the irony is that instead of lowering the stakes of failure he raises them. Though irony provides an excuse that he wasn't playing for real, in fact he is playing for keeps. He is not about to refuse the benefits he gains in social and self-esteem for being good company, nor will he fail to feel chagrin at the losses he suffers when his shtick fails to gain him social credit. Unlike the person who plays it dully straight and goes home to a good night's sleep, our ironist worries how his act went over.

Though this kind of ironic style is meant to call attention to itself as a pose, it is still committed to good manners. Its practitioner means only to amuse or to be amused by introducing a whiff of drollery into simple encounters, not to make scenes or make everyone else awkward. Yes, a little more risk is introduced into the setting, but only in the interests of interestingness and of protecting himself from the risks of nonironic social interaction. This is not the freshman's view of irony, in which words are used in the opposite of their literal sense, and it is broader and subtler than merely saying one thing when you mean another but with an intonation or wink so that there is no blame for a lie or misrepresentation.[8]

This kind of irony can function as a fake fake, for it is hardly the case that he is not still properly filling the roles he is pretending to distance himself from. It is trite to observe that we suspect that certain people might also adopt this style to cover a deep seriousness that they think, at some level, it would be bad form or unsafe to reveal. They thus pose as ironical when they are dead serious. Part of the motive may be that they are shy or embarrassed by their own seriousness or afraid to give up the defense their irony provides. And what is one to do once the conventional markers of seriousness and sincerity have been polluted beyond repair by those given to new-age "I hear you"-style signs of concern, by politicians, by people who believe themselves serious and sincere because they have learned to look you in the eye, or into the television camera, and not smile, except with unctuous empathy?

I do not mean to delve very deeply into the various styles of ironic poses except to mention a few of the most common types.[9] There is the knowingly defensive ironist, anxious about his position. He can be a high-status person desperate not to seem snobby; or she is the anxious middling soul uncertain of precisely where in the hierarchy she is; or they are those self-conscious occupiers of the marches and border regions of full personhood, who are never quite sure whether they are in or out: the Jew, the affirmative-action admittee, the fat among the thin, and so on.

There is also an ironic style we associate with snootiness, usually adopted by people who think themselves brighter than they are, and hence their irony often becomes the failed irony of a would-be ironist. Incompetent ironists have a moral failing we tolerate about as well as we tolerate a completely humorless person. The latter we avoid as a killjoy, the former we fantasize we might enjoy killing. The sins of the bad ironist are numerous: they insult us by their lamely hostile comments, which are all the more offensive because they radiate superciliousness, excessive self-regard, and contempt. If their irony is a defense to cover various fears, those fears are buried deep indeed, for these are usually very self-satisfied souls.

The ironist is not quite the licensed fool, the court jester, although he runs the risk of becoming one if he cannot modulate his pose from time to time. Unlike the ironist, the fool has a privilege to overstep the bounds of propriety because he is already deemed a nonperson. His privilege, ironically, comes from the fact that he has no other privilege but to be a fool, and this means he must speak the truths that politeness refuses even to the ironist. He is compelled not to fake it, to tell the whole truth and nothing but that truth that Mrs. Harold Smith found so hard to do even when freely resolved upon. He must expose pretense, whether he wants to or not, and that is another reason the fool is harmless – not only because he is counted no person, but also because his truth is constrained, not freely told, and hence dismissible as compelled and not meant. Contrast the constrained truth of the jester with the constrained unfelt apology of the impenitent wrongdoer. Coercion makes the apology work as compensation, whereas coercion makes the jester's truth a joke.

Cultivating an ironic sensibility as a way of handling one's own anxiety about faking roles, or failure to get into role, or one's anxiety about one's own seriousness, or as a means to prevent getting hoist by excessive immersion into one's roles, is, ironically, a petard waiting to explode in your face. For being an ironist is a pose. It too is a role, an amusing one if played well and very conventionally within the array of acceptable social roles. But the ironist takes on risks that other presentations of self do not take on in the same degree. He had better be good at it. It takes very fine adjustments to mock without offending, to self-mock without self-aggrandizing, and to assume ironic posturing without calling into question whether there is any nonironic self that is left to be protected by the pose. It can also become excruciatingly tiresome. The risk is that irony ends in self-involved shallowness, irony all the way down, a chronic refusal to take anything seriously. Ultimately there may be no there there.

But I wonder. If being an ironist is itself a role, like other roles, then it can be taken off, if not quite at will, then stripped off involuntarily. It is hard to be ironic all the time. One must eat, sleep; and one complains and means it. More than anything one gets bored, not in the style of ennui, which forms an unholy alliance with irony, but plain old bored as when listening to people discourse on where their kids are applying to college. Irony also beats the rats off the sinking ship, long before life itself is threatened, when things are getting to you. Furnaces break down, pipes burst, your spouse's needy friend just rang the doorbell, and you see no humor in it at all: nothing but pure unaccommodated reality.

Most ironists in our day are not the kind of ironist a saga hero was; he would joke in the face of his own violent death, and he could do so because his irony worked in the service of his sense of honor.[10] A saga character named Atli remarks dryly on the fashionableness of the spear used to run him through; Hrapp congratulates the person who chopped off his arm as doing the rest of mankind a service. Honor was not a joking matter; but death was. Our kind of bemused irony – "I am above losing my entire being in any role I play, I have a proper critical perspective" – doesn't have great staying power in the face of serious humiliation or pain. It does fine with small-stakes embarrassment, but not with bigger issues such as betrayal by someone you love or the discovery that you are physically revolting to the person you have a crush on. You may put on a mask of irony to hide the pain, but you are no longer an ironist when you do so, for you are recoiling in misery, buying time until you figure out how to reconstitute your being, desperately serious, hurt, vengeful, and bitter.

### Experience: Becoming What You Pretend to Be

Not all merging with role has an unhappy ending. A law student graduates. Three years earlier she knew nothing about the law. Now she knows something, but not very much. She is not deluded on this score. She knows she knows very little. She did well in law school, gets hired by a big firm at a big salary, and is assigned work that sometimes has her talking to clients. Each encounter with a client is a real test of her ability to put on a show. She must exude confidence and competence. People are paying big, and the last thing a client wants is someone assuming a light irony about how she is fresh out of law school and doesn't have a clue. So she fakes it.[11]

She feels painfully aware that she is faking it. She fakes confidence; she fakes a kind of tough directness to cover her fears of not knowing anything. She is completely aware that these are poses, even ironical ones, but without the appearance of irony to make it bearable, to give it a lightness of touch. Because what client would accept that? Imagine the resident surgeon joking to you about this being his first time removing a disc, but big deal, got to do the first one sometime on something other than a cadaver or a cat.

To her mind the chief irony is that she is a lawyer; the state bar says so. That's the joke. She is, but she isn't. She feels as if she is winging it, all pretense, a pure fraud, though she prepares with care for each meeting. She fears nonetheless that she might have overlooked the most obvious of things, the most obvious of theories, because what does she know? After a meeting she is drained, not quite relieved, because she is not sure the client didn't see through her. After a couple of months of faking, she gets more daring; she risks sounding knowledgeable when she has not looked the stuff up, just guessing but with an air of assuredness. She can't believe she is running a risk like that, and after the meeting she races to look up what she had so blithely been BS-ing about. To her great surprise, she finds she basically got it right, but then what if she hadn't? How would she have covered for that? Well, she would harrumph about minority rules and majority rules, splits in jurisdictions, confuse the client a bit. And she survives yet again.

We know the end of the story: after faking it like this for six years, something has been happening. She is now what we call a possessor of experience. She has become what she was faking. She is so good at faking it that she is no longer all that anxious. She might even not feel like a fake anymore, but surely some days it must dawn on her that so much of what we call expertise is in fact expert faking it and never having been caught, and that we will have an excuse or answer ready when someone calls us on it. But no one ever does, until one day...

On bad days she cynically suspects it is an unwritten rule that no one calls anyone's bluff unless someone pretty much dares you to. The whole world is faking it, and everyone is complicit in everyone else's frauds. That is not fair. She has acquired real judgment. She knows she doesn't know everything, but she knows something; she sees people who indeed know much more than she knows, more than she believes it is humanly possible to know; and she genuinely respects and admires such people more than she fears them, but fear them she does, for surely they must see through her. These are the people who are "the real thing," truly knowledgeable, who she imagines must feel secure in their mastery of their subject, though perhaps they never do either. She comes in the end to believe that her anxieties about faking it and exposure are the very form her respect for mastery takes. On good days she lets herself believe that she might not be faking it; she is truly what she once had to fake being; she is one with the role, a lawyer and a pretty good one at that.

The analogy with the lawyer is not quite apt, but it suggests that if someone plays being an ironist long enough, a mocker, a person who fancies he is deep and needs to protect his depths – with humor when he is charming, but with sneers and superciliousness when he is not – he eventually becomes his defensive system and nothing more. A walled town, with everyone inside dead of the plague.[12]

No sooner do I write that than some part of me stands outside myself and says, come off it, Miller, what pretentious overdramatization. You really are not ready to defend the implication that somehow the nonironist has any more people alive inside her town. It is the letter, remember, that slayeth, not irony. That metaphor about everyone dead inside the walled town suggests there is a lively core housed within that needs defense. Just what is at the core? One true self, a town full of clamoring burghers, or nothing at all?

# TEN

# The Self, the Double, and the Sense of Self

SUPPOSE THE NOTION OF AN AUTHENTIC core self is an illusion or little more than what Edith Wharton called a "fugitive flash of consciousness";[1] at least she thinks it is there even if gone in a flash. Much respectable opinion doesn't think the self is really there so much as it is a fiction that keeps us roughly the same person from one day to the next, or a convenience adopted because it is useful for us to think that way. Thus, for instance, Hume.[2] Very respectable philosophers still argue for some form of his position.[3] The debate continues apace, and I merely intend to gesture in the direction of it after my own fashion to get at various social and psychological anxieties that suffuse certain aspects of identity, self, and role.[4]

There is also a long tradition that we do not have one self, but many. This view was offered in various forms, from something as simple as the idea of good angel/bad angel, a kind of Jekyll-and-Hydism, to a view of multiple selves recently resurrected in rational choice theory to help account for the myriad human behaviors that make us continually act as if models of economic egoistic rationality were silly inventions of bizarrely robotic minds.[5] Even the words we use to describe aspects of the individual, if not the self itself, such as "person" or "character," are evidence of a deep belief as to the fictional nature of our psychological, social, and moral selves. "Person" comes from the word for mask, a theatrical term, still imbuing the word "persona" with its sense of an assumed character. "Character" is the name we use to refer not only to our moral essence but also to an eccentric person and the fictional denizens of novel or play, and to the very letters of the script that create him.

The anxiety that our self may be constantly threatened by doubling and replication is an ancient one.[6] The horror of cloning is only its most recent form,[7] and cloning itself can be seen as a continuation of the theme of doubling so central to the nineteenth-century Gothic imagination.[8] But one can see it in the Bible too. The chief article of faith in Judaism is embodied in a commandment called after its first word, Shema: "Hear O Israel, the Lord our God, the Lord is One" (Deut. 6.4). The literal meaning is clear: it basically repeats the first commandment prohibiting setting up other gods before God. But it is more than that: it also says that you Jews shall not evade that prohibition by making Me into myriad emanations of Myself. Angels OK, but no avatars. But the Shema also looks as if the people are giving an order to God to hold Himself together, to keep himself One, as against the threat to multiply implied by his name "I will be who I will be" we touched on in the first chapter. The Shema is thus a kind of mutual command and compact between God and the people to work together to keep Him One.

But no sooner does Judaism make God one than its daughter religion gives Him three selves, and that not being enough, each village and monastery claims its saint, and we are pretty much back to Baals in the groves and on the mountaintops.[9] All the king's horses and all the king's men in the Reformation got Him back to three, and then the Unitarians get Him back to one, but with an accompanying tolerance that let everyone else have their God too, which meant He pretty much disappeared as a unified being. You can have your God; I got mine, and I bet they are not quite the same guy; yours may not even be a guy. Our views of God's own self are a mirror of our uncertainty about the unity, even existence, of our own self – am I one, none, or many? The self, not unlike God, may be something we *sense* more than something that *is*, and we sense it in more ways than one.

The anxiety regarding multiple selves also manifests itself in the fear that the self or selves we think we have may not be ours, but may be imposed on us or borrowed from without. George Herbert Mead has us introjecting various selves from others into our own version of our "me."[10] Much of Mead's position is already set forth in the role played by Adam Smith's impartial spectator, who variously resides within and without. Hume goes so far as to imagine our minds to be mirrors, set up to reflect the mirrors that are other men's minds, with the effect that our opinions and emotions are located in a kind of no-man's-land of infinite regression, an image Smith also resorts to.[11] Without too much stretching we can see in Hume and Smith a highbrow form of the theme of the double.

In a different but related matter, both Hume and Smith can be understood to suggest that our emotions are not our own either, but are caught from others because they are contagious, reflected, or generated by mechanisms of sympathy that require the projection of emotions into others before we can feel them ourselves. One can see in these views a justification for taking allegory seriously as a genre of psychological realism. Those ridiculous personified characters – Anger, Temperance, Sin, Prudence – in poems and narratives we no longer have much taste for are what we ourselves become when we say we feel anger, grief, and so on.[12] Rather than merely feel these sentiments we often become them, or they, like spirits from beyond, come to take over and occupy our bodies. We thus register our emotions not only by saying we feel them, which may or may not be the case, but also by saying we "are" them: I am sad, mad, glad as if I were Sadness, Madness, and Gladness in an allegorical poem.[13] We even raise our kids to see themselves as allegorical figures. Mary, you are the Messy One; Anne, you are the Organized One; Jim, you are the Hot-Tempered One; and John, you are the Quiet Guy. We find ourselves at times feeling put upon to play an allegorical version of ourselves because that is what the company expects from us. Time to be the me they invited me here to be, and that means, generally, they want an overstated version of the type, just to make sure that it is utterly recognizable and what they bargained for.

In the West, however, a philosophical and primitive fear of core-lessness flies in the face of the strong psychological sense of having a unique self at the core. At a minimum this sense of self is the point of consciousness from which I have thoughts that are felt to be mine and mine alone; it is that feeling of being inside my head and not somewhere else. This *sense of self*, which we believe mostly to be a feature of sanity, is assuredly there. Whether the self that the sense of self senses is there, too, is probably not susceptible of proof.

Most of us, even when sitting with 60,000 identical souls at a football game or when packed into a subway car, except in brief moments of dissociation, feel quite certain, self-deceiving though it may be, that we have a uniquely indelible core – embattled perhaps, but still special and our own. Me, a mere subject position? My foot. But why my foot? Is that foot part of my self, or merely attached to it? Would I cease to be me without it? Does my self need it? Surely if I am a serious sprinter it does. And why did I utter "my foot" as an expletive? Is it because it is even lower by one measure than the arse, which stands halfway between foot and head but still is understood to be the bottom – even named "bottom" or "bum" – spiritually lower than the foot? And thus the foot, because physically the lowest, is able to work as a euphemism for the lowly arse, which I, in a gesture of politeness, substitute prissily for ass, opting for the English form as against the American. And why is it that in biforms such as arse/ass, curse/cuss, burst/bust, horse/Hoss, it is the short-voweled r-less form that is lower in social status?

Desperate to distinguish my self from others I am thrown back on the fact that whoever I am I cannot tickle myself. I am also the only sighted person in the world who needs a mirror to observe the progress of my hair loss, and I am thus the only person in the world who can construct a self that forgets how thin my hair is in back while still caring desperately about it. But that's a start. Not even my clone or double can say that. My self is intimately tied up with my being embodied in a way that distinguishes me from others so that I am aware that I see their bodies differently and more fully than I see my own. That means the only full view I can get of myself requires others, for how can I see myself whole unless I see myself as others see me, a view I can guess at pretty reliably based on my experience of how I see them? I also need human culture to manufacture mirrors, because mere nature with its reflecting ponds will not do the trick of letting me see the back of my head.

This also raises complex questions of whether my body needs to be a particular type of body for me to be me. My view is that it does, for though I have been envious of other body types a good portion of my life, I have not been all that envious, for I fear that a body too different from what I got stuck with genetically would make it impossible for me to have the same inner life, which, such as it is, I would prefer to keep. Not because I find it all that interesting, but because without it my self as I know it would cease to exist, or so I fear.[14]

My self, then, to the extent I have one, seems to require some kind of embodiment, and not just any kind. Is the same always true of my *sense* of self, the feeling of being a thinking thing with thoughts that are mine alone? It has been forcefully argued that the sense of self is a purely mental phenomenon, for which the body is merely a vessel:

> The early realization of the fact that one's thoughts are unobservable by others, the experience of the profound sense in which one is alone in one's head – these are among the very deepest facts about the character of human life, and found the sense of the mental self. It is perhaps most often vivid when one is alone and thinking, but it can be equally vivid in a room full of people. It connects with a feeling that nearly everyone has had intensely at some time – the feeling that one's body is just a vehicle or vessel for the mental thing that is what one really or most essentially is. I believe that the primary or fundamental way in which we conceive of ourselves is as a distinct mental thing – sex addicts, athletes, and supermodels included.[15]

You recognize what the author, Galen Strawson, is describing. Yet isn't it the case that so many of those thoughts take the form of talking to oneself or to imagined others? The effect is to "embody" that mental self ever so slightly. Much of what we call thinking is carried on as a conversation within or with ourselves. Mead goes so far as to claim that self-consciousness can arise only via such a conversation: "It is only after the child has reached the point of communicating with himself that his own self-consciousness can arise. This process largely takes place through vocal gestures."[16] We need not see in our mind's eye a mouth talking and ears listening, but this internal talk is experienced not much differently from routine real talk in which there is an assumption of mouths, tongues, and ears and hence bodies. For instance, real external noise will prevent us from hearing our inner conversation. Once we cannot hear that internal conversation we get confused, says Mead,[17] and his observation is roundly confirmed by the reports of combat soldiers. Ford Madox Ford in *Parade's End* has his main character note the effects of the noise of exploding shells: "If you cannot hear your thoughts, how the hell are you going to tell what your thoughts are doing?" Civil War soldier Abner Small agrees: "The shock from a bursting shell will scatter a man's thoughts as the iron fragments will scatter the leaves overhead."[18]

Who is talking to whom when we talk out loud to ourselves? Who is the talker, and who the addressee? Mead says it is the self that is addressed; something he calls the "I," which is not the self, is doing the talking. But even if we do not subscribe to the Meadian analysis, it seems we do experience a sense of something less than unity when we speak to ourselves, something very much like the sensation we have of being a person who must play so many different roles. We surely split ourselves when we talk out loud to ourselves, so that the person speaking is directing words to the ears of a person listening. Internal monologues split us this way too, do they not? They might thus be better understood as internal dialogues, or at least as soliloquies addressed to ourselves as audience.

Might it be too that anxieties about doubling are simply a byproduct, or detritus, of the fact that self-consciousness is generally experienced as a conversation within ourselves, requiring speaker and listener? We find ourselves praising and blaming ourselves, silently and out loud: *Way to go, Miller*, or *Miller, you idiot*.[19] My sense of self can be a disembodied mental thing but not totally so, not all that differently from the way that I can completely disattend the bodies of real people when I talk to them on the phone or via e-mail. To the extent that language and conversation are involved, we assume certain necessary body parts to be doing their work unobtrusively. And from this minimal sense of embodiment, some – those who put gender first, for instance – would no doubt claim that the sense of self can never be experienced independently from the gendered body.

This is clearly true of the self, but as Strawson would understand the *sense of self*, that sense would precede any notions of gendered bodies or gendered minds.

Self-monitoring requires more than just talking to ourselves; we also use imagined visual inputs. We think of much of self-monitoring as *observing* ourselves. This observing is a strange thing, because it is only partly visual (much of it is listened to) and then is carried out by eyes (and ears) not quite our own. When we talk to ourselves, often in the form of approval or disapproval, it is because that talk is tied up with watching ourselves as if we were another, but not quite – a kind of quasi-other perhaps. And the entity doing the watching is also cast as a quasi-other in a dizzying sci-fi feat in which each is partly responsible for creating the other. Smith is clear that we must split ourselves to carry out the task of self-judging:

> When I endeavour to examine my own conduct, when I endeavour to pass sentence upon it, and either to approve or condemn it, it is evident that, in all such cases, I divide myself, as it were, into two persons; and that I, the examiner and judge, represent a different character from that other I, the person whose conduct is examined into and judged of. The first is the spectator, whose sentiments with regard to my own conduct I endeavour to enter into, by placing myself in his situation, and by considering how it would appear to me, when seen from that particular point of view. The second is the agent, the person whom I properly call myself, and of whose conduct, under the character of a spectator, I was endeavouring to form some opinion. The first is the judge; the second the person judged of. But that the judge should, in every respect, be the same with the person judged of, is as impossible, as that the cause should, in every respect, be the same with the effect.
>
> (TMS III.i.6)

Smith combines jural images of judge and criminal with theatrical images of spectators and actors. It is perhaps impossible to keep theatricality out of trials, and it has pretty near been impossible to keep criminality from coloring the lot of the demimonde of the actor. Funny, too, how certain forms of self-consciousness have the form of show trials. Smith assumes for the most part here that these internal trials of ourselves are not marred by overt deceptions and self-deceptions, but he well knows that the impartial spectator is bribable, suborned by the various tricks of self-love, envy, and interest – the log in the eye again.

## Stripping Off the Layers

I have been mixing up a set of complicated issues about self, sense of self, emotions, identity, and consciousness, and to unravel it properly would make this a book I could not and do not intend to write. The literature on continuity of character in response to Hume alone can fill shelves. For purposes of faking it and our anxieties about our own fraudulence and authenticity, it makes little difference whether or not the self is there. If the self is really there, it could still be doubted as Hume and others have, and if it is fictional it could be believed in as most of us do. The crucial test the fiction must pass is that it be plausible and sane given the truth about our abilities, looks, body type, words, deeds, and cultural attributes such as race, religion, and gender. The self, fictional or not, must measure up reasonably well as a legitimate self, given the social constraints imposed on selfhood.

The anxiety persists that, even if there is no real core of an authentic me, what part of me is making me a nervous wreck about those roles anyway? Is that anxiety an unfortunate but unavoidable byproduct of proper socialization, a sign of caring to play my role well, to good reviews and favorable mentions? Still, who the hell is running the show?

Those who sing the praises of authenticity, of being true to oneself, are of little help. The highbrow advocates are no less embarrassing than the middlebrow exponents; no one escapes sounding hokey.[20] The highly self-conscious poses of authenticity in the self-indulgent romantic egoistic style are about as silly as primal scream therapy. Manfred on the mountain, Zarathustra in Sils Maria ever so proudly escape hoi polloi on the plains below and then seek to be admired by them for contemning them as they lecture on self-realization and authenticity, posing as Moses, no less, laying down the law. Vanity oh vanity.

Authenticity? True to myself? And what does that mean? Am I merely the sum of my roles: father + son + husband + professor + American + Jew + next-door neighbor + writer + teacher + jester? What if I am good enough at some to qualify as the genuine article but am pretty much a fraud at others? Is it only the roles I am good at for which I can claim authenticity? Yup, that Bill Miller, fully one-fifth authentic. Or do I get credit for being fully authentic if I own up to being four-fifths a fraud? Or do I get credit only if I determine to improve the four-fifths of me that is a sham? The self-realization and authenticity babble assumes an ultimate unity. And I want to agree. Surely I am more than the actors in the play that bears my name. But I do not feel myself to be the director of that play either, for I am hardly calling all the shots. I experience myself as both more and less than the director. I am also the role I am playing, the repertoire of roles waiting to be donned at a moment's notice, and the roles I have played in the past that I am still hated or loved for. So am I an incorporated theater company?[21] I am more than that too, because I am also in the audience watching my performances. Moreover, I am never turned away at the ticket booth for a sold-out performance; I am condemned, unless alcohol or true fun intervenes to put self-consciousness to sleep, to play the smalltown newspaper critic to my own performances in the high school play, while bitterly wishing I could make a living as an author rather than as a critic.

I am not in despair about this, merely befuddled. Erving Goffman paints a much grimmer picture. He has often been accused of having no theory of the self, or of seeing the self as just a bunch of roles largely imposed from without, but in fact he has a view of the core stripped self and it is bleak.[22] Here he speaks of what is revealed when an audience is "inadvertently given glimpses behind the scenes of a performance" and gets a view of the performer it was not meant to have. What they discover is a "fundamental democracy that is usually well hidden":

The individual who performs the character will be seen for what he largely is, a solitary player involved in a harried concern for his production. Behind many masks and many characters, each performer tends to wear a single look, a naked unsocialized look, a look of concentration, a look of one who is privately engaged in a difficult, treacherous task.[23]

Goffman, ironist extraordinaire, antisentimentalist, plays against type here, moving from satire and irony to tragedy and high seriousness. And I don't quite believe him. Why think a harried look or a look of concentration is unsocialized? Just because it was not meant for the audience who is catching the inadvertent and unwelcome glimpse does not mean he doesn't put it on for himself or some imaginary audience. Are not those harried looks part of the show he plays to that judgmental audience he carries within?

Even if that look is really stripped down, naked, authentic, and unsocialized, the despondent soul may, in an access of self-consciousness, launch into playing Harried Desperation, an allegorical role to which he cannot find an exit. Goffman's use of "naked" to describe the look of the person stripped at last of all his masks suggests that stripping away the masks and roles culture imposes gets down to a real unaccommodated core. But the image of nakedness doesn't quite work. Whether the real me is real or a fiction, I know it is not the naked me. When Lear strips off his clothes to find man to be nothing but a bare forked animal, he is posturing. Once culture makes clothes the norm, taking them off is always a ritual or Ritual.[24] Getting ready for bed, taking a shower, getting examined by the doctor, sex.

I know I am exaggerating to make my point, but I am not fabricating. I can get ready for bed out of pure habit, without being racked by anxieties about how ridiculous it is to be human, yet when I turn my attention to the thought of those who sleep naked, I can't help thinking that they are putting on an act, a pretentious one, playing the liberated soul, freely experiencing animal freedom. Ya, right. Who are they trying to impress by thinking themselves superior to pajamas? I own to feeling a bit foolish when I put on my flannel pajamas; they seem one step up from pajamas with feet on them, like the ones my toddlers wore. At least there is no pretense in them, just utility, and a necessary accommodation with an imperfect world in which you must endure, no matter how careful you are, your share of looking foolish.

But where is the feeling of fakery, you ask, or of faking it when you are naked all by yourself? Before others yes, but not alone. Even Goffman would say you are backstage, and though you can't quite relax because you will soon have to be on stage again, for the moment you can catch your breath. I answer partly thus: I don't see my naked body as a mere representation of raw nature. No sooner is it looked at when I dry myself off after showering than all kinds of anxieties intrude, or are felt to be knocking at the door of consciousness, as to its increasing ugliness. There is a temptation to blind myself to the truth of it so that it will appear less disgusting. But I lack the imagination to do much of a makeover and fear those attractive students I teach would get the giggles or get sick at the thought of that body sexually. Worse, the dog just wandered into the bathroom and that makes me more self-conscious than if it had been my next-door neighbor. I feel embarrassed not only for myself, but for our entire species, which I am representing at that moment to the canine world. The cat makes me feel this way too, the turtle only a little bit, and the guinea pig, tree frog, and Siamese fighting fish not at all. I am still not at the naked core, but in the next chapter I suggest where it might be uncovered.

# ELEVEN

# At the Core at Last: The Primordial Jew

SO I ASK AGAIN: where amidst all these roles lies the true self, that core of authenticity, that real me behind the masks and veils, that authentic Bill Miller, not the guy who signs this book William Ian Miller? How I got the Ian long before that name became pretentiously fashionable is a story in itself, an innocent one of my dad doing honor to the Scotsman Ian McPhearson, who commanded the ship on which my dad served in the war. I was named after William Isidore Miller, my father's dead father, really Velvel or Villkela Yitzhak Miller in the Yiddish that was my namesake's native tongue. When you are Bill Miller there is always a good chance you will be sitting next to another one on the airplane; you get the mail of several others on your campus, and most recently you lost five years of accumulated frequent flyer miles because some other William Miller in Ann Arbor took a trip around the world on them. So you posture as William Ian Miller purely as a practical matter. But had my middle name been Seymour, I see you thinking, you would not be signing your books William Seymour Miller, would you? Spelling out that Ian, latching on to it as a veil of sorts, shows I know very well who and what I am at the core.

## A Bowdlerized Jewish Joke

Maybe the core naked me lies in certain identities, ineradicable identities. Let me try to get at it in a different way. Freud tells a joke, a Jewish joke, which he bowdlerizes in an important way. The joke – like most jokes, and especially Freud's, who had all the sense of humor of someone who thinks a squirting flower on his lapel is a fine jest – is

not very funny, but given Freud's usual fare not bad enough to pro-
hibit retelling:

> The doctor, who had been asked to look after the Baroness at her
> confinement, pronounced that the moment had not come, and sug-
> gested to the Baron that in the meantime they should have a game
> of cards in the next room. After a while a cry of pain from the
> Baroness struck the ears of the two men: "Ah, mon Dieu, que je
> souffre!" Her husband sprang up, but the doctor signed to him to sit
> down: "It's nothing. Let's go on with the game!" A little later there
> were again sounds from the pregnant woman: "Mein Gott, mein
> Gott, what terrible pains!" – "Aren't you going in, Professor?"
> asked the Baron. –"No, no. It's not time yet." At last there came
> from next door an unmistakable cry of "Aa-ee, aa-ee, aa-ee!"
> The doctor threw down his cards and exclaimed: "*Now* it's time."[1]

The joke is put through quite a sea change by Freud's censoring
and emending the Baroness's last scream. It was not a prelinguistic cry
of pain, "aa-ee," but, obviously, "Oy vay iz mir."[2] The point of the
joke is that for the Baroness, an assimilated Jew, each increase in pain
strips away the most recent accretion in the process of assimilation,
the *drang nach Westen* of the Jew. She is still able to maintain her
role as a French-speaking German aristocrat in the midst of minor
pain. Jack up the pain, and she starts drifting eastward back across
the Rhine to echt German, until agony rips off this last mask to reveal
the inescapable core of her being, east of the Vistula. Freud's bowdlerization is not motivated by scruples against telling unvarnished
Jewish jokes, for right before this joke he had been regaling readers
with them, some making much the same point as this one.

We can explain Freud's rewriting the last line this way: every-
one knows this is a Jewish joke, that the last line has to be oy vay.
It advertises its bowdlerization because it is so unfunny as told; it
has no point except a cheap misogynistic one not worth the telling.
Childbirth really hurts; you going to mock the woman for screaming?
But as a more complex commentary on Jewish pretensions to escape
Jewishness, it has some social and satiric bite. It just may be that
Freud's bowdlerization is itself a rather clever joke. Suppressing the
Yiddish of the last line is an attempt to make the joke pass, just as

the Baroness is trying so hard to pass. But the joke is that neither a Jew nor a Jewish joke can be anything but what it is. Their cores are ineradicable. No amount of culture will change the Jew; his Jewishness will burst through at embarrassing moments. That is the surface point of the unbowdlerized joke, and the deeper one of the bowdlerized version. All those parapraxes, those Freudian slips, are so many lapses into Yiddish or into a telltale accent. The point of the joke is that there is no risk that a Jew desiring to pass will ever fake so well as to become one with his new role.

John Murray Cuddihy argues powerfully that Freud's purpose is to war against the goy, to rub his face in the uncivilizable Jew. Because the Jew could never make a good civil Christian, show the Christian instead that underneath his veneers, his politeness, civility, decorum, restraint, and good manners, he is at his core nothing more than what he thinks the Jew is: a bestial, filthy sexual thing, precultural, neither civilized nor civilizable. The bowdlerized Jewish joke says that at our core we are instinct and beast, prelinguistic and precultural screamers.

But that aa-ee, aa-ee is also a mask for Yiddish, Jew talk. The suggestion is that the first human sounds of agony are not just nonsense syllables, that they are not a pure manifestation of unadorned nature that comes with the purity of pain, but that those pure unadorned natural vocalizations are Yiddish, or some kind of masked Jew talk. Jew talk in the Western tradition was the ur-talk, the first talk, the natural language of humankind, and the language of pain. The point is not the humanist one that at root we are all mere forked animals, but a more hostile one that at root gentiles are no better than a bunch of Jews trying to cover it up with perfume and manners, a claim that is a horror to Christians, too nauseating to contemplate.

Among the many hypotheses offered to explain anti-Semitism, at least in part, has been a supposed Christian bitter envy of the Jews for having been chosen as God's people. This view would then propose that the Christian could resolve the pain of his envy by making the lot of the Jew unenviable; make it so unpleasant as to breathe a sigh of relief that God had not chosen Christians like you to be tortured by the likes of you. But the one thing that must have still stuck in the craw was that during that period of history when God cared to speak directly to human beings at all, He had chosen to speak to Jews. No mediation, no translation necessary.[3] Though Christians insisted that from the time of Jesus God was veiled to the Jews, who in their blindness could not *see* the One Way to the Lord,[4] that loss did not quite assuage the envy of the fact that the Jews could talk directly to Him and He to them. He was a co-linguist of the Jews. The Jew could *hear* God and understand Him, argue and bargain with him, as Abraham, father of the Jews, did in Gen. 18.23–33. Christians, however, had to secure translators to hear God or his son, for both spoke in a Jewish tongue, whether Hebrew or Aramaic.[5]

Imagine, though, how to explain that God became man as a Jew. You could argue that God chose the most telling way to humble himself. Incarnating himself as Achilles or Socrates rather than as a Judean would have carried a very different message. But God, like pagan deities, cannot shake completely a habit of tricksterism; there are more than a few ironies in choosing to enflesh Himself as a poor Jew. Can we suppose a deep Christian anxiety that God, instead of masking Himself as the Jew Jesus, in fact, was stripping Himself of all His own veils and masks, revealing the naked truth about His own core identity? It turns out that God's indelible self, in the Christian exegetical tradition, his core, is the Jew Jesus, harbored deep inside His bosom until the time was ripe to loose him upon the world.[6] Like man, like God: Jew at the core. "Aa-ee, aa-ee, aa-ee!" For the anti-Semite, and for Freud, the Jew has a fixed self beneath his masks; it is Western civilizing Christian culture that is the costumery of roles and poses, fronts and fakes.

## The Jew at the Core of Christian Identity

If there is a core that is the pure us, that purity is subject to contamination. A researcher on disgust asks us to consider the effects on a barrel of wine of adding a tablespoon of raw sewage compared with the effects on a barrel of raw sewage of adding a tablespoon of wine.[7] The wine is magically transformed by the sewage, rendered disgusting and undrinkable. The sewage, however, remains just what it is despite the addition of the wine. Pollutants are thus powerful in a way that the pure is not; purity is much more vulnerable to pollution than pollution to purification. To war against the most routine types of moral and spiritual pollution, recourse must be had to majestic notions such as Plenitude of Grace. But the exceptional nature of Grace merely underscores the underlying sense that only the truly exceptional can do battle with the most ordinary types of pollution. The deck is stacked in favor of degradation by the low as against elevation by the high. Purifying agents thus must give themselves up in the process of purification in a kind of suicide mission, like the soap that is rinsed away in mutual scummy embrace with the dirt, going down together so that we can put on clean clothes again. But the pollutant infiltrates, thrives, and multiplies, transforming whatever it touches into, it is feared, what it is.

The power of the pollutant is the power of the Jew in the eyes of the anti-Semite, and in the eyes of Cuddihy's Freud and many another Jew, not all of whom need be crippled with self-hatred but who cannot avoid knowing how they are seen, loathed, and feared by the dominant order. Take the case of medieval Spain, which cajoled, threatened, and forced its Jews to convert during the fifteenth century, finally expelling those who remained in 1492.[8] Judenrein, right? Then the anxieties set in. What if these conversos really were Jews in secret? They are passing for Christians, marrying our daughters, and we marry theirs. And handy-dandy who is a Jew, who a Christian?

In the end, in a form of poetic justice that would make a Jew smirk if it had not come at such a price, instead of making Jews into Christians as they had thought and intended, Christians feared and believed that they were being turned into Jews. One drop of blood did you in. What power. Who could be sure he was pure? Under the law of *limpieza de sangre* (purity of blood) those suspected of converso origins had to prove their purity of blood, and surely this led to false testimony, to fake genealogies, to all kinds of posturing as not being the Jew you feared you were and suspected all your neighbors to be. The proof of converso falsity? They appeared to be Christian, and that was exactly the appearance that could not be trusted, for wouldn't it be just like a false Jew to counterfeit his Christianity?[9]

Converso blood filled some of the most pious and powerful of Christian veins: Ferdinand of Aragon, St. Teresa de Avila, Diego Laínez, friend of St. Ignatius and second General of the Jesuits. So the most damning appearances were – as per Goffman's brilliantly paranoid essay "Normal Appearances" – precisely those that looked perfectly fine.[10] You were either a fake, or, if a pure old Christian, you could never be sure that you were not, perish the thought, a Jew "at heart," for who knows what truth might lie beneath the falsity of your invented genealogy?[11]

Not only anxious Spaniards but also anxious Germans and anxious Protestants from St. Louis. This is not a sweet case with a happy ending in which Jews fake being Christians long enough and become Christians in the end. This tale is not one of an apprentice becoming a journeyman becoming a master, as with the lawyer, doctor, or laborer, who starts by faking and ends by becoming the real thing. This is a vision whose claim is that the indelible core will win out in the end, the Jew at the core, at least the Jew as he is imagined to be by the most paranoid of anti-Semites, thus captured by the distasteful sensibility of T. S. Eliot:

> But this or such was Bleistein's way:
> A saggy bending of the knees
> And elbows, with the palms turned out,
> Chicago Semite Viennese.
>
> A lusterless protrusive eye
> Stares from the protozoic slime
> At a perspective of Canaletto.
> The smoky candle end of time
>
> Declines. On the Rialto once.
> The rats are underneath the piles.
> The jew is underneath the lot...[12]

The Jew, whom Eliot refuses to accord the respect of a capital letter, in Eliot's disgusting vision is primordial ooze. Jews are nature at its most disgusting, representing the disgusting fecundity of rot and pond scum. They are both the rot eating at the foundation of Christian civilization and that civilization's rotten foundation. Venice has become Shylock's, though Shylock was forced to convert as part of the "mercy" shown him.[13] Unlike Iago, who warns us that he is not who he is, Shylock can be only the Jew he is at the core, even if he is not allowed to be the Jew he is on the surface. Bleistein is his modern avatar, now a tourist, having oozed further west from Vienna to Chicago, passing back through Venice, polluting vistas that Canaletto painted, ostensibly getting cultured and acculturated in the process. Eliot lets us know that though he is passing through, Bleistein is not passing. Eliot is thus in accord with a view that it has been claimed the Jews have of themselves: that Jews shouldn't even bother to fake, we do it so poorly. This is one way of putting Cuddihy's argument: the core of Jewish identity is the Jew's belief he can never really pass, because he can never learn the rules of civility; civility is a way of acting in the world completely at odds with his true self. Freud's joke about the Baroness is not a joke by an anti-Semite, but a Jewish joke composed by Jews.

Then why did Christians fear Jewish infiltration if Jews were so easily exposed? Would anyone "do it" with Bleistein? Here, I suppose, is where anti-Semitism converged with misogyny. Women, Christian women, could not be trusted not to do it with Bleistein. And what of the trustworthy ones, the Portias? Surely they would not give way to the vile Bleistein. What if, though, Bleistein were not so readily discernible because he had a Christian mother and maybe two Christian grandmothers and a Christian grandfather; in fact, he may have had no more than one Jew way back in his family tree, but such is the power of that Jewish blood that it a Bleistein makes. Bleistein is the horrific reflection in Eliot's worst nightmare of what he himself might be in the grand scheme of things: the barrel of wine in which some wag poured a tablespoon of sewage.

I SEEM TO HAVE LOST my sense of humor and have retreated into ethnic insularism. Am I just using Freud's bad joke to make a bitter one of my own? That if we are made in God's image and God humiliates Himself by becoming a Jew from Galilee, then the joke is that all of us are Jews at the core, a core Christianity has cloaked and veiled? I have taken an unfrolicsome detour, abandoning the psychological and vaguely philosophical approach for a literary one, because, I suppose, it allows for poetic license. My claim is fanciful and exaggerated but not necessarily false for being so. The point is not the banal one that identity is a matter of history, which of course it is, or that the self is an historical construct, sensible as such a point would be. The bitterness in the exposition is my quasi-serious suggestion that not just any history an indelible self doth make. I don't mean to be privileging a victim status, nor claiming an experience available only to persecuted people, for we are not, say, Gypsies or Potawanamie at the core, though a not altogether fanciful claim could be made for American identity being black with a dab of Irish at the core. Please do not think I am whining, though whining is one of the more authentic behaviors we engage in, despite its being so easily put on or faked. This foray of mine is a sociological fantasy, not a personal revelation or complaint.

Sartre claimed about half a century ago that the anti-Semite makes the Jew, and there is some truth to that, but not the whole truth. The lot of those with stigmatized identities is not just self-hatred but that that self-hatred coexists in some complex way with a pride that both opposes it and is in part caused by it. You lament the injustice of your group's inferior status in the larger ordering; you can wish for admittance or just to be left alone. You can also turn your back on the larger order and be proud of what you are. But when low-status groups talk up their pride there is suspicion all around, by insiders and outsiders, that it is all sour grapes and wishful thinking, a shrinking of aspiration to coincide with what you are or what you can actually get, that the whole thing is one barely disguised charade, one big fake.

Or if you cannot find much to be proud of, you can turn your back on pride, declare it to be a sin, and proclaim yourself to be exalted by virtue of being low and in the dirt and then, perversely, be proud of that. This is Nietzsche's well-known account of the transformation of values, motivated by cunning, meanness, and vengeful envy that inform an emotion he called *ressentiment*. He blamed the Jews for inventing *ressentiment* but blamed Christianity for perfecting it.[14] Weakness becomes a virtue, strength a sin. Not fighting back comes to be called courage, ugliness means beauty.[15] For Nietzsche the transformation of values is the con of all cons. It means a total refusal to accept the truth about your real motives and real lack of merit. *Ressentiment* is real, not at all a fake, but it motivates a massive self-deception.[16]

When excluded groups claim to be proud of what they are, we might want to test to see whether it is based on something more than wishful thinking and self-deception. Real pride is indeed available to them, handed to them on a silver platter by the moronic imbecility that is so often a salient feature of pompous or brute power. Thus the Jew's contempt for the *goyische Kopf*; the black's for the white's lack of physicality, humor, cool and grace; women's for men's psychological fragility; the child's for adult dullness (and bad breath). And this contempt funds a corresponding pride in one's own superiority on precisely these grounds.[17]

This kind of pride, though, is parasitical on the politics of contempt that gives rise to it. There is another, simpler feeling of pride, the one you feel when you see your kid do something special, or when you actually achieve something yourself that not even you can prevent yourself from feeling proud of. Pride, the rush of innocent pride, is another one of those experiences, like shame, that fills our entire being, uniting body, self, and soul. The rush of pride suspends self-criticism; pride can also exist in less intense forms, in a quiet and perhaps not unjustified satisfaction. But then the divisions start to reappear; we start wondering whether we are not deluded. And should we conclude that our pride is merited, we must take care not to impose it immodestly on others. Within seconds, then, unless alone, we are back to the world of poses and faking it.

THIS IS MUCH TOO GRIM; it too smacks of being a pose. I in fact have had it good, for which one must mostly praise the deep decency and expansive freedoms of America, and I am bitter only in bursts: when I think of how unfathomable the depths of hatred are for what my family and kids are, what I indelibly am and my ancestors were.

# TWELVE

# Passing and Wishing You Were What You Are Not

ONE OF THE MOST INSISTENT PRESSURES to fake it big occurs when we are ashamed of what we are seen to be. Shame can have a salutary social effect when it pushes us to be lawful, mannerly, and civil. Or it can become rather morally suspect when it tempts us to disavow our religion, nation, race, or some aspects, not all by any means, of sexual desire. In those cases in which there may be grounds for distrusting the moral quality of the shame felt, we can blame the person as a self-hater, as someone culpably not at ease with himself, culpable because he is cowardly and disloyal to what *we* say he is.[1] (Funny how we are often so much surer of the identities we impose on others than of the ones we feel we can claim for ourselves.) Or we can blame the unjust order that makes him have to mobilize courage simply to be black, a Jew, gay, or a member of some other group condemned by the dominant order to be pariahs. Or, as is often the case, we blame both – the pariah no less than the unjust order.

Hard to believe that turning my attention to self-hatred, very mild forms of it, will be my amends for the bitterness that leaked out in the preceding chapter. I undertake to present a lighter heart, and a droller tone. There is significantly less temptation now for a Jew to pass than there was fifty years ago. Temptations, though, there are still, and they are not completely resisted. Why do I really spell out that Ian, even though there is nothing Jewish about William I. Miller, unless it lowers the odds even further and in fact makes a false claim for not being so? There is less temptation for blacks and gays too. For some who could have passed under the older order, the ideal of diversity offers inducements to claim and publish identities they had abandoned or had the option to abandon or keep hidden in closets.

Yet few would deny that the shades and taints of stigma linger; the scars are discernible, and the people who bear them are occasionally tempted by plastic surgeries, figurative and real.

I will stick mostly to Jews in this chapter, with a preamble about Americans abroad, because I am a Jewish American and that gives me some license to say truths that if said about other groups would be deemed unprivileged. Truth is not accepted as a defense in such cases; in fact, one of the chief themes of this book is that truth is an offense, seldom, if ever, a defense. I especially want to get at the moves we make to disavow certain identities for the nonce, not for all time – small cowardices perhaps, but nothing major. It is about roles again, and fitting in, and trying to avoid petty embarrassments. Big shames and humiliations I put to one side.

Distancing oneself from others whom one is lumped with often involves a set of motives we loosely call self-hatred, but it needn't be as grave as that. Self-hatred, like love, lumps together a lot of different phenomena. The emotion directed against oneself may not always be hatred but rather contempt, or disgust, guilt, or shame, or simply a vague dissatisfaction, not even as bad as low self-esteem. It may be more or less durable, no more than a passing moment at one end or an immutable trait of character at the other. The loathing can be for traits that are yours alone or yours only to the extent you belong to a disfavored group.

Self-hatred can thus have different styles depending on what you hate yourself for. You might hate yourself in one way for being short, in another for being fat, in another for being skinny, black, Jewish, crippled, blind, old, or cowardly. And because self-hatred often takes its cast from the hatreds of those who hate you, it matters greatly by whom and for what you are hated, and the ways, means, and history of that hatred. Presumably the self-hatred of American blacks, to the extent they are self-haters, would not be structured in the same way or take on the same style as the self-hatred of Jews, for whom self-hatred seems to lurk at the very core of diasporan identity.[2] Not all the powerless and disfavored dislike themselves in the same way, if they dislike themselves at all. Nor are sentiments of negative self-assessment solely the curse of the powerless.[3] I might feel embarrassed

by privileges I have that I feel I hold unfairly or are not quite legitimate but that I am still not willing to relinquish: so-called liberal
guilt, a sentiment that can readily be blamed as merely sentimental,
no more moral than Claudius's weak or self-indulgent guilt noted
earlier.

## An American Tragicomedy

Take the case of a certain kind of American self-hatred that is motivated by class and regional biases, and also by a snobbish antidemo-
cratic impulse. The fear is that one belongs to a people that proves
itself consistently to lack sufficient insight to loathe itself for its beer
bellies, for coming from the prairies, for utter obliviousness to pretensions regarding coffee and wine, for enjoying tractor pulls and pro
wrestling, for bad sexual politics, for being drawn to drawing a bead
on furry creatures with beautiful brown eyes, for being more religious than is seemly, for having no culture, and, in a very restricted
and bad faith way, for being white, for this kind of self-hater is himself inevitably white. What he loathes, in other words, is that these
average people seem so damn authentic and at ease with what they
are, and he cannot believe they should be. Those sorts were supposed
to be shepherds playing flutes and lyres in Arcadia, and it turns out
they are tailgaters eating brats and blasting boomboxes in the parking
lot before the Packer game.

No self-hating American of the kind I am describing feels that
American blacks harm his *amour-propre* in the same way as does a
white frat guy or a yahoo tailgater. Not because he is not racist, but
because he feels he will never be held accountable for loud fat blacks
in the same way he will for loud fat whites. Indeed, he is willing to
concede with some sincerity that blacks have style.

There is no self-hatred, quite the contrary, for coming from
Berkeley, from Greenwich Village, from unproductively pleasant-
looking settings in Vermont or on Cape Cod, or from any other place
deemed suitable for a second home. This self-hatred, though distasteful, is not as morally defective as, and should be distinguished from,
the self-hatred that characterizes much of the American left as when

it responded to the terrorist attacks of 9/11 with a barely disguised Schadenfreude.[4] The self-hatred I am talking about, though, is different. It is mostly snobbish and patrician, available to hoity-toity conservatives as well as to limousine liberals. That these types are understood as being pretentious by everyone including themselves matters not; they seem to cultivate and delight in an affectation of having these kinds of affectations. This kind of self-hatred, in other words, is really a way of congratulating oneself on being above the others who happen to be your countrymen. At home it is a cause for self-congratulation. Trips abroad are the problem, to Europe primarily, rich Europe, and this means that Slavic areas and certain circum-Mediterranean regions don't count, nor does much of the rest of the world. Any number of anxious Americans are eager to show these qualifying Europeans that they are neither as vulgar, fat, nor twangy as they suspect they will be expected to be, for, of course, these Yanks agree entirely with this unkind assessment of their fellow citizens even as they also believe in their own individual exceptionalism.

Here is a fairly classic situation. My wife and I were in a pub somewhere in the Cotswolds, seated at a small table. To write "Cotswolds" rather than "England" is of course an affectation, a code for speaking to those in the know, even if "the know" here represents little real knowledge. Six middle-aged American women were seated nearby, speaking loudly, laughing even more loudly, drawing disapproving looks from the natives. One announced to the others that the Lake Country from which she had just come was nothing compared with the Finger Lakes. Both my wife and I sat in silence, afraid to open our mouths for fear we would be known for what we were. I even thought we might try to pass with our small amount of German, enough to have us carry on competently about beer and potatoes, which was exactly what we had in front of us anyway. Imagine the sorry state of a less than self-assured American tourist, a Jewish one no less, who feels tempted to pass himself off as a German. In a gesture of complicity, a young Englishman at the next table leaned toward us and said, imitating the ladies by exaggerating their nasal vowels, which he heard as a high-pitched whine, "Yes, nothing to compare with Rochester."

Shameful to tell, we were flattered that he colluded with us, even more flattered that we weren't immediately identifiable as Americans. But such flattery was purchased at the price of not being able to answer without embarrassing *him* for his having insulted what we were, to say nothing of embarrassing ourselves for speaking the way we would once we opened our mouths. Our own American tongue would sound especially grating to us at the moment, now that we knew how painful it was for an Englishman to hear it. Hadn't Trollope complained of "the well-known nasal twang" as early as the 1870s?[5] How were we to answer this Englishman to save him and ourselves the embarrassment? Moreover, as luck would have it, my wife was born and raised seventy miles south of Rochester. How contemptible we were. We laughed in bonhomie and pardoned him and cravenly said we knew what he meant, but we were painfully self-conscious of our o's and a's. Disgraced and disgraceful as we might have been, however, we did not stoop to an Anglophilic accent, Katherine Hepburn talk – self-hatred of this sort has its limits. In my trade that accent seems to be an occupational hazard of anyone who has spent more than three months in the United Kingdom some time in the past forty years.

The best we could claim is that we had been counted as the right sort of serviceable American. In this setting that meant being an American who registered proper embarrassment for what he was, joined in mocking his countrymen, and accepted the greater desirability of passing for something else, though in the end we were still as American as apple pie, forever kin with the ladies from Rochester. But I can hardly trust my reading of the situation. Maybe that Englishman could readily see or hear that we were Americans before he leaned over. In that case his speaking to us was not an act of collusion with us as against the ladies from Rochester, but revenge in the form of getting one American to betray another by flattering them into agreeing with the most unflattering interpretation of what an American looks like to a cultivated Englishman. He had forced our hand; and we were doubly shamed. Shamed by how we were seen as Americans, and ashamed for being so ashamed. But that Englishman also did us a small favor: he let us know that it was not our self-hatred that made us attribute to the English such an unflattering view of Americans. No. He confirmed that the English indeed looked upon us just as we feared they did.

American self-hatred, though it knows other forms, is mostly about measuring up to the English first, then to high-style European sophisticates in general. Any old Englishman and especially an English woman can prompt it,[6] for they can make us feel awkward speaking our own tongue, though I must confess I have felt that way when speaking with North Europeans whose English as a second or third language achieves an elegance in accent mine lacks. We are still beset with Francophiles, too, though their number is shrinking, mirroring the decline in French culture as a standard-setter. "Slavophile" is not really available to designate a possible American attitude, having been taken over by nineteenth-century Russians concerned to battle what they took to be Russian self-hatred. The grim comedy of the Slavophile movement is its implicit supposition that only a Slav could love a Slav and then only after a heavy dose of consciousness-raising. And as to Latins, Asians, Africans, and so on, we don't even have a discernible syndrome ending in "phile" to describe a craven anxiety to be accepted by them.

The same American who squirms when witnessing American boorishness abroad, nevertheless feels prouder than hell of being an American when he hears pathetic Euro-rock or French rock 'n roll playing in a Parisian disco, or notes with self-delighting contempt that all the anti-American demonstrators are in jeans and baseball hats and sport t-shirts advertising various American products. He may lament that American pop culture seems to be driving out quaint contrived localisms, from Morris dances to Passion plays, but he revels in the feeling of dominating, of having immediate and natural access to what all those European wannabes think of as cool. One's self-hatred as an American is manifestly not the self-hatred that plagues the weak, the defeated, the poor, or the downtrodden. It is the self-hatred, if even that, of the parvenu. Few indeed are the number of this kind of American who would ever trade nations with anyone (you would have to be nuts to do so), preferring instead to think of the rest of the world as so many vacation spots, some of which may even offer a picturesque third world experience of mercifully brief duration.

I must retreat. Self-hatred, self-loathing, shamefulness are too strong and too pretentious to capture the quality of the emotional experience. This is not the self-hatred that Jews or blacks (perhaps) experience, the self-hatred of those actually dealt a bad hand in the social and moral order, who in fact are demonized, stigmatized, and made to suffer. This American sentiment of negative self-assessment is mostly a matter of pretty small-stakes embarrassment, not shame, except for shameful sorts such as T. S. Eliot and others, who have cultural pretensions that involve them more closely in self-loathing; they actually do rush to live elsewhere, speak differently, and be something else. Standard American anxiety abroad, and then mostly in the face of Brits, operates in the comic mode; it does not owe its origins to having been beaten, murdered, spat or shat upon, and discriminated against in myriad humiliating ways. It is fairly small potatoes and marches to its own tune. This kind of embarrassment is completely consistent with arrogance and power and certainly consistent with the kinds of self-satisfaction that flow from wealth and armed might.

As contemptible as my wife and I felt we were, we still felt superior to the ladies from Rochester, if not to the Englishman at the next table. Those damn English, we thought. They have no anxieties on account of their Englishness. They feel unanxiously superior, with a self-confidence that others, against their own interest, confirm and defer to. They never have to fake being anything but what they are anyway, at least in front of the likes of us. We slavishly defer to them, intimidated by their self-confidence, their reserve, giving them the benefit of about thirty extra IQ points simply for having the accent they do, even when the accent is Manchester working-class.

How many Englishmen are ever embarrassed by, let alone ashamed of, being English? I expect some English person, in response to this, to remonstrate that he, for one, is embarrassed by being English and that I have concocted a fantasy that is just another symptom of my anxieties about what it means to be American as against a stage Englishman. But should such a soul be embarrassed he would carry it off with such poise.[7]

So secure are Brits that they are barely embarrassed by their soccer hooligans. I suspect they are just a little prideful that they can set the standard in boorish and violent self-assertion as well as in matters of poise, tact, and reserve. Since when did any Brit mind that one of his countrymen beat the living daylights out of a Belgian or a Frenchman? There are some groups that are seen as winners no matter what, and one never hears of the problem of English self-hatred.[8] Something about them makes others accept their mildly self-mocking self-satisfaction as utterly justifiable, something most would agree seems much less to be the case for the French, whose self-love seems indecorous, it not possessing the boisterous and generous innocence of the American version of the same. Funny too is that I feel no inconsistency in being manifestly proud of being an American and admitting how nervous those damn Brits make me about it.

## Passing

I know I am making some cavalier, maybe offensive, assertions, parading American anxieties and prejudices as if they were getting at Truth, but they are getting at some kind of truth, one many of us have to own up to, however grudgingly.

Take the case of passing, as in light-skinned blacks, closeted gays, and delicately benosed, blondish Jews. Passing involves, whether intentional or not, disguise and dissimulation. In one sense, all faking it is a form of passing, but the idea of passing is properly reserved for big fakes. It is not about being polite when you don't want to be. It is about faking what most people feel are essential aspects of identity for which all would agree the stakes are high: thus a woman going off to war as a man is passing, but not a sixteen-year-old boy lying about his age, because the recruitment officer is trying to sign up bodies, not expose and refuse kids eager to fight. It is about faking gender, ethnic affiliation, sexual orientation, race, and religion. That doesn't quite capture all the cases either. Goffman would include anyone whose natural identity is stigmatized in some way and manages to conceal it. We might also want to consider that a spy must pass, as must many an infiltrator the basis of whose passing is ideological and political, but it would seem an expanded use of the term to apply it to an unfaithful spouse keeping an affair secret. Con men of the more mundane sort seem to fall on the nonpassing side of the line, too.

What makes passing full-fledged Passing is that it is undertaken in relation to what is perceived to be a low-status default identity. Motives can vary. Self-hatred need not play much of a part. Coleman Silk in Roth's *The Human Stain* is a purely opportunistic passer who simply decides not to correct people's mistaken assumptions about his identity. Coleman harbors no special loathing for his people. Some people, in other words, pass without trying to; they fake out others without faking it. Consider the turmoil of self-blame this could lead to for the very non–Jewish-looking Jew or very straight-acting gay who fears he might look cowardly or self-hating if he took advantage of not being immediately recognizable as a member of his pariah group.[9] He may thus find himself searching for decorous ways and occasions to leak out the information as "naturally" as possible.

Assimilation can be viewed as quasi-passing, as a willingness to adopt the styles and manner of the favored group without disclaiming the low-status identity.[10] Even here the lines get fuzzy. The assimilator does not see himself as a deceiver in the way a secretive passer is, yet he may be seen as trying to pass, both by conservative members of his original group and by hostile members of the favored group. In other words, he will be blamed as a Passer or an attempted Passer.

Assimilation could be understood to be a strategy of passing at the level of the genes rather than at the level of the individual; the first generation assimilator will fool no one, nor does he mean to, but his children and grandchildren will intermarry with the favored group and eventually will merge with the nonstigmatized population. The first-generation assimilator begins the process of identity laundering.[11]

Many in the favored group fear assimilation as a plot ending in a bastardization of their blood, while many in the assimilating group fear the dilution of theirs. The two fearers thus share a common interest, and one need not be too paranoid to imagine a despairing Jew, sick at the thought of his people surviving so many persecutions only to be digested and dissolved in the undiscerning maw of the American suburb, bizarrely seeing in the uncanny lunacy of the anti-Semite the last hope of Jewish survival. In a minor readjustment to Sartre's thesis, this despairing Jew bitterly supposes that even if Jews disappear, anti-Semitism, sempiternal, will re-create them, vesting their invented Jew with the same phantasmic powers Jews have always been accused of possessing.

Groups that fear themselves subject to infiltration by plagues of passers develop methods to keep them out. Some also feel it is important to hone techniques of unmasking those who have gotten inside the perimeter; others prefer to turn a blind eye, believing it best not to know how impure the blood of the so-called bluebloods is. Techniques of keeping the stigmatized out are sometimes very crude, such as forcing Jews to wear yellow badges, an open admission that it was harder to spot or sniff them out – and I do mean sniff out, given the belief in the *foetor judaicus* (the Jewish stench)[12] – than the ideology of their self-evident repulsiveness would have it. More interesting strategies of defending against passing, because they are more complex, are the ways aristocrats and upper-class people manipulated and elaborated codes of manners and fashion, posture, and linguistic markers to catch up the parvenu. Then, when the parvenus became expert at mimicry, the high would turn around and violate the strictures with casual nonchalance, a luxury they could in security indulge but that the parvenu was hardly secure enough to risk without being charged with vulgarity or immorality:

> The Rich arrive in pairs
> And also in Rolls Royces;
> They talked of their affairs
> In loud and strident voices.[13]

Classifications based on skin color allow for passing, too, for wherever one drew the line, at one drop or at one great-grandparent, there were going to be many who fell just to the wrong side who were indistinguishable in looks from those who fell just to the right side. Whatever race was conceived to be, it wouldn't always be easy to *see*.[14]

The passer runs the risk of exposure that in some regimes could have more serious consequences than being chucked out of a country club, painful as such a humiliation would be.[15] The passer is faking it big time, and he must fake out others completely or else the jig is up. It may be, however, that the anxiety of being discovered is more than compensated for by the delights of knowing you are bamboozling those on the inside, not to mention the obvious benefits of not suffering the indignities of being an open member of your low-status group.[16] Not that the glee of putting one over need always run in the passer's favor. The dominant group may have set you up, letting you believe you are passing though they have seen through you from the start. It is their secret kept from you that they have let you believe you have a secret kept from them. Your expulsion will come at a time of their own choosing guaranteed to make a cautionary example of you, which they (and your own) will regale themselves with from beyond your grave.

Sometimes, strangely, the dominant culture abandons its surest defenses against the passer. I was seven, the year 1953, in Green Bay. We were one family in a small Jewish community of about thirty families. I was the only Jew in my school class until fifth grade, when two others joined me. The night before I was to attend my first swimming lesson at the local YMCA, my father and his brother sat me down for an earnest discussion to prepare me, they said, for what I would face the next day. They hemmed and hawed, but the upshot was that I would notice that I was different from the other boys, who, they said, would "not have a ring around their penises" as I did.

That night I peered closely to inspect the ring that had heretofore escaped my attention. Nothing I saw looked like a ring to me, but then, not to worry, for once I had checked the other boys the next day the matter would be resolved. At the Y I tried ever so discreetly to catch a glimpse of the other boys as we undressed and then as we swam naked. I saw short penises, long ones, skinny ones, fat ones too; I saw crooked ones with a bend sinister, some dexter, some up, most down, but I could not for the life of me discern what the ring was that they didn't have that I did. God knows I wouldn't have been such a close observer of these facts, nor would they have seared themselves into my memory, but for Dad and Uncle Gene trying to spare me trouble on this score; they meant well.

How could Dad and Uncle Gene have been so wrong? It is embarrassing to confess the number of years that passed before I discovered what the ring really was, even more embarrassing that in deference to my father and uncle I believed it to be the skin within a half-millimeter of the urethra. Within the twenty-five years that separated my father from me, Christians in Green Bay had exchanged Pauline figural circumcision of the heart for Yahweh's literal circumcision of the flesh.[17] Making circumcision the norm worked to deny male Jews a stubborn sign of exclusivity while at the same time giving them a kind of passe-partout, a foolproof means of evading ultimate detection if they had already managed to remain undiscovered with their clothes on. Why would Christians give this up? Why would they so easily cave in to *their* doctors? (This change took place long before Jews had penetrated the medical profession in significant numbers.)

It has nothing to do with guilt over the Holocaust, for the practice had already begun shifting in the late nineteenth century, apparently taking its good-natured time getting to Green Bay, something it had yet to do by my father's boyhood there in the 1920s and 1930s. Various voguish late–nineteenth-century medical theories argued for circumcision as a health measure whose time had come; it promised all kinds of benefits – cures for compulsive masturbation, for paralysis too, to say nothing of the virtue of having cleaner and less odiferous genitals.[18]

Science was also operating, it has been suggested, in response to anxieties of Protestant America, which was concerned to distinguish and insulate itself from the filthy teeming masses streaming into America, more of whom were Catholic – Irish, Italians, and Poles – than were Jews. If there was a colorable argument that circumcision was cleaner (and surely the elimination of smegma should clinch the case for those inclined to be fastidious about such things), then the circumcised Protestant could still feel he was not mimicking a Jew in his heart, for his motives were secular. His conscious motive was hygienic; his unconscious motive was social and anti-Catholic, albeit no less hygienic for that. The advocates of circumcision took great care to distinguish their hygienic procedures from the dirty Jewish way of getting the same result.[19] The Jews, in their view, were still behaving barbarically, for their motives were superstitious, not progressive in the best modern style.

With tongue pretty much in cheek, I can't help half entertaining the suspicion that another unconscious motive might have been at work. What if Christian men didn't want to know how many Jewish men their women were sleeping with? (Christian men sleeping with Jewish women posed less of a risk to Christian purity, for by conventional understandings of the sex act it is the male who pollutes, the woman who is polluted.) Or was it that they wished to preserve for their women the excuse that they had not done so knowingly? "That's funny, you don't look Jewish" could now be a line said to a guy in complete nakedness who got himself in that position because the line was also accurate with his clothes on. But it cannot be denied that by circumcising themselves, Christian men decided to make their bodies Jewish, thereby, bizarrely, making my earlier, rather aggressive suggestion – that at least as far as the Christian anxiety goes, humanity is at core nothing more than a Jew – true in body as well as in mind.

IN SUM: though nothing as firm or pretentious as a conclusion seems warranted, might we not draw from these last three chapters an unsettling sense that when our mission is to find our core self we know we are in its near environs when our consciousness of it sets off unpleasant sentiments of shame, self-doubt, and suspicion? Yes, surely, it may also trigger pride, but the prideful, one suspects, are more likely to cheat in their own favor. Feeling good about oneself tends to depend, in fact, on having licked the compulsion to self-examine very insistently, except perhaps for Socrates. Maybe, just as a brain researcher gets at how the brain works by examining its pathologies and lesions, so too if we want best to understand the notion of a core self, and its relation to one's core identity, it may be best to look to damaged identities.

# THIRTEEN

# Authentic Moments with the Beautiful and Sublime?

MAYBE THE AUTHENTIC SELF, should it be there, is not discoverable by a conscious effort. Self-consciousness, inescapable posturing, cognitive biases all interfere with finding it. What if, however, the authentic self is less a thing to be known than an experience to be had and, bizarrely, an experience of that true self's own escape from self-consciousness? Losing track of the self as self may be a way of finding it. (Sounds kind of flaky – if, like me, you resist it as so much chuckle-headed nonsense – or Buddhist if you wish to vest it with worthier authority.) There has been floating around since the romantic period an idea that one can achieve certain grand epiphanies of self-realization in moments claimed to have a supra-authenticity to them, and that these in turn are often triggered by confrontations with the beautiful and the sublime in nature and in art. But since when does the contemplation of the beautiful or the sublime necessarily lead to escaping self-consciousness any more than it is likely to bring in its wake instead a whole assortment of worries about whether you are feeling deeply enough or whether others will think you a phony for looking as if you are feeling too deeply? The pure experience of the aesthetic does not escape the long shadow of faking it. Unmediated unself-conscious immersion into the beautiful is often something that must be worked at, struggled for, or, if we are lucky, achieved as a gift of grace.

## Phoniness by the Sea

It has been fashionable for some time in the humanities to argue for various species of cultural and historical relativism. Suppose a programmatic cultural relativist or, as the more pretentious cant would style him, an antiessentialist. Let us grant that the fashionableness of his position makes him hold it doubly sincerely; sincerely because he believes it, and sincerely because he wants to be fashionable. Even such as he may experience a twinge of anxiety that his experience of natural beauty suggests he is in the presence of some essential grandness whose grandness will impose itself on a third worlder no less than on suburbanite, on black as well as white, on woman as well as man, on Muslim as well as Christian, on ancient Greek as well as modern. Moreover, the very grandness of his experience depends on his suppressing any thoughts of its localism and relativity, for its grandness is felt as indisputable, even to him.

But then his intellectual positions start to interfere and gum up the experience. Am I awed by that mountain view, our antiessentialist wonders nervously, only because my culture makes me see the mountains this way or because culture, as I seem to be, is helpless before the grandness of that mountain? But then, he counters, what is it that makes the mountains on average more sublime than the plains, or the sea more sublime than Lake Superior? We can predict, he continues, given the culture, the likelihood of which member of these pairs will be considered more scenic and sublime than the other. Were not the Alps often viewed well into the nineteenth century as jagged deformations of nature, not beautiful but grotesque? Trees? Did not the Talmudic sages 1,800 years ago require that no trees be grown within twenty-five cubits of a town, and that carob and sycamore trees were to be banished to fifty cubits' distance, along with carcasses and tanneries: "To preserve the beauty of the town, every tree that is found nearer to the town than that must be cut down"?[1]

If someone were led blindfolded to Lake Superior, would he know it was not the ocean? You cannot see to the other side of either one, and, like the sea, Superior is in constant roil and its waves can rip apart ocean-going vessels. Sure, the salt-free spray is a giveaway, but that is no longer an issue of visual beauty. Doesn't our knowledge of maps influence our decision? The cachet of the sea and the coast, in the United States at least, is fraught with all kinds of pretensions that would deny to those in the middle of the country any access to culture or beauty, unless it be in the form of mountains. No doubt the majesty of the sea moves them. They are not faking that, but there are all the other status gains to be had by communing with the sea that makes their refusal to have the same experience at Lake Superior a form of vanity.

That is why I distrust those who claim too much for salt spray because I suspect that some of what they like about it is the proof it provides that they are on the coast and have not been tricked by the Great Lakes; olfaction is needed to save their culturally imposed ranking system for the sublime. Is there really anything inherently more beautiful about a mountain than the plain, about the sea than Lake Superior? If the flat infinite expanse of the ocean makes it, why can't the flat infinite expanse of the plains? There are ugly mountains, too, and ones that are kitsch, that are less sublime than a field of wheat, with the wind stirring the expanse into iridescent waves stretching as far as the eye can see.

So why is the sense of infinitude a selling point for the sea, but a reason to dismiss the plains? Is it because the sea and mountains are scary in a mighty way, whereas the plains, to these sophisticated appreciators of beauty, are scary only because they are believed to house boring people? Yes, says Edmund Burke, who specifically addresses the point and claims that the plains are not sublime like the sea because the plains do not generate terror. Laurence Sterne suggests that the very commodiousness of a fertile plain can terrorize only the travel writer, not travelers, because the absence of danger and risk makes for few good stories: "There is nothing more pleasing to a traveller – or more terrible to travel-writers, than a large rich plain."[2] Sterne, living in the eighteenth century, assumes that the flatlands are preferable to the scenic route to the extent they make getting from point A to point B pleasant and easy, with their good inns and level roads that don't tax the horses exceedingly. "Pleasant," notice, is not the adjective one uses to describe the experience of the sublime. For us, though, who do not have to worry about where we will sleep (there are Motel 6s in every godforsaken place) or whether our horses will founder on the next steep climb, sublime scenery along the route is costless and safe as long as we are not so mesmerized as to go sailing off into it after missing a turn in the road.

Fear for our lives, even fear as to whether we may run out of gas before the next gas station, has a way of pushing our attraction to the beautiful and sublime well off center stage. We must, as Kant says, "see ourselves safe in order to feel this soul-stirring delight."[3] The perception and appreciation of beauty in the fearsome, as Kant and others have pointed out,[4] requires our safety and well-being and even is dependent in some nontrivial degree on pacification and reasonable security, on political and social order. In other words, we cannot really be afraid, except in a kind of virtual, fake way, if we are going to be moved aesthetically.[5] Even trivial interferences with our sense of well-being can reveal just how fragile our willingness to be moved aesthetically is: vistas of breathtaking fall foliage were insufficient to overcome my kids' sense of ruination brought on by the collapse of the car's CD player at the outset of the trip. And scenery, no matter how sublime, cannot elicit much aesthetic attention when we are beset with a desperate urge for a restroom.

The incredible lethal beauty and awesomeness of a volcano or tornado or jet fighter is usually apparent to most of us safely on film, and those of us who have actually witnessed them still worry first about getting to a safe place from which to indulge our awe or, in the case of the jet fighter, of making sure it is friendly. A soldier is more likely to indulge his sense of the sublime at the vast array of his own fleet behind him than of the enemy's array in front of him. But there is something to those suggestions of lethality. The plains of wheat never seem to overcome the comfortable story implicit in them of well-being, habitability, fertility, and subdued and defeated nature.

The relativist wavers: here on the fjords with mountains coming down to the sea, his experience, he knows, will definitely be improved if he can suspend his disbelief and let himself be overcome by the feeling that there is something essentially sublime in the setting, something primordial, precultural and grand beyond all obsessive human intellectualizing. Did the Vikings find the mountains coming down to this fjord at sunset sublime, or did they merely look at them as barriers to be sailed around and see the setting sun as a practical indicator of tomorrow's weather? Our cultural relativist finds it hard to believe they did not experience the beauty – "Sophocles long ago/ Heard it on the Aegaean." He is now even less sure that his relativism isn't a pose and something of a position he adopts because of the pleasure it gives him to assert it against philistines or the man on street. And he is quite thankful the fjords overpowered his intellectual commitments. These come back later to nag at him in the hotel room, but they did not interfere with his experience when he was having it. Though it provides small solace, he feels that his affectations do not quite render him as obviously phony as those who think that when it comes to the sublime Lake Superior must be inherently inferior to the sea.

## Anxious Experts

There are other sources of self-consciousness in the face of the beautiful or sublime, as sufferable in a museum before a famous painting as when dealing with sunsets or fall foliage. These latter add the frustration of our never being quite sure we have captured or can identify the optimal moment when the sunset and leaves are at their most glorious.[6] With art we have the added anxiety as to whether we are enjoying it properly and whether we can convince others we enjoyed it properly without seeming either too simple or sillily pretentious. For a painting this means enjoying it intelligently, whereas the intelligent enjoyment of natural beauty – say, a sunset – seems less a matter of the essence of sunsets than of our own response to beauty. There is no special expertise in observing a sunset. We wouldn't think someone a philistine who said that when it comes to sunsets he just sits back and enjoys them.

But with a painting one knows that there are experts out there who could tell you so much more about it; you may have read them or may even be one of them, and still you are not sure your appreciation is the finest appreciation possible. You still could do better. You start to feel vaguely deficient for not knowing more or, if you do know more, for needing a boost to make you feel the power as you once felt it or as you think you are supposed to feel it. Though your knowledge may have increased and the sophistication of your appreciation with it over the years, the cold fact is you suspect that the painting moved you more when you were younger and knew less. You are now reduced, if not quite to feigning awe, to paying mere lip service to awe once felt.

Or are you playing the role of a melancholic, deriving more pleasure from present self-doubt than from any misremembered prior ecstasy? You have reason to believe that your prior ecstasy might be misremembered. You know it is not beneath you to have repressed the memory of your anxieties as to your ignorance when young, anxieties that you could dredge up if you wanted to. You suspect that your recall of the earlier ecstasy is in fact something of an invention fashioned more for the purpose of casting doubt on your present experience. For you suspect you were posturing back then, too, faking feeling awed because you were afraid of being seen as too dumb and dim not to feel it. But that is not fair either, for the memory of a prior ecstasy is a pleasurable memory, and it has served you well when it flashes upon your inward eye. So what if that purer ecstasy was in fact constructed later, that it is really something of a fake? Fake memories may enhance the authenticity of the present moment, and we are never sure that there is not always a whole lot of faking going on in even our truest memories.

Adam Smith (TMS I.i.2.2) observes, "When we have read a book or poem so often that we can no longer find any amusement in reading it by ourselves, we can still take pleasure in reading it to a companion;...we enter into the surprise and admiration which it naturally excites in him, but which it is no longer capable of exciting in us." Recapturing or reproducing all the emotions of your best experience with a particular object often puts you to a kind of parasitical appreciation, piggybacking vicariously on the joy you see others experience when they first discover it, especially when as parent, friend, or teacher you introduce them to it. Without that last proviso their pleasure may simply cause you chagrin, as when you suffer the view of the young in one another's arms. Yet your pleasure is more than just witnessing their pleasure, for you find yourself re-experiencing your original zeal because you have worked yourself up trying to convince them to feel the power. Nevertheless you need the other person in order to *feel* the greatness of the work again. This is one of the great services students provide their teachers, who might otherwise feel as if they are faking their pleasure in their chosen field.

## Faking It in the Museum

This piggybacking of your appreciation on another's can work great wonders; but the presence of others whom you are not teaching or linked to so as to use their pleasure to prompt yours can produce petty miseries. You cannot help but be aware of their reaction, not just to the object of appreciation but also to your watching of it. They will be judging, you feel, whether you are being a proper appreciator. Your reputation – for having a soul, for having taste, for being a worthy object of love, and for not being either a pompous prig or a hopeless philistine – is in some way engaged. There is competition even in the watching of a sunset as to who is feeling the most, let alone a painting, where the competitiveness is more clearly the case. True, the others may not in fact be judging you, but you suspect they are, because you are certainly judging them and comparing their responses with yours. It is a rare day that a trip to the art museum doesn't leave you feeling something of a moral failure for not liking Picasso as much as you thought you should have or as much as the others faking liking him are liking him.

A certain obligatoriness undergirds the awe and admiration we give to the sublime and to simple beauty too. Some of the obligatoriness is the very experience of the sublime, as when the awesomeness and splendor render nonobeisance to its wondrousness impossible. But there is also the obligatoriness of being properly appreciative of those things we are supposed to appreciate, and that can provoke resistance as well as feelings of inadequacy and failure. If we fall right in line and admire what is admirable we wonder at how slavish we are; nor would we feel any more original if we made typically avant-gardiste gestures of rebellion and resistance. All paths have been well trodden in this domain, in which the distinctly unconventional is totally conventional. The pretensions and self-satisfactions of the avant-garde have succeeded in giving the charm of authenticity to the simple philistine who tells the empresses of performance art that they have no clothes on, which in fact they often don't. Philistinism is no great shakes either; it comes in varieties ranging from naïve to studied, and its charms tend to have a short life.

How long are you obliged to pay homage, to stay looking at the Vermeer? There is the niggling worry about when we can declare ourselves properly released from having to attend to it. The painting stubbornly stays there, available to be admired or studied until the museum closes or until your companion urges you to move on in no uncertain terms. When can you say, "OK, enough" and feel you have paid proper homage? The problem of release is especially acute in certain social settings. It is the exhausting demand made upon us to admire someone's new home, or garden, or collection of butterflies. Leave it to the always-insightful Jane Austen to capture the sentiment:

> "That [Fanny] should be tired now, however, gives me no surprise; for there is nothing in the course of one's duties so fatiguing as what we have been doing this morning: seeing a great house, dawdling from one room to another, straining one's eyes and one's attention, hearing what one does not understand, admiring what one does not care for. It is generally allowed to be the greatest bore in the world, and Miss Price has found it so, though she did not know it."[7]

Sublime scenes in nature raise the same problem. How long do you have to look at and commune with the scene? When can you turn away? Taking a picture or buying a postcard of the scene offers a way of weaseling out of cutting our ties completely with the scene; taking a photograph lets us pretend that we are not turning away forever and thus are turning away respectfully.

## Postcards and Memories

Have you not also experienced the small shame of having felt more for a photo or reproduction than for the thing itself? It seems we often prefer the fake. Nature can be at its best in postcards or nature documentaries. When *en scene* I am never quite sure I am positioned for the best possible view, with the best light, in the right season, to say nothing of the vexation of bodily discomforts and the insects (and tourists) who claim the outdoors as their own. I am determined too that the kids had better enjoy it because I paid a small fortune to bring them here. Better not waste such an opportunity. At least I can blame some of my failures to feel exactly the awe and delight I think I should feel on the kids, and that may be why it was a good idea to have brought them along. When one has paid money for the view, there is pressure to get one's money's worth – felt ever the more keenly because I feel I have to make up for the kids' lack of interest – and that complicates the pure aesthetic experience with yet another distracting intrusion, another demand upon me to perform or else. I am assaulted from two directions: I worry not only that the kids are not feeling it as they ought to but also that I am coming nowhere near my wife's quiet appreciation of the scene. Going alone doesn't solve the problem either because of the need to share your oohs and ahs and have them confirmed by another. There is sometimes an overpowering urge to confess the depth of your experience, if you think it deep, within seconds of its occurrence.

But the sublime seems to invite the ridiculous. We, for instance, often consider the expedition a success when we find that the scene lived up to the postcard, that the expectations it raised were met. The postcard (or the nature documentary) can't help but be a reference point, a standard we erect to orient and gauge our aesthetic judgments of the scene. We also seem almost bent on knowingly sacrificing the present moment to make sure we get a good photo of it, or we hurry back to a souvenir shop to peruse the collection of postcards, deferring the appreciation of the present to a more tranquil appreciation of an epitomized version on film viewable at whim in the future.

I am being unfair. The photo could just as well be an homage to the grand moment just lived, an effort to memorialize it. But taking a picture often ensures a less than optimal experience as we fumble with the settings, wait for people to get out of the way, puzzle over which is the best segment of the panorama to settle on, and then steel ourselves to commit and click the shutter. The photo can also have the unpleasant effect of diminishing the positive memory of the experience if it in fact turns out not to reflect the exquisiteness of the setting adequately. You end up having to apologize for it when you show it to a friend: "It's not really a good picture, but you get the idea, don't you?" And though a mediocre photo works well enough to produce a very active memory of the original experience the first time it is viewed, it becomes less able to do so as the event recedes in time and the photo itself becomes more and more the primary source for the memory. You end up seeing the scene forever as you ineptly photographed it.[8]

Memory also acts like a postcard in those scenes and paintings we actually revisit in the flesh; it can enhance the experience, but it can also make it disappointing. The memory, contaminated by the pictures we took and the postcards we bought of the scene, sets a standard by which we judge the present and sets up various interferences with present enjoyment. Good memories, as I noted earlier, may be especially good because you have selectively forgotten all the anxieties that attended the experience when you had it. This may be a kindness offered by memory's fallibility and malleability, but it is a mixed blessing, for it risks making the present fail to match the imagined past.

Stonehenge moved me when I first visited it as I never thought it would. The sheer size of the stones, the unfathomability of transporting them and raising them given the available technology, the uncanny perfection of the way some were knocked over and how perfectly they fell, looking significantly more sublime as ruins than had they been preserved in their original glory – all this gave me the heebie-jeebies.[9] I dragged the family to it because I wanted to treat them to the awe. I told them that it surpassed all PBS specials, all postcards, and this was a recommendation indeed because they are well aware of my preference for reading about places rather than seeing them, or for watching them on TV rather than dealing with the people and clumsy changes of position that come with visiting them in the flesh.[10] I expected to be moved again myself; I was disappointed. It looked so much smaller, and I could not decide from which point of the circle it looked most like Stonehenge. What was the optimal point from which to view it? And what was "most like Stonehenge" to mean?

The second trip made me doubt the authenticity of my memory of the first trip. Had I really been moved by it to the extent I recalled, or was my memory a fake I constructed to make the first trip worth it, a self-deception I concocted to avoid the self-contempt of having wasted the opportunity to be moved? Was it that, in Wordsworthian predictability, the memory was the experience to cherish, not the actual provision of the raw material of the memory, the experience itself? What was my present experience but a reassessment of my prior experience, which now, too, suffered for having played its part in ruining the second trip. There was no bittersweetness of nostalgia or wistfulness to add texture to the loss, only a vague annoyance at Stonehenge for not backing me up in front of my family.

Not only natural beauty or the sublime suffers the postcard effect. The museum brings you face-to-face with grand paintings you've seen in art books and on the big screen in your introductory art history class. Sometimes the real thing wins hands down, and not only when it is bigger. The Vermeer is even more amazing for being smaller than you imagined it would be, and you discover that it has a luminosity that is beyond reproduction, while some large paintings don't live up to the gasp you emitted when they flashed up on the screen more than thirty years ago. Such moments in art history class had all the elements of surprise: a darkened room, the big screen, the feeling you were finally getting educated and cultured. In the museum you have to deal with the crowds in addition to the painting, the annoyance of having your view blocked, the concern that you are blocking someone else's, the fear that you may be looking foolish as you try to figure out precisely how to look appreciative and awed without looking pretentious; and pathetically hoping the gorgeous soul a few feet over chooses to notice you as well as the painting. You suffer feeling foolish for worrying about looking foolish, especially when you know that nobody is watching you anyway (but someone might; better be prepared, just in case). Unless you are really misbehaving or are the best-looking woman in the crowded room, you will be playing to an audience of one. But that audience of one can be quite demanding and will insist that you put your best foot forward.

You know these are foolish thoughts, yet you still worry, especially about when you can declare yourself released from paying attention to the painting. That is more than a matter between you and the painting. In a museum there are many other masterpieces housed in the same building, in the same room even, jealous of your attention, getting impatient and insisting you attend to them. Not only does your companion want you to move on, but the other pictures are asserting their demands too. Then, when the day is done, you feel somewhat defeated by the experience, by the fact that you were cowed into granting your not-quite-sincere homage completely predictably, paying attention only to paintings you already knew were to be admired.

You may be tempted to dismiss this as a highly personalized neurasthenic account, not worthy of being generalized. Sure, there are people, you will say, who are this agonizingly self-conscious, and we will even grant that many of us have experienced similar sentiments in some settings. But most of us do not find nature and museums as agonizing as you, Mr. Miller, would make them, nor the appreciation of beauty as fraught with constant self-defeating self-monitoring as often as you claim. A good number of us go to museums and are wholly absorbed, not giving a damn about what others think, other than looking around occasionally to see whether we have been occupying the best viewing position too long. Some of us know we are posturing and love the posturing, love any offense it may give or any status we may achieve by it. Posturing as an appreciator of art can put us in the proper mood to be pleasured by it and to appreciate it; posing as appreciative helps mark the moment as an appreciative one, and what is wrong with that? Others of us like the fact that we are in Florence or New York or Amsterdam or Madrid and love that what it means to visit those places is go to the museums they are famous for. So how, we say, do you get the right to use "we" or bully us with that "you" with such a presumption of authority? If you, Mr. Miller, can be so anxious about a trip to a museum or looking at the trees in their autumn beauty, how can you be so complacently unanxious about claiming universality for your inner states?

I allege in partial defense that the sensibility and anxieties I have described look typically Western, and its typicality outside the West seems confirmed in a negative way by various Eastern philosophies that are centered on the desperate effort to train the spirit out of experiencing reality the way I have suggested we, or many of us, often do. The competitive, unsatisfiable, anxious sensibility that informs this book is the hobgoblin of Buddhism; it is the sullied sensibility that must be overcome and exorcized. That tormented sensibility, at least in Buddhist thinking, is taken to be the default setting from which humankind must work to free itself. And in my defense too I ask you to consider the ubiquitous museum shop. Were the epiphany before the original grand work all that it was cracked up to be, a postcard or a replica would blaspheme the experience. The shop exists as a testimony to our guilt for having blown it before the original. It is not as if we just stumble on to the shop at the end; rather, we feel ourselves pulled, even hurrying toward it, so that we can get a manageable version, one that is less intimidating because it won't raise such unfulfillable demands to appreciate it more than we are capable of. And we owe those shops a true debt of gratitude, for those reproductions do teach us to admire the greatness of the original that made us too self-conscious to appreciate when we had our chance in its presence.

# FOURTEEN

# The Alchemist: Role as Addiction

THE BULK OF THE VEXATIONS dealt with so far have been about fears of not getting into our roles or experiences as deeply as we feel we should be. There is perhaps a more compelling problem at the other end of the scale: getting into them too deeply to get out.

## Elster's Alchemies

Some faking, we have seen, openly acknowledges that you are trying to bootstrap yourself into a preferred disposition, set of beliefs, or character traits by acting as if you had it or them. Such is the case of Pascal's wager, which has acquired a classic dignity because the initial risk-averse bet to believe in God's existence is relieved of its actuarial small-mindedness by being a necessary first step to commit yourself to a serious regimen of observance. The habit of acting as if you believe ends, eventually, in belief.

Some faking has no goal other than for you to survive the moment with dignity intact and to let others preserve theirs; this is the case of routine politeness and tact. Even these scripted moments of faking can bend the mind to play it up all the way, so that instead of faking sorrow at your guests' departure you actually end up feeling a twinge of melancholy when they depart; or, as noted earlier, if you give what you think is lip service to a position you are too cowardly to oppose, you end up coming to believe the position.[1]

Jon Elster describes a variety of transmutations of motivation in which the initial motive cannot be publicly avowed because of its offensiveness or inappropriateness. You start with a conscious lie, a hypocritical assertion of a noble motive. Then you begin to believe the lie and think yourself (falsely) nobly motivated. And the last step: the lie ends up becoming true as you actually come to be moved as you initially had falsely claimed. The intervening false belief as to your motivation might be a necessary middle step in the process of transmutation from knowing hypocrisy to unknowing hypocrisy, to an actual change of motivation. Elster seems right when he says, "Durable and consciously hypocritical or cynical stances are probably quite rare."[2] Or in Orwell's formulation: "He wears a mask, and his face grows to fit."[3] More effort is sometimes needed for us to stay separated from our roles than to merge with them.[4]

These transmutations of motive, of nasty passions into generous ones, of self-interest into generosity, of sham sorrow into real sorrow, are what Elster calls alchemies of the mind. "Transmutation" is an alchemical term of art; it means the changing of base metals into silver or gold, a transformation of essences from mean to noble, from low to high. Elster, rightly, also reminds us that not all such transmutations are upward. Some work in reverse, turning gold to lead, as in the classic case of sour grapes, when we downgrade our desires by imagining that the unattainable thing we desired was no good anyway; or as in the case of congenital pessimism, such as characterizes the spirit of my dear father. He finds a dark lining to every fleecy fair-weather cumulus cloud and succeeds in metamorphosing the fear that things might go wrong into the expectation that they will.[5]

For Elster, alchemy provides an evocative metaphor, a way of conceptualizing the transformation of mental, not metal, essences. The alchemical image means to suggest that these transformations take place in the world of deception, wishful thinking, and self-deception. They are magical, at least appearing so, because they seem to be effected by a mental sleight of hand, operating mostly "behind the back," as Elster says. The magic is not psychosexual; it involves a mix of mechanisms, but the most crucial seem to work in service of what moralists would call vanity: our desperate need to look good to others and ourselves.[6]

I want to put the metaphor aside and treat the real thing, to look at a tale of an alchemist when alchemy was practiced – a tale of deceptions and of self-deceptions too. If the Freudian system is tied to the deadly sins of gluttony and lust, alimentary and sexual desire, the alchemical world hovers between what medieval moralists called pride (refusal to humbly accept the limits of human knowledge) and avarice (the quest for goods, not the hoarding of them). The tale also raises the interesting case, very relevant to our central themes, of people who know they are con men but believe, or do not disbelieve, the line they use to bilk their marks – the televangelist springs to mind in our culture, the shaman in shamanistic cultures. It is not so much a matter of being hoist with your own petard; it is about mental states composed of, in Goffman's terms, "mixtures of cynicism and belief." He cites the anthropologist Alfred Kroeber:

> Probably most shamans or medicine men, the world over, help along with sleight-of-hand in curing and especially in exhibitions of power. This sleight-of-hand is sometimes deliberate; in many cases awareness is perhaps not deeper than the foreconscious. The attitude, whether there has been repression or not, seems to be as toward a pious fraud. Field ethnographers seem quite generally convinced that even shamans who know that they add fraud nevertheless also believe in their powers, and especially in those of other shamans: they consult them when they themselves or their children are ill.[7]

These people, even when perpetrating their frauds, are not standing outside the structure of beliefs they are manipulating to their own advantage. It might be that "*even* when perpetrating their frauds" should be changed to "*especially* when perpetrating their frauds." It is because they believe in it that they are so good at conning others.[8] A remarkable and perfectly insightful comment from an Icelandic saga has the thirteenth-century Christian author remark that his tenth-century pagan ancestors rigged judicial ordeals "because [they] felt their responsibilities no less keenly when performing such ceremonies than Christians do now when ordeals are decreed."[9] I did not mis-copy that. The point is that pagans were just like Christians: both rigged their ordeals because they feared they would reveal the un-welcome truth if not rigged. This is something rather different from a pious fraud. The cheating is not designed to maintain the belief in ordeals; nor is the rigging mere manipulative charlatanism; it is just as likely, as our author notes, to be motivated by a belief in the efficacy of ordeals, a kind of perverse homage to them.

## The Canon's Yeoman

The special situation of the alchemist raises these and other issues, and they are the substance of a confession of an alchemist's apprentice in Chaucer's *Canon's Yeoman's Tale*. Chaucer's tale depends on alchemists in his time not having a generally nefarious reputation. They thus can gull their mark not merely by playing on the avarice of the victim but by playing on the respect they command as learned men, as "philosophers." The tale is especially insightful as a study of the effects specialized jargon has, not only in giving people an air of authority and mystery so as to hoodwink others but also in its capacity to fascinate and thus hoodwink its own users. The alchemist's "termes" – terms of art, complex and specialized diction, jargon – are employed sensuously and lovingly in this tale, not least because they intimidate others and serve as a special sign of election, conferring too much advantage on its users to be questioned critically by them (compare in our day the jargon-driven and jargon-dependent morass of deceptions and self-deceptions that have taken place in psychoanalysis, postmodern literary theory, and postcolonial studies, as well as in other suspect discourses).

To be sure, people in the fourteenth century knew there was an alchemy racket. From the earliest of times the average person has mistrusted the smart. Because to the middling mind there is no point in having brains and wisdom if they are not good for getting rich, the general belief is that the intelligent need to be regarded with circumspection. Smarts means cons. Thus the fear and loathing in various times and places of Jesuits, Jews, and lawyers, but not college professors. (We academics are deemed more fool than knave by the laity – the view is that if we really had brains, we'd be a whole lot wealthier than we are – and though many of us are quite good at conning each other, cunning is something we are believed to be without.) Hence too the double meanings of "craft" and in Middle English "sleight" to mean both skill or expertise *and* trickery. Smart people are always suspect, but by the time Ben Jonson wrote his *The Alchemist*, the racketeering alchemist of fiction had suffered a loss of prestige; he was no longer scientist or philosopher, but a lowlife con man, a pimp, a small grifter.

Chaucer's alchemist and his assistant, the yeoman, are more complexly engaged in their craft than Jonson's alchemist. They are crafty; but they are craftsmen, too, and the word already had this double meaning in the fourteenth century. They are searching for the Elixir-stone, the substance that can transmute substances, altering their essences and extracting their quintessences, turning lead into gold. They are crooks and they are believers. They deceive others, not to get rich but to fund their researches, so committed to and so enthralled are they by the quest for the philosopher's stone.

To the extent that the sin of avarice motivates them their avarice has been so alloyed with other motivations as not fairly to be their chief motive, if ever it was. They seek gold, but they care desperately about how they get it. They do not want to mine it; they do not want to sail ships and discover worlds and slaughter people to obtain it. They are not satisfied merely to plunder their marks, for no sooner do they con a mark than they invest the gains in yet more equipment and raw materials, impoverishing themselves in the process. They are truly curious souls who are obsessed with gaining a special knowledge, with cracking a code, with solving nature's mysteries. When they swindle their marks they are really engaged in an activity completely analogous to a modern scientist applying for a research grant.[10] And it is clear that though they are driven to distraction by their failures, in one sense they love their work.

Chaucer's tale is a triumph of poetic virtuosity, spoken with a breathless intensity by its narrator, the yeoman, as he confesses to the pilgrims that his master is a swindler and an evil man. He cannot, however, hide his admiration for his master, not for his crookery but for his learning. The yeoman launches into his confession while in the hate phase of his love/hate obsession with his alchemical craft, and as he tells his tale he seduces himself again into the trade, though it promises, as he knows, nothing but prospects of frustration and failure: "But unto God in heaven, I confess, that for all our 'craft' and all our 'sleight' in the end it [the Elixir-stone] escapes us" (865–867). It is not the charlatanism of the craft that calls him back, but that he believes in it; he too is faked out, at a much profounder level than his marks. He is hooked: "For all my sorrow, labor, and trouble, I could never leave it" (713–714).

Try the Middle English for which I provide a translation. Chaucer's dialect became the basis for most of modern English, so it is not that difficult. Ezra Pound, that charming, kindly soul, correctly offered this opinion: "Anyone who is too lazy to master the comparatively small glossary necessary to understand Chaucer deserves to be shut out from the reading of good books for ever":[11]

> He [the philospher's stone] hath ymaad us spenden muchel good
> For sorwe of which almoost we wexen wood,
> But that good hope crepeth in oure herte,
> Supposynge evere, though we sore smerte,
> To be releeved by hym [the stone] afterward.
> Swich supposyng and hope is sharp and hard;
> I warne yow wel, it is to seken evere.
> That futur temps hath maad men to dissevere,
> In trust therof, from al that evere they hadde.
> Yet of that art they kan nat wexen sadde,
> For unto hem it is a bitter sweete, –
> So semeth it, – for nadde they but a sheete,
> Which that they myghte wrappe hem inne a-nyght,
> And a brat to walken inne by daylyght,
> They wolde hem selle and spenden on this craft.
> They kan nat stynte til no thyng be laft.
>
> (868–883)

> The philosophers' stone has made us waste much property,
> For sorrow of which we go almost crazy,
> Except that good hope creeps in our heart,
> Supposing ever, though we hurt a lot now,
> That the stone will in the end relieve us.
> Such supposing and hope is hard and sharp;
> I warn you well: it means to seek forever.

Trusting in that future has caused men to part with
Everything they ever had.
Yet they never get their fill of the enterprise
Which is bittersweet to them
So it seems, for even if they only had a sheet
To wrap themselves in at night
And a coarse cloak to walk around in by day
They would sell them and spend it on this craft;
They cannot stop until there is nothing left.

That stone "has caused us to waste much property (that is the primary sense of "good" in the first line, though the added moral meaning colors the sense), for sorrow of which we go almost crazy." The property whose loss they grieve they consider their own, and that indicates that when the yeoman says that for all their "craft" and "sleight" Elixir escapes them, he means "craft" and "sleight" in their positive sense of expertise and skill, but the overlay of cunning and deceit in how it was obtained is also suggested. That the alchemist and his yeoman are conning others is not the yeoman's concern; it is his own getting sucked in that is his theme. He is an addict and an obsessive. The yeoman's understanding of his addiction takes a different tack than that of one influential recent theory, which argues that the crux of addiction lies in problems the addict has in properly evaluating and ordering his preferences. According to this view, his desire for a fix in the short run intercepts and overpowers the desire for the long-term rational goal.[12] Short run beats out long run. But the yeoman understands his curse differently. It is the long run that does him in. His problem is to be constantly chasing a future he knows to be distant against a present stated resolve to kick the habit. "That futur temps" defeats him, he says, makes him squander everything he has, waste his "good," in all the senses that term had in the fourteenth century.

The modern theory could still press the yeoman into its service by interpreting him as follows: what the yeoman is calling the "futur temps," it could be argued, is properly to be understood to refer to an *immediate* overpowering bad desire for the philosopher's stone that will defeat his rational long-term goal of an alchemy-free life the next time the temptation arises. The yeoman suffers from a gambling addiction that takes the form of believing that this time he will hit the jackpot or, if not this time, then surely some time soon. Each time the bug bites him, he thinks the future is very near at hand, that is, he fails to discount adequately the probability of his hitting the jackpot this time.

The yeoman, though, sees it differently. Let's instead take him at his word: he says it is the "futur temps" that causes him to succumb to temptation. He is not some benighted medieval person devoid of psychological sophistication. To his mind, he is not undone by thinking the future is now. He is not a victim of his own bad math or of irrational discount rates; his is not an ordinary case of weakness of the will. He never forgets that the shot at Elixir is a long one, almost an impossible one. He is not driven by a belief that this time will be the lucky one but, on the contrary, by prospects he despairingly sees as ever remoter, ever more postponed to some rapidly lengthening future. And still he cannot stop.

He has a sophisticated theory of his addiction that is emotion-based. It is less about the ordering of his preferences than about the peculiar workings of particular set of emotions. These lines hold the key:

> that good hope crepeth in oure herte,
> Supposynge evere, though we sore smerte,
> To be releeved by hym [the stone] afterward.
> Swich supposyng and hope is sharp and hard...

He sees his compulsion to chase chimeras to be caused by two closely related emotions. It is "good hope" and "supposing" that do him in. "Supposing" is meant as more than an elegant variation of "hope." Though of an ilk, it is not a synonym; it brings with it a very differ- ent set of associations. "Supposing" is a sentiment common to these men of learning; it is part and parcel of philosophical disputation and argument. "Supposing" is to enter the counterfactual world of hypo- theticals, of totally imaginary, even far-fetched cases. "Suppose," for example, we added brimstone to urine during a lunar eclipse, when Mercury is ascendant. Philosophers "supposed" in this fashion all the time; and in fourteenth-century usage an alchemist was a philosopher, the same name being applied to both. Philosophy and alchemy had not yet parted company; the philosopher, the alchemist, was concerned with gaining access to remote knowledge, access to essences of matter and spirit. Supposing was a tool of this intellectual trade. It meant using imagination to come up with hypotheses.

The yeoman says his problem is born of hope and supposing. They creep into his heart, causing great pain, and there is only one remedy for the pain: the Elixir that turns all matter to gold. Supposing generates improbable fantasies, and hope sustains them. Hope, a virtue in the Christian scheme, is a vice to the hard-nosed rationalist, for it is a form of self-deception, a way of not facing up to the most probable implication of present facts. Hope, by necessary implication, means desiring in the face of pretty long odds; otherwise, hope is not the sentiment felt. When the odds get better, hope gives way to anticipation or expectation.

Hope makes these men persevere; it is part of the emotional drive that informs their love of the very process of searching for Elixir. Hope also helps drive a propensity to make errors in the math of probability in their own favor; it often finds itself playing a part in a progression of sentiments that ends in wishful thinking. As that most eminent of psychologists, Jane Austen, would have it: "What Marianne and her mother conjectured one moment, they believed the next – that with them, to wish was to hope, and to hope was to expect."[13] But our yeoman's mind doesn't work in this way. Hope itself remains for him a sign of the remoteness of fulfilling his desires. Otherwise, he would not be hoping, he would be awaiting or expecting. Hope, though, is its own kind of reward. It provides enough motive to keep plugging away. It fuels perseverance. Is this any different from the scientist in search of a cure for cancer? If we called the yeoman a chemist instead of an alchemist, we would not describe him as addicted but as persevering, committed, and dedicated. The yeoman, however, is hostile to hope. He sees it as his undoing because it keeps him persevering in what he suspects is a hopeless cause.

Easy to see why this emotion is a virtue in the Christian order. It is asking a lot of anyone who is suffering injustice, who sees evil thrive, not to despair and curse God. Hope keeps him in the fold, keeps him faithful, on the long shot that somewhere in some other world, in some eternity, he will see justice done. The yeoman sees hope the way a lot of cultures did that weren't as high on hope as Christianity is. The ancient Greeks made it the evil of what was left to humankind when Pandora's box was opened. Nietzsche reminded us of the proper meaning of that tale – hope is "blind and deceitful" – but our pious cultural commitments to hope as a theological virtue make the tale of Pandora baffling to us to this day.[14]

Consider the yeoman's blaming "*good* hope" that creeps into his heart. Why is the hope good? Hope is what he knows is ruining him, destroying his sense of well-being. The "good" is there, it seems, as a nervous gesture of piety or no more than a rote honorific that is unfelt, as when one addresses a "right honorable sir" or, more pointedly, a "my good man" in which the "good" often works as a mild form of reprimand or admonition. The yeoman pays homage to hope as a virtue in his cultural order just as he is about to curse it.[15] Hope ranks with the most energetic mechanisms of self-deception, not quite beating out vanity and self-love but coming close. Vanity might stake the claim to being the chief source of self-delusion of those who do not have to worry about their basic needs, such as food, clothing, and shelter. Hope takes over as the chief source of self-deception among the poor and among victims of suffering beyond all reason.

The canon's yeoman represents a limiting case, the other side of the faking-it coin. The yeoman too is anxious about his relation to the roles he plays, but in a different way from the cases we have been dealing with, which mostly involve anxieties about inadequate immersion into a role. The yeoman's problem is that he is drowning in his role; there is no self left over to let him regain the shore. Full immersion in a role is a true delight as long as we can still come up for air and choose when to dive in again. Though the yeoman might appear to have regained dry ground in his lament to the pilgrims, it is still the alchemist in him that is calling the shots. The lament is not a respite or relaxation but a phase in a cycle he cannot escape.

What is especially interesting about this kind of addiction is that it leaves enough of its victim's critical capacity intact so that he can understand exactly what is happening to him. But that understanding is itself part of the problem; it is the part that creates the sense of powerlessness, the sense of despair, and it fuels the sense of urgency that is the compulsive characteristic of the alchemist. The case shows that self-deception can coexist rather well with a critical purchase on one's condition. It is just that the critical purchase is never consistently available, nor available when it is needed to break the cycle. It arises only when it will not dictate action. For now come hope and supposing, and he is undone again.[16] And besides, he really loves the process itself, complain as he may.

# FIFTEEN

## "I Love You": Taking a Bullet versus Biting One

THERE IS NOTHING QUITE LIKE *Tristram Shandy,* the most deliciously prurient book ever written. You will find yourself returning to read it again and again, always discovering dozens of new jokes that flew by you the time before; nor will you ever cease to be amazed at the cleverness of the ones you get, how surprising they are though you have read them before and even expect the surprise. You will lose yourself in wonderment and laughter until you start worrying about how dim you are, not compared with Laurence Sterne, for you concede he has it all over you, but compared with the intelligence of the average eighteenth-century reader he was pitching his humor and wit to.

Almost nothing in all literature has quite the charm of Tristram's Uncle Toby. Toby is simplicity itself, with an *idée fixe*. He was a soldier, wounded in the groin at the siege of Namur (1695), and since his retirement, together with his devoted servant Corporal Trim, he has occupied his time building models of the progress of the War of Spanish Succession on his bowling lawn. Toby is at one with himself; he is, as Sterne says, his hobbyhorse (1.24). He is totally a creature of his obsession with battle, armament, fortification, and drill; he is an allegory of himself, meant to be a conventional comic character with one motivating humor or trait that informs all his behavior and conversation. Despite his hobby and notwithstanding his benevolence and sweetness of soul, Toby acquires depth in spite of himself. Much of the depth is owed to the wound to his groin: can he do it, or can't he?

This is the core question for all the males of the Shandy family, who have the hardest time with their "noses"; either they are too small, or unresponsive, or getting inadvertently circumcised by window sashes slamming down on them because Trim had removed the window weights to employ as cannon for Toby's sieges. "Nothing," says Tristram of the window, with more than a hint of wider meaning, "was well hung in our family" (5.17). Even the family bull is impotent. Except, it is faintly hinted that, just maybe, Toby, sweet, modest, and sexually innocent Toby, with his wound in the groin, might be fully capable. Sterne dies before the Widow Wadman and we can find out the definitive answer to her researches on the matter, but Corporal Trim, who is not cursed with the Shandy curse, vouches fully for Toby.

The Widow Wadman has besieged Toby for years with every wile and stratagem. The innocent Toby is oblivious until he finally succumbs when she asks him to check for a speck in her eye; he, of a sudden and for no reason he can fathom, declares that he is in love. Walter, his philosophical and equally endearing brother, in a disquisition on the forms of love, offers the following opinion on how Toby will behave in his new condition of love:

> Love is not so much a sentiment, as a situation, into which a man enters, as my brother Toby would do, into a corps – no matter whether he loves the service or no – being once in it – he acts as if he did; and takes every step to shew himself a man of prowess.
>
> (8.34)

Toby will perform his role in the world of love as he did in the world of arms. He will behave admirably. His inner disposition is beside the point. He acts *as if* he loves the service, whether he does or does not, and because love is not so much a sentiment as a situation, Toby will acquit himself as a man of prowess.

## It's the Word "Love"

The word "love" is not only an emotion term but also a term, as Walter said, that indicates a certain situation. Love, that is, is a state of affairs. No, dear reader, Walter does not mean that love is *the* state of *an* affair; where doth the prurience of thy mind lead thee?

179

The situation called love brings with it expectations, claims, rights, and duties that have moral force, and also a kind of quasi-legal force, independent of whether love also means marriage. Even when "love" is used as an emotion term it seems to be applicable to a multitude of rather different sentiments and moods. It is not like disgust or anger. When you say you are angry or disgusted, I am pretty confident that I know what you are actually feeling; but when you say you are in love or that you love X, I know only what kind of general claim you are asserting, but I am not about to vouch for what you actually feel.

Words frequently have multiple meanings that context usually makes clear, but the stakes are higher for love because of the centrality that some version of it has in our moral, social, and emotional lives. Put aside cases where the word "love" merely indicates an enthusiastic preference: for example, I love the Packers, I love real ale, I love revenge stories. The problem is this: we use the same word when we say, "I love you" when courting. We apply it to our relation with our spouse – assuming a reasonably good marriage, meaning one in which though the battles are frequent the swords are dull and have buttons on their points. But love hardly means the same thing the first time it gets said as on the first, tenth, twentieth, or fortieth anniversaries, when it might not get said. We say that we love our parents, our children, our dog; we say it too of certain friends, of either sex.

Why think that any of these loves is the same phenomenon? Of course each one of them comes with an instant context supplied. When I say I love my kids, that should pretty much take sex out of the picture. When you say you love your dog, that is doglove; when you say you love your mother, that is momlove, which is manifestly not dadlove, as my six-year-old recently informed me; dads, he said, get loved every third day. We know this about love, yet we don't know; we know that the particular contours of what we call love depend greatly on the object of that love, whether it be parent, spouse, lover, child, dog, country, faith, or friend; yet we are never quite sure which is the love that is the purest or deepest or that should set the standard for the others. Somehow all are felt to be paler versions of the love

celebrated in fiction, the passionate quest for a mate. We are put to
ranking these loves, in part, because the word "love" applies to all
of them and forces the comparison upon us. We think of them, if not
exactly the same, as being of the same species.

Walter's perspicacious observation that love is not just an emotion
but a situation plays havoc with our expectations for both situation
and sentiment. Each somehow, falsely, suggests that it demands the
forms and feelings of the other, or makes us feel we are falling short
now at one, now at the other. In the situation of love, however, as
Walter suggests, the sentiment we call love may be felt only occasionally or not at all. We are not sure what it feels like anyway; it is
always getting confused with other things. A big part of the problem,
as usual, is sex. Passionate sexual love seems to set the standard – at
least for the past eight hundred years in the West it has. Love worth
having is Eros with a little *philia* thrown in; *agape* is for when you
are older and need to do penance for Eros.

Examine, in your own life, how many times you have said "I love
you" in and around the sex act, only to decide later or even as you
were saying it that it meant something more, less, or different from
what it was supposed to. You either didn't mean it fully or said it
to convince yourself, or to prime the other to say it to you, as when
it was said as part of the seduction game, or you meant it but in
the sense of "having a very intense preference for" or in the heat of
the moment as a synonym for "wow" or "zow." True love in the
hyperpassionate stage usually feels pretty awful most of the time, as
many a poet, novelist, and teenager has lamented. La Rochefoucauld
offers this: "If one judged love by most of its effects, it looks more
like hatred than friendship" (M 72). You constantly fear not being
loved as much as you love; you are insanely jealous of every past
lover, of friends, pets, brothers and sisters, his or her job. You feel
sick, constantly seeking reassurances. And you long for the day when
you can take your beloved for granted and get back to dull grazing
and snoozing.[1]

When I try to decide for myself what the "feeling" of love is – I am
blushing now at my sentimentality – it is that sensation of wanting to
burst at what appears to be a glowing specialness of the other, seeing

the other abstracted from the usual clutter, vaguely transfigured and usually across a room or a table, or at some intermediate distance, or just as often in the mind's eye or when looking at a photo, the person not being there to spoil the glow you now see emanating from him or her. Usually you do not communicate the sentiment, too embarrassing, or if you do it is via a smile, a hug, or certain restricted forms of teasing. If it were taking place in the movies the soundtrack would let the other know what was going on. But in real life the communication of the sentiment often fails to register with its object.

## Winding the Clock Once a Month

The sentiment of love is not my theme, it is Walter's love as a *situation* that is, and why that state might generate anxieties about faking it. Walter does not use the term "faking it"; the word "fake" in the sense I have been using it is first recorded in the early nineteenth century, almost a hundred years later than Walter's conversation was to have taken place. He says "as if" – that Toby will act "as if" he feels love. If Toby's military service is any indication, as Walter says it is, Toby will occupy his role so thoroughly as to have that "as if" not really be discoverable to anyone, least of all to the sweet Toby, and in fact Toby will become his role in both senses that the word "become" bears: as a transformation and as doing honor to it.

We can conclude, I think, that the proper sentiment, if it is to occur, is powerfully linked to the commitment to play the role right, to play it like a man of prowess, to play it convincingly, with complete respect for the setting. Considering that it is Uncle Toby, Walter is right: no one would play it better, no one could find a sweeter mate. There is but one cause for concern: in war Toby was injured in the groin, and in the situation of love, as far as Walter is concerned, a Shandy is also likely to be injured in the groin. The situation of love has a certain noisome chore associated with it for which there is no proper "as if"; when it comes to sex, Toby has got to deliver. The as-iffing has to stop the once per month Walter deems it necessary to engage in this activity (and combine it with the other importuning chore of winding the grandfather clock) and still be fulfilling the obligations the situation demands.

To others not possessing Toby's benevolent simplicity of spirit, the state of love invites all kinds of anxieties. For it seldom "feels" like much of anything other than the usual array of feelings it takes to get through the day. That would bother no one if we didn't feel that being married, being a parent, a friend, or a brother or sister, even a lover, didn't mean we were supposed to *feel* something more than the usual flux of daily feelings. Anxieties about faking it in these matters are like the Eumenides to Orestes. I would bet it is an anxiety most have experienced: how come the most routine character in a novel or a movie seems to love better than I do? You worry that you fall short, too selfish, too easily annoyed, too impatient. Are you a total fake, a fake spouse, parent, sibling, son? You can fool some of the people some of the time, something probably made easier because they have lowered their expectations to accord with what they can get from the likes of you. But mostly you fear they are disappointed in you, not just that your kind of love doesn't stack up very well against that of fictional characters but that it cannot even make it against the next-door neighbor's. You mean you don't have these worries? Oh what I would give to have your talent for confident love . . . or your capacity for self-satisfaction.

Love as a quasi-juridical state still demands ritualized displays of certain gestures; above all it demands the expression of something we think of as "concerns." The state of love demands, it seems, oc-casionally professing to third parties your love for the second party, of paying public lip service. This is often easier than expressing it to the loved one. Love often ends up cowering behind embarrassment's burly back. There are those moments when love actually is verbalized in an overwhelming access of sentiment, yet even then embarrassment is not so much left behind as suffered to come along for the ride.

Routinized expressions of love don't often require being acted out "as if" they were an expression of feelings; they are so conventional-ized as to be little more than a "see ya later" on parting; no feelings are expected. Many people, however, cannot get themselves to say these conventional I love you's. If you didn't start the practice early on or come from a family that made a habit of it, then all of a sudden to begin would elicit suspicion as well as discomfort. Those I love you's (not quite as meaningless as love-ya's) are of an ilk with those little pecks on the cheek, which are the equivalent of air kisses between spouses. I must admit I never forgive anyone who gives me an air kiss, or anyone who gives one to anyone else either; but why should I not be able to return the favor without feeling awkward and silly, given that these kisses are, like the apology, openly a fake? Why is everyone else so good at faking these things, or really meaning them?

Maybe I am attributing too much virtue to these others who seem so good at playing the role of love. I do not have access to their self-doubts. I may doubt another's motives, but I cannot always know that he doubts them; I know, however, when I doubt my own. Self-doubt is more than doubt turned inward, for it not only undermines my own performances but also seems to give everyone else the benefit of the doubt. The effect of my blaming my own motives is that I flatter theirs. Maybe to them I look pretty good. Says my wife in the margin: don't flatter yourself.

Is it the sheer conventionality of these rote I love you's that brings on the fit of self-consciousness? That can't be, for conventions in other domains don't do so as readily. Might it be that love, even when completely expunged of sex, makes as much a demand on our capacity for reticence as it does on our capacity for expression? That is why public displays of affection strike me as little different from people not having enough shame to go off into a corner to talk on their cell phones, and also why it might not always be easy to play the part privately either. Yet there is surely a case to be made for these trivial displays. They are small reaffirmations of one's commitment to Walter's love as a situation.

But a certain embarrassed reserve and stiffness can have its own charm. Especially now, when it comes as relief from our new-age style of verbalizing invented feelings we are "getting in touch with" in favor of suppressing verbal expressions of real emotions we are completely in touch with. A friend's father, described without condemnation as "an uptight and embarrassed Scot," said to his Italian bride, my friend's mother, at their wedding ceremony: "I love you and I will always love you. And I am never going to say that again as long as I live. You will have to see it in my actions." He kept his promise and never said it to her or to his kids either, but they loved him like crazy for that line especially. The line became famous, because Mrs. McClean and his kids regaled everyone with it for years, the joke thus being that the one time the poor man did say "I love you" it followed him as an embarrassing echo for the rest of his life. Had Mr. McClean dwelt, not in America, but in the Highlands, where reticence is the norm, he might still have loved just as well for being reticent, but he surely would not have been so endearing for being so.

We tell ourselves that love, the situation, is about commitment, faithfulness, caring, and being there when the big crunch comes, though something worthy of being called a big crunch might never come. You tell yourself you would take a bullet, knowing full well that that is unlikely to be put to the test, and besides, you might then get into a tiff: "Look dear, you take the bullet this time, and then next year I will take it." For the kids you don't argue, but for each other...? But saying you will take a bullet, actually saying "bullet" and not using another less metaphorical assertion of commitment, is a kind of faking it. It is exaggerated, and it is said knowing it is playing a role, casting yourself as a hero in your own film. Face it: in suburban middle-aged life, it ain't going to happen. Still it registers a fantasy that pays lip service to grand commitment, and, as I have said, lip service is a kind of service. For if big crunches don't happen in a pacified society, little crunches do, and if you said you would take a bullet when the big crunch comes you would look not just like a cad but also like a fool if you did not put your own desires on the back burner and engage in the sometimes irksome process of being responsible and unselfish, at least for the sake of appearances, if nothing else. That's right: bite the bullet, Bill. And to be fair to the taking-the-bullet metaphor: it is a less embarrassing way of declaring love than "I love you."

# SIXTEEN

# Boys Crying and Girls Playing Dumb

THE STORIES I AM ABOUT TO TELL are a prequel to the preceding chapter; they are about the faking that goes on when we are first experimenting with what it means to be in love as an adolescent and about the presentation of self in courtship.

The tale that follows is also one of great gender anxiety, and it is true. I even think it happened exactly as I will relate it, for the events are so vivid in my mind's eye. I know – vividness has no necessary relation with veracity, at least where memory is concerned. I have told stories about myself that were largely true, but I remember altering the details to make them funnier, more suspenseful, or less boring, or to present myself as either wittier or more endearingly pathetic than really was the case. Now for the life of me I can no longer construct what really happened. I see it as I have told it, though I remember – no, I *know* – that I fabricated parts, but I no longer know which parts. My intentions are good, and, even if they were not, I take the refuge of the postmodern scoundrel: whether true or not it makes no difference. The tale raises the same points whether it happened exactly as I remember or not.

One day the acknowledged toughest kid announced to a group of us fifteen-year-old guys that he had had a fight with his girlfriend and that he had cried in front of her. I cannot recall the reaction of the others, but I remember mine to have been something like, no way, impossible. The impossibility was not that boys, especially ones for whom toughness was the chief virtue, could not cry; hell, you were on the verge of tears all the time, every boy-on-boy confrontation being a dare not to shed them. But what could possibly prompt you to shed them over and in front of a girl who could not beat you up?

Yet over the course of the next month, one by one, boy after boy announced a big breakup with their various girlfriends in which they had broken down in tears and had begged to be taken back. I could see I would have to take my turn in this new rite of initiation; I either had to make a confession of tears spilled for love or be forever cast out among the uncool. Unfair, I thought, to keep changing the rules of cool like this. Was Ron, the guy who started all this, just trying to see how much of a trendsetter he could be; was he even telling the truth? And if he was, could it be possible that all the other guys were telling the truth? Had they really cried?

As I try to access what I truly felt through the distorted lens of memory, it seems that whatever distrustfulness I had of Ron was muted. In short I believed every outrageous tale these guys told, and the consequences of my naiveté were that I often got into more trouble than they did actually trying to do (and failing) what they only said they had done. I was too uninformed and naïve to lie about sex. My lying was restricted mainly to how many beers I had downed, and in another year I would add tales of how fast I had taken the corner in the car, though I still accepted everyone else's tall tales as gospel, and probably even deluded myself into believing my own fabrications. But maybe they did cry, and my retrospective suspiciousness is as naïve in its own way as my gullibility was back then.

My turn, I saw, had arrived. It is clear to me now, and I think it was clear to me then, why I was the last to join the new emotion display fashion. I was barely holding it together in my act as a would-be tough guy. Pretending to be tough took all my energy and resolve; I had no margin of error. These guys could afford to announce they had cried, because no matter how hard they got hit in a game or fight they would never shed a tear or show signs of fear. They could actually benefit from the thought that people would mistrust their tale of having shed a tear over a fight with their girlfriend, but should I tell the same tale, they would believe it with no discount for whether or not I was lying. Of course Miller cried. For I suspected they suspected me of being a fake real guy. I leaked unacceptable truths about myself more often than I would have liked. I couldn't, for instance, disguise, in junior year, much as I tried, my excitement over *Hamlet*, a guy whom I understood to have been as nervous about sex and revenge as I was. That I tried to cover for my interest by getting kicked out of the class fooled no one, though I was accorded some grace for it.

Why not put my unmanliness to good use? Because few would doubt I had shed a tear, I could make up a tale that I had had a fight with my girlfriend (who dumped me shortly after these events took place) and forget actually having to worry about generating false tears, or a false occasion for real tears. I was not sure, either, that these guys hadn't actually shed tears, and if that is what toughness had become in our high school, then I guess I had to go along.

What did I do? I picked a fight with my girlfriend. I cannot recall precisely the grounds. No doubt it was some jealousy that you were never quite sure you weren't faking anyway. Strangely, it was the guys who insisted you feel jealous. Hey Miller, I saw Ellen dancing with Zawatska at the CYO. No way I was going to bring that up with her; Zawatska could kill me with both hands tied behind his back. Ellen was surnamed Hickok and she claimed Wild Bill as a distant kinsman and would have insisted I address myself to Zawatska if I had any complaints. Whatever the grounds, the moment had come to shed my tears, but none appeared. I was thinking of everything I could to coax them out, but nothing worked, not even the thought of my dog getting run over. I was obdurate; me, who had faked his way through every minute of my public life since the onset of puberty and a lot before that too, could not generate tears.

Desperately I embraced Ellen – I am ashamed to confess this – so that I could poke my eyes real hard behind her back, all for the sake of telling the truth that I too had shed tears in this new cursed regime Ron had inaugurated. Real tears, genuine fake real tears. But no tears came. I took some solace in the thought that she was not expecting tears from me anyway. I just hoped she hadn't noticed all the ridiculous commotion behind her back. The truth is I was so worried about what to say to the guys that I can't remember anything else about the interaction except a small sensation of cowardice over my inability to gouge my eyes hard enough to provoke the tears I desired.

I never wondered – and if I didn't wonder I doubt the other guys did – though surely it must have been the case, whether the girls were also commenting on the new regime; unless, that is, Ron and every other guy had made the whole thing up and no girl had seen any of the boys in tears. Maybe she was faking going along with it too, knowing only too well that I was playing a role. Besides, I had a distinct feeling I was not playing convincingly any aspect of this postpubescent daily trauma. Who was I playing this for anyway? Not for her, but for the guys, but not the guys either, because I could have lied. It must have been my homage to the dominant adolescent social order, and I was a member of that audience, judging my competence in proper emotion display.

If this was how emotions and courtship were to proceed "naturally," why didn't nature operate a little more automatically? Had any evolutionary psychologists – who blithely come up with just-so stories to show why it is written in our genes that attractive undergraduate women must inevitably find middle-aged male evolutionary psychologists sexy – ever been teenagers? None of this was coming naturally. I was learning a part that I only wish had been better programmed into my genes (and jeans). We were acting; mimicking actors in the movies or enacting what the older kids lied about doing when they were our age that they had got from the movies: life imitating art.

I was utterly clueless, operating in a fog. As I dimly recall, the whole game was played with alternating senses, alternating fast as a strobe light, of an acute awareness of fumbling cluelessly through a role not fully understood, and of being so totally immersed in it that my parents started sending away for brochures from various military academies as threats to get me to cool it with the fair Ellen.

I was thrown back on my first plan. Tell the guys I had had a big fight with Ellen and that I couldn't help it, but that I had broken down and cried. That is what I did. I was lying through my teeth, but no one called me on it, for there was in fact a real truth to my lie. I had committed myself by it to the new order; I was giving it the homage of paying it lip service.

IF FAKING IT IS SO MUCH of what masculinity is, it is surely no different with femininity. So much of early feminism was staked out precisely on this ground, of the revelation of and the resentment for the playacting women had to do to be women for men: putting on makeup, feigning desire, faking orgasm, playing dumb, and, above all, veiling their contempt and disgust at the insipidity of the roles they were asked to play. The most powerful passages in de Beauvoir's *Second Sex* have this as their theme.

In other words, what about Ellen? In this tale she is a mere prop in a performance primarily directed to the guys who were engaged in a competition with each other about who was having the most tumultuous relationship. I am sorry about this. Men no less than women posture before the other, posture before their own sex too. Surely masculinity, no less than femininity, is about appearances, about strutting and hiding stuff. Men fake being men no less than women fake being women. If we still feel that women have it worse in this charade, might it be because what men must fake is less contemptible than what women must fake? Pretending to be tough is not as demeaning (though it is often quite as silly) as pretending to be dumb or scared of a mouse (which has nothing to recommend it). Or is it because what women are working so hard to fake is devoted to supporting the male's fragile pose, whereas his faking is less likely to be devoted to supporting hers except to the extent that it helps her to keep him believing in the success of his?

Yet in this tale of woe I had to fake the equivalent of being scared of a mouse to add to the many hundreds of times I also had to play dumb to be one of the guys. But I had to shed tears to maintain what? My manhood? My sense of belonging? Belonging to what? A group of tough guys who cried over girls and were probably lying anyway? This coming to manhood was still about boys relating to boys, but now it meant boys relating to boys with regard to how they related with girls. No tears before boys, but tears before girls were now fashionable, which meant imitating what we thought the girls did (I doubt any of us ever witnessed one crying) right to their faces.

Goffman quotes this tale of a college girl from the 1940s reflecting on the distasteful role she finds herself playing on dates:

I sometimes "play dumb" on dates, but it leaves a bad taste. The emotions are complicated. Part of me enjoys "putting something over" on the unsuspecting male. But this sense of superiority over him is mixed with feelings of guilt for my hypocrisy. Toward the "date" I feel some contempt because he is "taken in" by my technique, or if I like the boy, a kind of maternal condescension. At times I resent him! Why isn't he my superior in all ways in which a man should excel so that I could be my natural self? What am I doing here with him, anyhow? Slumming?

And the funny part of it is that the man, I think, is not always so unsuspecting. He may sense the truth and become uneasy in the relation. "Where do I stand? Is she laughing up her sleeve or did she mean this praise? Was she really impressed with that little speech of mine or did she only pretend to know nothing about politics?" And once or twice I felt that the joke was on me; the boy saw through my wiles and felt contempt for me for stooping to such tricks.[1]

This woman has no doubts about her own intelligence; she is smart enough to suspect she might be getting outsmarted occasionally. She is alert to the risks of looking foolish in this kind of faking it. She doesn't like playing dumb in the first place; she wishes rather that the boys were "her superior in all ways a man should excel so that she could be her natural self." She lives in the 1940s, so pardon her articulation of her wish. Besides, she is not giving much away. She is asking only that he be sufficiently smart and secure in his intelligence so that she can be her natural, manifestly intelligent self, so that she can give up this particularly contemptible role of playing dumb for him.

Demeaning as it is to have to play dumb, it is not as bad as being dumb, like many of her dates, though we should not underestimate how often boys have to play dumb too – before other, tougher boys to be sure, but for the girls too. Being a dumb frat kid does not come as naturally to some of them as to others; some guys have to work at it and never succeed in playing the role without evident embarrassment. Our girl though is pretty sure these guys are dumb, not just playing at it. She wishes they were smarter, not that she were dumber. Except sometimes "once or twice," the guy, she suspects, is smarter than she initially thought and sees through the act and thinks it demeaning for *her* to put it on. For this perspicacious and self-reflective girl, what could be worse? It is not just being seen as dumb for playing dumb that is so humiliating, it is being exposed as thinking you are outsmarting someone by playing dumb when you should have been smart enough to have read the guy better. Now you fear he has real contempt for you, contempt you would agree with him for having, not the kind of stupid contempt that a stupid guy has for a "dumb" girl who is making a fool of him. Yet we do not know whether these guys have really seen through her either. She may be suffering a bout of paranoia.

An even scarier thought: only one or two guys made her suspect that her dumb act was unbecoming to them. What if others let her continue to think she was getting away with her act and sat back and played along, outplaying her at playing dumb, either because of some pathological misogyny that makes them like it when smart girls play dumb, or because they had too much contempt for her to signal she should give it up? What if, that is, the joke had been on her seven or eight times, when she thought it was so only once or twice?

What about the boys dating this girl? They would have to know she has been getting straight A's. How faked out are they; are they not scared of her? Are they really unaware of the contempt she has for them? This girl suspects they may have such an inkling. In one sense they are in a less enviable position than even she is. The boy playing smart and the girl playing dumb do not have the same risks when their cover is blown. If the smart girl playing dumb has her cover blown, she falls, if "falls" is the right verb, not very far for being revealed as intelligent. The guy, though, if exposed, turns out to be revealed as a dimwit. Neither playing it smart nor playing dumb is an especially attractive pose, but the risks of the former are the great humiliation of punctured pomposity; the risks of the latter are that the pose will be believed or that you will be disapproved of for betraying your own virtues.

Presumably it is easier to fake being dumb, most of us having been so at various times, than to fake being smart if you don't have the equipment. Playing dumb is not easy though; it takes a certain

amount of intelligence to get it right. It might in fact be easier to fake
out the smart than the dumb with a dumb act, for, just as this girl
suspects, the dumb cannot be reliably counted on to be so stupid as
not to know when they are being talked down to, whereas the smart
are only too willing to believe you are as dumb as you appear to
be. And if you fake being smart, you had better make sure you are
smart enough to know how smart the people you are playing it for
are. Smart people are experts at faking smartness, that being one of
the surest proofs of it. Nonetheless, there are all kinds of cultural
supports to back up the pompous male and pump him back up when
he is deflated. Indeed most of the cultural support will come from
women who will tell him the lies he needs to hear and even, perhaps,
come to love him, if he turns out to be an amiable buffoon. What
upsets this girl, however, is getting caught putting on the dumb role
for someone she feels she should have been smart enough to see would
have preferred the "real" her.[2]

Why shouldn't she recognize in those one or two guys, if not in
the others, their anxiety at the role they must play? She thinks of
them only as dangers to her, as sources of her humiliation. Surely she
must know that they are scurrying about desperately trying to defend
themselves from being made a fool of by this smart girl, while at the
same time, and with equal desperation, trying not to make fools of
themselves without her helping them along. They too have to perform
and may not be into or up to it; they may feel their natural selves are
also light-years away.

Goffman does not say much about the girl's comment. He takes
her confession to indicate a "special kind of alienation from self and
a special kind of wariness of others" that is a cost of maintaining
"a show before others that [she herself] does not believe." He says
nothing more about it except this: "Shared staging problems; concern
for the way things appear; warranted and unwarranted feelings of
shame; ambivalence about oneself and one's audience: these are some
of the dramaturgic elements of the human situation." For someone
usually so reliably perspicacious, Goffman disappoints us here.

I am inclined to be less melodramatic about her "special kind of
alienation." There is nothing very special about it: it is business as

usual when the risk of looking foolish is high. Courtship is one of those domains in which our self-esteem is especially vulnerable, in which we can look the fool and not feel it, or feel a fool and not look it, or both feel it and look it. The roles we are forced to play, men and women alike, are often badly written parts, and few are up to authoring their own original scripts. A date, a first date, has such a vulgar plot. Two people audition for each other, or are making a judgment as to whether even to hold an audition. Each inspects the other to judge desirability, availability, accessibility for the act of darkness, and the probability that this person would be worth talking to after doing it. The encounter is either, as we have discussed, an elaborate indirect statement of a vulgar desire, "wanna ****?" or, worse, a periphrasis meant to convey the brutal message: "with anyone but you, buddy (baby)." Painful, but not the stuff of tragedy; it is dark comedy.

# SEVENTEEN

# Acting Our Roles: Mimicry, Makeup, and Pills

RECALL WALTER SHANDY'S STATEMENT: "No matter whether [Toby] loves the service or no – being once in it – he acts as if he did; and takes every step to shew himself a man of prowess." Walter is not just proposing a theory of love but also, by implication, a theory of acting. It says a proper actor need not feel the emotions he is portraying to portray them well; he need only act *as if* he felt them. It is all about adopting the outward signs – the visible postures, words, and behaviors – and getting them exactly right. Inner states will either come along for the ride or not, but that is not the actor's concern, only the justness of the visible and audible form, of playing the role as it should be played from the viewpoint of an audience. Contrast this with the view that a good actor should enter his character's psyche so as to generate the feelings the character would feel; that the best way to get the outside right is to get the inside right first. This was an actively fought battle in the eighteenth century and continues to be disputed.

## Diderot and Actors

It was the philosophe and encyclopedist Denis Diderot who took the strong position that acting is about mimicking gesture, posture, expression, about external representations of feelings and motives, not about feeling.[1] He even argued that it is better not to have the feelings should you be able to generate them. The conventions of drama ask for quicker shifts of sentiment than real feelings could possibly keep up with; it is best to keep cool on the inside and perfect your mimetic technique. Besides, the actor must perform the same role night after night (in the theater), and for consistency's sake technique is more reliable than mustering feelings on demand.

Yet Walter's comments also hint at anticipating the famous view of emotions articulated by William James, which is usually (and a bit unfairly)[2] boiled down to this: "I do not weep because I am sad; rather I am sad because I weep"; "I do not tremble because I fear, I fear because I tremble." James's view is that the feeling we call the emotion is nothing more than our awareness of certain changes that occur in the body in response to external stimuli. Diderot's actor, by this account, need not generate the feeling to represent the emotion on stage, but by representing it he may trigger the feeling. Diderot, we have just seen, would prefer that the actor not develop the feeling; it might interfere with the performance.[3] Though the James theory has problems (it is making a comeback),[4] it embodies a certain folk wisdom that some experience seems to support. The put-on-a-happy-face doctrine is a practical application of the theory.[5] Postures of the body, expressions of the face, by some mysterious mechanism, seem to push the sentiments to accord with the outward display. Toby may indeed come to feel love if he acts as if he loves. Whatever the mechanism that accomplishes this accord between gesture and sentiment, it is hardly foolproof, for it is not uncommon to feel completely dissociated from one's gestures and actions, to feel and know them to be fake.[6]

Like Diderot, Walter does not care about inner states. It is all form, throwing oneself wholeheartedly into visible forms when propriety demands it. That is what a man of prowess such as Toby does. It leads to deeds of bravery on the battlefield and acts of kindness in the drawing room. The bedroom is another matter, but there is hope even there. Walter is not a cynic. How do we teach our children to have the inner state of the emotions of sadness, guilt, regret, disgust? We cannot verify that they really feel what they are supposed to. We are satisfied that they have the proper sentiments if they are making the proper facial expressions, adopting the right tone of voice, making their bodies accord with how that sentiment is to be properly displayed, carrying out actions that such a sentiment properly prompts, and last and most importantly, doing those things when it is appropriate do so. That much we can teach them and monitor whether they have learned the lesson.

When changing your two-year-old's diaper, you go "Yuck, ech, how disgusting." You make exaggerated disgust expressions, and the kid thinks you're a real comic genius, but the child is also learning the facial and oral signs of the emotion and learning that they are properly associated with excrement. (A significant number of those kids never cease to associate broad comedy with excretory functions; the joking shows that the disgust response is doing its work with a vengeance.[7]) It is all about getting the acting down, and we assume that the feeling in the gut will follow to keep in step with everything else the body is doing. Even if it doesn't, as is often the case with the apology, who cares as long as the proper deeds get done with the proper display of emotion, whether felt or faked?

Parents put on performances to teach their kids emotions, performances the parents recognize as performances, which they play up in the campiest of exaggerated styles. By the time the toddler is old enough to be taught to be disgusted, the parents are such old hands at dealing with his excrement that they are not all that much disgusted; they are faking the degree of their disgust. Parents have to fake it big to raise their kids. They fake anger, shock, interest, and indignation. What, you punched the neighbor kid in the nose?[8] One ex-hippie I know, who was unstoned possibly three whole days from 1967 to 1970, assumed a high-toned, Puritanical "absolutely not" when asked by her fourteen-year-old daughter whether she had ever taken drugs. Parents must put on shows for their kids, just as kids come to learn that it is best to put on shows for their parents, especially when the kids have something to hide. They then get punished for lying, if caught, but it is hard for them sometimes to discern the qualitative difference in all these fictions, especially when faking it is itself often a virtue.

Sometimes they get punished for telling the truth, not just when the truth is not good manners but when the truth flies in the face of other expectations. Truth telling in formal settings in which telling the truth is the actual substance of the ritual, as in confessions or judicial trials, is itself a performance in which in the interests of the "truth of the ritual" the particular truth being admitted must be a lie, or made to look like a lie. A story told in a student paper I received makes the point nicely. The tale is of a fifth-grade girl who gave the finger out the classroom window at the back of a hated playground attendant on the grounds below. She was soon to discover that in rituals of truth telling, truth is something more and less than the truth, the whole truth and nothing but the truth:

> V. J. Parmley and Chevy Zinder saw it, and ratted me out. [The teacher] called me into the hallway and asked me if it was true. "What is truth?" I should have answered . . . But, in my naiveté, and in the grip of my conscience, I thought that this was a crossroads moment. I felt that there was a right and a wrong thing to do. And there was, but telling the truth wasn't it. I knew instantly that I should have lied. Whether or not she suspected that I had done it, she never expected me to own up to it. She was more outraged by the fact that I had the audacity to admit my misdeed, than that I had committed it.[9]

We perform, but we are not professional actors. They are a caste unto themselves, and there is something unsettling and uncanny about them. We have raised their status considerably in our celebrity culture, but they still are of an ilk with the circus performer, carnies, and prostitutes; they occupy a demimonde. Diderot likened actors to an unsavory lot: to courtesans faking orgasm, to beggars faking their meekness and deformities, to seducers faking love, and to atheistical priests faking belief.[10] "The greater the actor," says one commentator on Diderot, "the more pointedly he reminds the public of what powerful instruments nature has placed in the hands of the deceitful."[11] One fears they constitute the limiting case we worried about earlier: is there any core to them? Are they only the sum of their roles? Is their hollowness the perfect and uncanny image of our own hollowness? Thus Diderot:

> It is said that actors have no character because by playing so many roles they lose the character nature gave them, and thus they become fakes (*faux*), in the same way that the physician, the surgeon,

and the butcher become callous. I believe that that mistakes cause for effect: it is rather that they are suited to play all roles because they have no character.[12]

Actors might chafe at such an unflattering description, but then many of them, at least the Hollywood sorts, seem bent on proving Diderot right. All surface glitz, most look like drag versions of themselves. One suspects that the tabloids do not make them as superficial as they do the tabloids. When stripped of clothing, which the female ones often obligatorily are, they are still in full costume, sometimes in the form of a faked body double. Other people play them in stunt scenes too, so that even as actors they are pulling a sleight of hand as to their assumed identity. You think they are playing others, but in fact others are playing them playing others. Some movies, none more so than *Sunset Boulevard* (1950), are very smart about the general theme of the illusionism and proteanism of an actor's self and sense of self, with directors interchangeable with butlers and husbands, narration by a corpse who is a would-be scriptwriter (fitting for a movie about the death of silent film and its stars), real people playing themselves, or characters playing vaguely disguised facsimiles of themselves watching earlier movies of their "real" selves and fantasizing that they still are what they once were, which was merely an image in the first place.

Thin-lipped moralists are usually on to something when they sniff out sources of temptation and corruption. Even should we grant, against Diderot, that there is nothing especially wicked about the souls of people drawn to acting, acting, it is feared, will soon make them so. People who must declare love and show expressions of it in the theater or take off their clothes and simulate erotic passion on a sound stage will be tempted to finish offstage what they started on it. Indeed nonactors may seek to become amateur actors and put on small theatricals as an amatory aid. Neither Mr. Bertram, nor Jane Austen, was wrong that an innocuously innocent attempt to alleviate the boredom of daily life at Mansfield Park by staging a play was not so innocent. Something about openly donning masks or posing as another frees the character from moral constraints. An actor gets to be professionally what kids are taught is allowable only at restricted times, such as Halloween, Purim, or Mardi Gras, or only in restricted places, such as vacation spots catering to the spring-break crowd, Las Vegas, red-light districts – all sanctuaries of a sort in which one's proper identity is suppressed and, with it, the rules of responsibility and respectability.

My sixteen-year-old daughter wants to be an actress; visions of Broadway musical theater dance in her head. She is not too young for me to begin seriously worrying that she is serious, so I have already told her to hone her table-clearing techniques, which she so far has shown little aptitude for at home. But do I want her waiting on tables? The culture of the restaurant or bar is somewhat theatrical, not in the way life is theatrical but in being a setting in which certain kinds of vices, amiable and not so amiable, are abetted and thrive. The young waitress of today occupies much the role the actress did for the idle young man about town in the eighteenth and nineteenth centuries: an object of desire, attainable desire. But how naïve am I to think that love does not take place even in the coldest climate? Why, even the academy, the only place where sex is written about more than it is done, is a bawd.

### Pretending versus Faking It

Four-year-olds, not sixteen-year-olds, match actors in their uncanniness. They dress up in costumes, talk to themselves, invent whole lives and imaginary friends. "Child's play" we call it as they hone their skills of faking it with no sense of faking it, but of pretending instead. There is a difference: pretending allows you to play any role you want; you write the play, set it where you will, play the part you want to play. Faking it means playing a role that the larger culture has already scripted and that your inner being somehow feels is not quite your own. Faking it is forced upon us and gives rise to unpleasant accesses of self-consciousness. Faking it places us ever so much in the world. Pretending gets us out of it for a brief vacation.[13] Pretending is like a daydream or often takes the form of a daydream, adopted because of the pleasures it affords, pure escapism. Indeed, there is some marring of the pleasure by the knowledge that it is not really real, but most of us wouldn't wish it any other way for fear we would lose our moorings entirely or actually have to be the action hero we daydream ourselves into being for a two-minute fantasy.

Parents who watch their children totally lost in their fantasy worlds worry that their kids are nuts, only to see that the neighbor kid seems almost as crazy. When my aspiring actress was two she would proclaim that she was Cinderella pretending to be a mouse pretending to be Bess (her name) and then would proceed to do nothing different as far as I could tell. She continued to sit there with furrowed brow until she announced she was pretending to be another someone pretending to be something else. I am not sure what she was doing. Was it pretending to pretend? Or was it a complex nesting of roles to make pretending itself the subject of the pretense – she was starring as the Great Pretender?

I want to give this some pretentious meaning when it probably has no meaning beyond the ludic (ludic? thus I manage to be pretentious while pretending to turn my back on it). Giving grand significance to things that cannot bear the weight of the pretense is one of the most common forms of fakery academics engage in. Settle then for this, which does not quite evade charges of pomposity either: Bess was testing the durability and contours of the self she was in the process of acquiring, making sure it would be there to come back to. This kind of play is part of the process of coming to believe there is a self called Bess precisely because she could be X, or Y, or Z at a whim of *her* choosing, though the roles she plays will still be stitched together from the culture she is training herself to enter. This is long before she will feel as Orwell did when he shot an elephant he did not want to shoot because the expectation in the eyes of 2,000 Burmese natives watching him gave him no choice but to shoot the poor beast. As a toddler Bess felt the freedom of willing her role and would be as free in willing it as she would ever be again. She is already finding out that an actress, though she gets to play various roles, does not get to choose the roles she gets to play. The competition for being a professional assumer of roles is as stiff as any competition there is.

I would imagine that at age two she experienced no anxiety for complicating her relations to herself, though I know of one child who, when pretending at two, would turn to tell her parents not to worry, that she was only pretending. But by seven or eight can't you recall already feeling silly at some of the parts you were forced to play in certain games? It was more than the fear that adults or older siblings might stumble upon you and make you feel self-conscious or tease you; it was that you were embarrassing yourself in your own mind whether they showed up or not. I recall that playing war was, on occasion, not fully consuming, though it was still more fun than not playing war. I would feel a little foolish making the gun noises; maybe it was because I made them so poorly compared with the other kids, though my envy of them was tinged by a nagging disbelief that they could be so totally into all those pows, clicks, and saliva-thick explosion noises. That is not fair to them: they too must have been as disappointed that they could not really shoot me as I was that I could not shoot them, that it was all fantasy bullets and shells. Instead we argued over who killed whom first.

## Making Up Is Hard to Do, or Masking for It

We sometimes need external aids to get us through performances or prepare for them. Our roles need props and proper costumes as well as proper dispositions, though these be feigned. Thus rum rations are needed to help us through the minefields of so-called convivial social interactions. Actors get in costume and makeup; they go into training to lose weight or gain it. When does preparing, making up, getting in costume pass beyond mere preparation to play a part well and begin to shade into morally troubling misrepresentation – hoodwinking, conning, tricking? Must we own up to certain kinds of help we are getting to play our roles, help that if not revealed would be thought to be cheating? Surely we will trouble ourselves about hiding something that we think might raise a moral demand to disclose, or that requires an explicit limitation of warranties.

Actual cosmetics, face-painting, have long been held to be a legitimate prerogative of women; men quite frequently have dabbled in it too, and not only in decadent Rome or Weimar Berlin. Like all practices it is subject to a thick array of rules, some articulated, most not. Makeup that calls and is meant to call aggressive attention to itself tends to indicate an aspiration for, or the fact of, marginality: the whore or actor or super-hip or gender-bending male or weirded-out teenager. (Makeup that calls, but is not meant to call, aggressive attention to itself is usually the curse of the bumbling teenager or aging woman.) Long before that line was crossed, however, innocent rouging provided a basis for misogynists to lambaste the false seeming of womankind.[14] The woman who does not make up, or put on a face, is also sending a message variously ranging from indifference to not giving a damn (not the same as indifference) to thinking she is so beautiful she doesn't need it to claiming a certain style of feminism, and more. The woman who refuses makeup is no less making up for a role than the one who puts it on. The exact meaning of the positions changes roughly each decade or two but, again, very much within predictable ranges.

There is an honesty to cosmetics: the woman putting them on is not ashamed that she is doing so. Women in my mother's generation would pull out a compact and reapply makeup seated in a restaurant; not to do so was bad form. In that day a woman might never be so inaccessible as when she was redoing her face in public. And cosmetics work more magically for not being disavowed, for being so open; it draws men and frightens them; it is all so mysterious. The more makeup, the more it suggests a certain freedom from sexual constraint, a mask for carnival, while also suggesting a seamless self-involvement that blithely denies the existence of others present. The coding is complex: certain styles of making up thus signal primness and propriety better than would no makeup. I am speaking only very generally; these rules vary by social class and ethnicity and geographical region, and most of us are quite fluent in the language, at least in the dialect of our own generation.

Before Prozac and its ilk, before implants, Viagra, and Rogaine, the world of faking and pretense was about donning clothing and the vocal accent of a different class. Shakespearean comedy depends on the magical transformation that changes of dress can work on identity, and surely it was the case that clothes made the man and woman, hence the myriad sumptuary laws to regulate who could wear what, so leaky were the dikes separating the various social ranks.[15] You were to stay within gender confines too. Saga Iceland, for instance, loved its women tough, capable, good-looking, and smart, but they were not to dress like men, nor men like women. The penalty most frequently visited on cross- or ambiguous dressers in the sagas was immediate divorce, but the laws go farther and subject the person to prosecution for lesser outlawry – loss of property and three year's exile – at the suit of anyone who wished to bring it.[16]

What of the status of Rogaine, Prozac, or implants? Is there a duty to inform? A very bald friend suggested that Rogaine does not belong on this list because "it just retards hair loss and I wouldn't call that 'faking'; how about liposuction?" But I am retaining Rogaine; it tries to mask the truth of the disgrace that the course of nature has visited upon us. To confess to using it is embarrassing and forces one into a self-mocking mode to own up to it, for it is proof that our vanity has reached pretty near the depths of pathetic foolishness. Something still makes Rogaine more a form of deception, for instance, than using toothpaste with whitener in it, which is more, we think, like using soap. That aside, is there a duty to inform, say, that you have breast implants or use Viagra? And if you don't tell and the other finds out, will he or she accept you as the real you or as a discounted "you" or as a jacked-up YOU?

Would you not feel a little bit betrayed by a guy taking Viagra or a woman with breast implants? Wouldn't a guy, in the latter case, feel embarrassed if he got aroused by them knowing they were fake? He, however, would have a response to that: "Fake? What's fake and what's real? I have been reading the fathers of the church and various monastic writers, and they have always suggested that even so-called real breasts are fake, a false appearance, for all they are is skin covering disgusting goo, mostly fat.[17] Would a bowl of fat turn you on? No, it is only the location and the skin over the fat that transforms the fat into a breast. So what is wrong with skin over silicon or salt water? Rather better in fact." And he is not a fetishist, merely a medievalist. If men can get turned on by makeup, why not by a false breast with real skin on it?

Does a man who needs Viagra to perform have to avow it? Would a woman feel betrayed upon discovering that the man, whom she heretofore believed she was exciting so much that he never failed, owed his powers of penetration to a blue pill? Feel she got conned, made a fool of, not just a teeny bit hurt? Or would she feel grateful that he cared enough to take the pill? Doesn't the guy, himself, feel like a fraud? Or does he defend himself thus: until Viagra all the faking in sex was on the woman's side; their pleasure could be faked, and few men were ever the wiser, and none had any inducement to probe too closely anyway as to whether the woman was faking it for fear of finding out how unaccomplished he was. Now men get to fake it too. Admittedly it is not quite analogous. Women who fake don't get orgasms – that is what they are faking – men whose erections are in fact Viagra erections do get orgasms. But there is still a point to the comparison. Both are about playing roles convincingly and pulling a fast one. Is it the poor man's fault that he simply cannot fake it without chemical intervention?[18]

What of antidepressants? Depressed people, down-in-the-dumps pessimists, people given to ready annoyance at human foible, might find life easier, if not quite as interesting, if they use chemical aids to help them mellow out. These people are often types who need chemicals that really work – no faking them out with placebo. There have been a host of studies proving that depressive pessimists are not misreading the world. They tend to test out much better than happy people in intelligence and in seeing themselves and the world accurately. Their powers of discernment send them into a tailspin.[19] If, as Swift would have it, "[Happiness] is a perpetual possession of being well deceived," then the problem of these depressed souls is that they are not much given to self-deception.[20] For these depressed Westerners, yoga and Eastern meditative techniques won't work, except to the extent that their spirits get picked up for a few seconds to ridicule the hokiness of going east for spirituality rather than for food. Yes, they know this snake oil stuff works for people who believe in it, but there is no way they could ever overcome feeling foolish for giving it a try. They would sink even lower for having sunk so low. But a little yellow pill?

Here then is the problem. Suppose you court a person and win him or her over to love you because you are easy-going and sociable. True, some people would have loved you as a depressed and occasionally angry wit, but this person whom you love beyond belief loves you as you are on Paxil. He or she bought the act hook, line, and sinker. What if she should go up to the attic and find your true portrait? Should anyone feel anxious about matters of authenticity in this vignette? Should they treat the new, docile you as an amiable imposter, a new, better Martin Guerre returning from the wars? Good riddance to the old one, whom no one liked anyway. And though people know the new one is a fake, they prefer not to think of him that way; it is so much pleasanter to take the imposter as the real Martin.

Your old friends know that it is not the real you but may prefer the more tractable fake you anyway. But what of the friends you have made after you became Paxilman? Must you disclose? If you do, do you risk losing them? Or will they stick with you because it would make them look shallow to abandon you on such grounds?[21] But then you might suspect that the only reason they did not abandon you was out of a sense of duty. Would they trust you to keep taking your pills? Maybe they would love the old you too? Want to give it a try? These same anxieties are mirrored in the other person, who may want to live dangerously by finding out what the real you is really like. Nor is it all that unlikely that the person who discovers that your character is chemically maintained is also on an antidepressant and so may be forgiving. Does this make the situation exponentially falser or somehow truer and fairer?

Then there is hair. The rules are very different for men and women, because the former are desperate to acquire it except on the ears, back, and neck, and the latter are desperate to get rid of it, except on the head. It is male hair loss I limit myself to, not waxing, bikini lines, or electrolysis. Rogaine seems fair preparation for the public presentation of self. If it grows hair, which it probably won't, it is real hair, your hair. And though this makes it seem analogous to Viagra, which makes real erections, that is not the case, for she has no reason to believe that your love and desire for her caused your hair to grow. If Rogaine doesn't grow hair, you are out the money and look foolish only to yourself and to the check-out clerk in the pharmacy.

Rogaine is surely an acceptable preparation for presenting yourself in public in a way that hair transplants, with plugs that change a head into a doll's head or, worse still, a toupee, which justifiably subjects its wearer to infinite ridicule, is not. A toupee is by definition a botched performance.[22] You think you are playing in a serious drama, and instead you are the star of a farce. Rogaine carries a risk of humiliation too, though small. No one believes you want to be bald; they will mostly amiably laugh away the silly vanity you reveal for wanting to have more hair than you do. You give others a chance to tease you gently: suppose you say to your significant other, "Hey I think it's actually working" and the response is, "Yup, as an hallucinogen; just slip it into your students' water and they will see you with hair." Oh, the trials and tribulations of maintaining dignity.

### Surgical Masks

There is a tradition, often maintained ironically or with a sense of its shock value, that it is only when masked that we can speak truly, or if not truly, at least interestingly. This is Oscar Wilde's view. But there has always been a related belief that fiction is better at approximating truth than nonfiction and then, paradox upon paradox, that the "truest poetry," according to Touchstone in As You Like It, "is the most feigning" (3.3.16).[23] Real life often seems more fake than fiction. And acting styles as well as characterizations and plots in novels have always had to perform serious cosmetic surgery on true life to satisfy our demands for verisimilitude and plausibility. In a different vein, we know how to mobilize contrived fiction to flush out truth, as when the play is the thing wherein we catch the conscience of kings, or as when Polonius and law enforcement agencies entrap wrongdoers: "Your bait of falsehood takes this carp of truth" (2.1.62).

But the truthfulness of masks is not categorical; some allow truth to flourish, others suborn it utterly. It depends on what kind of masks, when and where donned, and what kind of fictions. To play being a polite person is to be a polite person. The mask is all that is asked for. There is a truth there. Sincerity supposes, in contrast, masklessness, but that presents an impossible bind stated succinctly by Andre Gide: "One cannot at the same time both be sincere and seem so."[24] One can play a role sincerely. I sincerely act out my role as a teacher. Playing the role of the sincere person sincerely, however, rightly raises suspicions. Recall the unverifiability of sincerity in displays of remorseful groveling. There is, as we have seen, more verifiable sincerity in the coerced spat-out apology than in voluntary sackcloth and breast-beating. In the latter case, but not the former, the apologizer is trying to sell the other on his sincerity and hence falls afoul of Gide's law.

Where, though, is the truth in masks that are surgically applied or achieved by ingesting pills, other than the truth that we are vain, ill, neurotic, and sad? These are not masks that allow for much artistry on the part of the wearer; all the art belongs to the surgeon or the chemist. What a crabbed moralist I have become. Is it because I feel conned by breast implants, Paxil, Rogaine, and Botox, but not by pretenses of gratitude, amiability, and modest applications of makeup? Or is there some deeper notion of fair play and cheating involved? Some ways of cheating nature have a long and venerable tradition; other ways look like crass innovations, part of an unrelenting move toward the moral horror of designer babies, cloning, and obscenely long life.

Is it that a breast implant suggests the mind of the whore, or a similar kind of pathetic pandering to male foolishness? Or is it nothing more than a slightly more expensive and invasive succumbing to pathetic vanity on the order of the man driven to Rogaine? Neither wants to be rejected as an object of desire because of having, in one case, small breasts or, in the other, thinning hair. Both evidently would prefer knowing they have been rejected on more substantial grounds, such as their dullness, shallowness, or moral failings. Incredible, but no small number of us, I bet, would rather find out another is turned off by us because he thinks us morally defective than that he found us so physically unappealing as to make sex with us either unthinkable or nauseating. Is it that self-esteem starts first with wishing to see ourselves as attractive rather than wishing to see ourselves as good? Or at some deep level, is it that we, like ancient Greeks, do not feel there is any distinction between the good and the beautiful?

Why is it that cosmetic surgery seems like cheating and cosmetics do not? Is it only a function of what our sense of the usual is? If I were thirty years younger and had lived a good portion of my life in southern California, I would probably be more liberal on these matters. Moreover, surgical interventions catering to vanity are not some newfangled innovation; they have an impressive historical pedigree of more than two millennia. A popular one for Jews trying to Hellenize themselves before the birth of Christ was to undergo an uncircumcision, an operation designed to make them look as natural as the day they were born, with penile skin stretched out enough to make it pass for a real foreskin. Locker room anxieties, it seems, are as old as the hills.[25]

Botox, the wrinkle remover, raises other issues. It works by paralyzing selected facial muscles, relaxing away wrinkles, thereby also destroying those muscles' ability to participate in the making of various facial expressions, such as furrowing the brow in a frown of annoyance or of concentration. Try this experiment. Concentrate intently on a difficult math problem or focus your attention on a picture of a painting in an art book without furrowing your brow or contracting it a little. Not easy, is it? It may be that we need the facial expression as an aid to the deeper thoughtful enterprise, that the furrowing is more than a mere sign that thinking is taking place. Now comes the Botox person, who not only can no longer fake a look of concentration, interest, or mental focus but also may, at the margins, lose the very ability to concentrate, focus, and think intently. Better, it seems, to be thought vacuous and indeed to be vacuous than to bear the signs of your age. Big deal, you say: people so apocalyptically vain as to sign up for Botox injections probably are not losing an ability they had before anyway.

Perhaps the draw of these surgical interventions and openly fake re-creations of our lost beauty – or new creations of beauty we never had – is that the embarrassment of being seen as that shallow has a short half-life. The same person who might at first give you a black mark for shallowness and vanity on account of your breast implants is soon likely to be very forgiving. Better attractive fakery than ugly truth. Besides, the fakery has its own kind of truth, the truth of beauty, which moralists of a certain stripe forever claim, to little avail, is false. Within a month, maybe even an hour, he will be putting the moves on you, and you will not reject him as readily as you would have months before Rogaine had its salutary effect on him, and, what with his Viagra, to misuse Yeats dreadfully,

> So great a sweetness flows into the breast
> We must laugh and we must sing,
> We are blest by everything,
> Everything we look upon is blest.

TRAITS ARE NOT ROLES, but they imbue roles with a certain style. And these styles can be faked too or can often look fake when they are genuine. The next chapter takes up certain styles of self-presentation: modesty, both true and false, pretentiousness, and a reprise of some issues raised by the ironies of self-mockery.

# EIGHTEEN

# False (Im)modesty

ROLE PLAYING, PERFORMING OUR PARTS, is what we do; we can hardly blame one another for playing roles. Suppose, however, the role is flavored in such a way that the player can be described as pretentious. We all pretend, but that does not make us pretentious, or even pretenders in a bad sense, or in the way of Bonny Prince Charley. Pretension can take the form of adopting a style of something you aspire to be, and may eventually be, but are not there yet – thus the grad student who postures as a prof. A variant version has the middling prof posturing as a prof of importance. He differs from the grad student because his case holds no promise of the pretense ever converging with reality. The third in the series is the prof of importance who postures as a prof of importance.

Unlike the first two examples, the prof of importance is playing a role he is entitled to play and is claiming a status he actually occupies, but in a way that reveals him to be too taken with the station life has assigned him. We can imagine a person exuberantly delighting in his high station who is not pretentious. It takes more than just loving his role to make the prof offensive. This pretentious person's delight is a smug delight. He is self-satisfied; he puts on airs, and we feel he is full of air, usually hot, a stuffed shirt, overinflated. As early as Chaucer, this kind of intellectual pretentiousness was conflated with flatulence, as an intellectually pretentious friar is stumped by the subtlety of how to divide a fart into twelve equal parts.[1] And images of gas (*flatus*) and overinflation invite corresponding images of vengeful deflation: we thus speak of popping or piercing their pretensions. One of the reasons I try to deliver lectures in what I congratulate myself is a comic style is that it allows me to interpret the laughter of the students as not being *at* me. But can't the pretentious prof think he is a really funny guy too, delivering what he thinks are fine jests?

Not all fakes are pretentious, and not all pretentious people are fakes. But so obviously unpleasant and affected is the style that one wonders why on earth anyone would adopt it outside the German academy, where it appears to be a necessary and often sufficient qualification of a professorship?[2] There are various cultural rules on this. In America, democratic norms should make a pompous professor more seriously morally defective than his pompous German or even English counterpart. Pomposity does have different national styles: the pomposity of the French, who think themselves witty and, more pathetically, sexy, is not the pomposity of a Herr Doktor who prides himself on taking more words rather than fewer to say something. The pomposity of Oxbridge dons is itself such an arabesque of affectations that it is hard to believe anyone can play the part without being aware of its comic implications. It is badly restyled in the American academy, the difference being that the English are secure enough in their pomposity to engage in pompous self-mockery about the pompousness of it all, whereas the Americans are sincerely pompous, like the parvenu who cannot run the risk of self-mockery.[3]

So distasteful is the style, given democratic assumptions, why on earth would any American adopt it?[4] Here is one reason that transcends the cultural: I have found over the years that students tend to confuse pomposity with knowledge and nastiness with smarts. Students thus force otherwise indifferently kind and modest teachers into being mean windbags to get the respect they crave. It may be less that pompous power generates toadies than that toadyism generates pompous power.

Pretentious people seem to inhabit their role in a unique way. They are fully immersed in their role, but not in the manner of people who lose themselves in a role out of exuberance, dedication, addiction, or simplicity. One of the peculiar forms of this pretentious style is that though the person never puts his role aside, he also never seems to relax into it. One imagines that they never cease thinking of themselves as Herr Professor Doktor when they fornicate and defecate. Yet such pompous souls, not uncommonly, believe themselves, in fact, to be rather deft wits and ironists; they thus take great care to enter their *bons mots* in their class notes for annual repetition. And it need not be that the pretentious person thinks he is more important than he is – he is often quite important. It's that he wants to make you feel his importance in an unbecoming way. He lacks what in the eighteenth century was called the virtue of condescension; he does not know when to give up on the privileges of his standing when he could gain credit by doing so.[5] Because he insists on extending his authority to occasions and physical spaces where it has no business, we treat him as if he were making fraudulent claims. And we are right, for his authority is not always properly to be on center stage, but only when the stage directions say it is.

There is no way to separate the sociological from the moral here. Modesty is a virtue that has very little to do with intention and very much to do with how you present yourself modestly. Like courage, modesty is about delivering the goods. If others feel you lord it over them, never letting them forget for a moment that you are pleased to be their superior in a way that makes them resentful, well then, despite all intentions, you got it coming. That is another of my over-statements, so let me clip its wings in the interests of accuracy. If we discern that the pompous person is otherwise decent, that when push comes to shove he is kind and generous and comes through on im-portant matters, we will tell ourselves things like, "He really is OK once you get to know him." In the interests of equity, we make the moral move of distinguishing between his style, for which we want to stone him, and his substance, for which we will commute his capital punishment into merely complaining about him behind his back or warning people who are about to meet him to cut him some slack.

Pomposity seems to be an occupational hazard of academics more than most professions, and I fear I am not always vigilant enough not to succumb myself. But is it really that the academy draws more than its share of pompous people? Or is it that the peculiar kind of preten-tiousness that thrives in the academy is one of gravity, gravity being much more prevalent in the ivy-covered walls than other equally annoying forms of oppressing people with self-satisfaction, such as the tough guy who won't let you forget he can kick the crap out of you; or the femme fatale who, depending on your gender, either won't let you forget you are to desire her or that she is more beautiful than you; or the rah-rah jock who is always too loud; or the cooler-and hipper-than-thou types, any number come to mind, people so thoroughly immodest in their style, so deeply self-satisfied? If the professor's offensiveness of style lies in its pomposity, the cooler-than-thou's offensiveness is his flippancy, in which a pointed detachment of a contemptuous sort pretends to wit, which even if directed at himself fails to do the proper work of false modesty or of wit.

## False Modesty

Pompous pretentiousness is one way of characterizing the vice opposed to the virtue of modesty. In the Middle Ages the opposed vice would have been understood to be pride, but we have long since reevaluated pride and blame only a pride that is too prideful, too showy, too pompous. Quiet pride is in fact how we have come to understand what modesty is. Not too quiet, though. What is more pretentious than the friend who does not tell you about winning a big award? So what if she is beside herself with anxiety about how to tell you or whether to tell so that she doesn't look as if she is bragging? To choose silence is the wrong move.

Modesty is another one of those virtues in which the faked version makes the real thing suspect, so common is fakery in this domain. Whatever false modesty is, it is not hypocritical any more than politeness is. False modesty is about taking care of others' feelings on the tricky terrain of envy. It is the concession we grant to a certain justice in envy that we not too far outstrip others, lest they hate us or we offend them. False modesty is thus an homage to envy, born not only of fear but also of fellow-feeling.

True modesty may have no motive other than its own realization. False modesty, though, is precisely what propriety often demands in the service of reducing envy. For this reason, real modesty that does the sociable work we ask false modesty to perform will get not much more credit than if it were false to begin with. What is being asked is that the fortunate person spare the feelings of others.

And this can often be accomplished by the falseness of the modesty, the very falseness, within decorous limits, revealing the effort being made to make concessions to the dangers of the situation. The proper performance, in other words, demands small leakages; the falsity should not be completely hidden. True modesty does not show effort, often because it doesn't take any for those to whom it comes naturally. If it were to take effort, the modest person would suspect that her modesty had failed for that reason.

Modesty is tricky: if you are a person of considerable ability and talent you can exemplify one minimal conception of the virtue by not calling attention to your virtues and position, by not being openly vain of them, or showy; one cultivates understatement. We even credit people with some facsimile of modesty if they quietly take their advantages for granted. As it is said of the two Miss Bertrams in *Mansfield Park*, "Their vanity was in such good order, that they seemed to be quite free from it, and gave themselves no airs" (ch. 4). Suppose, however, you are a person of "modest" abilities or station, no great shakes at anything. This person has one kind of modesty thrust upon him, and it is not a virtue, merely a statement about where he ranks in the relevant pecking order. He would get no credit for understating his abilities, for they are already sufficiently understated. For him modesty demands that he not overstate his modest talents, that, in other words, he know just where he stands. It would be a presumptuous arrogation for him to put on a show of false modesty. Nor do we want him pretending to be worse than he is, to indulge in a sentimentalized low self-esteem or a flaccid spiritlessness.

Modesty, in our time, has come to be tainted by a supposed relation between it and low self-esteem, either as cause or as effect. And immodesty, in the sense of bragging and talking oneself up, has gotten some cachet not only because of the self-esteem movement but also because of the draw of the energetic in-your-face style of trash talk, hip-hop braggadocio, a style that is hardly recent or black; it also is the style employed by Beowulf and the heroes of the *Iliad*, if not U. S. Grant or Clint Eastwood. Despite the decline in the value of its shares, modesty continues to be respected as a virtue by enough of us that it behooves us to cultivate our talents for false forms of it.

When I am being falsely modest, though, I am not really faking it. I am being sincerely falsely modest. The sincerity of it goes to the real concern it evinces not to want to give others grounds for hating you. You hardly want your pride to alienate your friends or mobilize your enemies. False modesty nicely unites motives of prudence with motives of benevolence. But woe to the person who acts falsely modest when he has no basis for gloating or inspires no envy in anyone. That is a fear that haunts more than a few of us as we feel oh so good about our managing to be (falsely) modest about precisely those virtues that we incorrectly believe ourselves to possess.

### Self-Mockery and Frank Confessions

Sincere self-mockery can do the work of false modesty. But it is falsely modest in a different way than feigning modesty is. False modesty must obey the time limits of true modesty. No holding the floor beyond the minimum necessary. Self-mockery, in contrast, is often meant to be a way of holding the floor, having the topic be yourself, and entertaining others with all attention focused on yourself. Self-mockery is not about *quiet* self-effacement or about self-effacement in any form.[6]

Self-mockery attempts to package vanity in acceptable forms. Thus you ridicule your hot temper, but you really are making a claim for the virtues of your recklessness, your daring and courage. Or you can ridicule your blundering failures in courtship as long as it makes desirable people desire to take you on as a work in progress, or at least to give you credit for being charming. Self-mockery is also a way of fishing for compliments on the cheap, because it dispenses with the expense of the bait of falsely complimenting others first so that that they will compliment you back.

La Rochefoucauld discusses another variation in which contrary to the self-praise effected by self-mockery we actually confess to real faults "sincerely." You decide whether "sincerely" needs the scare quotes: "The desire to talk about ourselves, to expose our faults from the point of view which we would choose, constitutes the great part of our sincerity" (M 383).[7] The way the maxim is worded indicates that the speaker is not using a tone of self-mocking raillery, but a more somber tone of self-criticism. It makes no difference that the self-criticism is falsely motivated; that, says La Rochefoucauld, is the strategy we must employ when it comes to posing as sincere about our own faults. The sincerity, though, is not quite a pose. One is indeed sincere about maintaining one's standing before others; what is false is the pretense that the sincerity is attached to remorse.

La Rochefoucauld's bemused oh-what-fools-these-mortals-be tone is more tolerant of our vanity than George Eliot's judgment of this kind of self-protective strategy: "The vicar's frankness seemed not of the repulsive sort that comes from an uneasy consciousness seeking to forestall the judgment of others...."[8] The good vicar is frank not in order to talk about himself or to put a favorable spin on his faults. But Eliot feels obliged to defend his motives because frank confessionalism looks like a pretense, a repulsive one at that. The uncharitable La Rochefoucauldian viewpoint has become the norm, so that no one believes that sincerity and frankness about one's own faults are anything but ploys.

Self-mockery has to be managed with care. You cannot ridicule yourself for all your failings without seeming undignified and shameless. If self-mockery descends into playing the clown one had better be sure that it is a fairly sophisticated kind of clowning. An unseemly self-mockery is a role foisted upon the powerless, stigmatized, and deformed: the Jew, the black, the Italian, the Irishman, the physically deformed, though these clowns often manage to turn the tables on their audience. It takes skill to play that role with enough leakage so that the dominant order understands the depths of your contempt for them, without giving them reason to chop off your head as an impudent rebel. There is no exact way to define the limit of the confessable, admittable, or own-up-to-able (these are not quite synonyms); some of the things your enemies would say behind your back are probably easier to mock yourself about than are some of the things your friends say behind your back, so the line between enmity and friendship provides no clear guide.

Finding the right faults for which to ridicule yourself need not be tied to whether you have them. A good portion of successful self-mockery is to do La Rochefoucauld one better and confess not just to modest faults but to faults we do not have. Engaging in the *forms* of self-mockery and frank confession is what is rewarded, not its accuracy as a self-critique. Clearly there are limits if it is to be successful. The absolutely good-looking person cannot be heard to self-mock about her ugliness. But she could tell stories of clumsiness, of slipping on the ice when she was strutting around thinking herself really something. It is probably best to tease the audience by having the false fault be one that they cannot prove you have or don't have, but whose substance gives you credit for modesty or proper false modesty either way. Thus the big strong guy can joke about his fear of bugs or bats, and people may or may not believe him, but the company appreciates that he is wearing his bigness in a way that makes it palatable for all who might resent him for it.

Do you as self-mocker suffer from feeling you are faking? Not at all, because you are one with your role: a performer holding center stage in a play about himself. That does not prevent momentary accesses of panic that people are not laughing with you, but at you. The thought often waits until 3 A.M. to pay you a visit, when it is too late. The various looks in the audience that encouraged you earlier that evening are now recalled as bearing a different meaning than you thought they bore when you were flushed with adrenaline in the midst of your performance; you now, with a sick feeling in your gut, recall seeing X cast Y a knowing look that their laughter did not quite hide. You tell yourself that this is frequent 3 A.M. fare for you, and as soon as the sun comes up you will have a more comforting picture. But that is an eternity away; so you hasten to your computer to e-mail apologies to everyone, thereby making sure you will have something to be truly humiliated about when the sun rises.

The truly modest person, however, unlike the knowingly falsely modest person, may fear he is faking his modesty, caught in the same bind as the humble person who may be proud of his humility. Or he may fear that his true modesty looks more fake than false modesty would and so becomes self-conscious about how to style his modesty to make it *appear* real, not just to be real. Maybe he thinks he would be better served by packaging his true modesty as false modesty. But he also fears that he will only outsmart himself and opts instead to stick with being his plain old modest self. Except that is now not so easy. How did he act when he was unconsciously modest? Can he reproduce it if he is self-conscious about it? Perhaps, just perhaps, he will manifest sufficient embarrassment and fluster trying to present himself as the modest person he truly is that his very embarrassment will be exactly the right signal to sell his modesty. And if it works this time, next time he can fake the fluster.[9]

# NINETEEN

# Caught in the Act

MOSTLY WE LIVE AND LET LIVE with our faking it. I won't call you on yours if you won't call me on mine. The agreement works quite well in domains of small encounters and routine politeness. But what if your faking is less about faking for a good cause – such as politeness, apology, being a dad, a teacher, a friend – than for a bad cause? And what counts as a bad cause? So much of our faking is done to satisfy our vanity, the bad cause par excellence in one well-established moral tradition: the sin of pride.

We have already seen that another nonnegligible moral tradition winked at vanity, even blessed it as the chief motive behind making us virtuous actors. The desire to gain the good opinion of others and the equally great desire to think well of ourselves drove us to do good deeds and cultivate virtue. Vanity of this sort, if not quite a good cause, surely makes the world a better place to live in. To borrow from Lord Chesterfield, why should we not wink at the small-stakes vanities that help people get through the day a little happier; politely flatter them so that they will politely flatter us, all to the advancement of sociability and amiability?

Most – but not all – in the tolerant second tradition would agree that it is a bad cause when our misrepresentations and self-delusions claim more for ourselves than is fair. We draw a line at some magical point when your attempt to fake it, to fool me – pardonable – makes a fool out of me – absolutely unpardonable, unless I have it coming. But we also find it unpardonable when you fool yourself to the point of making a fool out of yourself. And that is precisely the circumstance in which I can make a fool out of you, because you have done most of the work and you have it coming. When your vanity so blinds you that you feel yourself great and grand no matter how inept and unbearable you are, then you deserve precious little quarter.

I must immediately make a clarification. Not all self-duping is unpardonable, especially that kind of self-esteem that leads you not to quit at the first failure and persevere instead, or that keeps you performing at the highest level of your abilities. But when vanity moves in the direction of pomposity or self-inflation or ineducability, it dares us to pierce it with pin or pen. The implicit agreement not to expose each other's faking collapses in the face of our graceless and baseless self-love.

Because these themes are rather central to some of the essays I published in a book called *Humiliation*, I will take up only issues not discussed there, or ones that looking through the lens of faking it might lead to different observations. I want to deal with the earliest stages of self-consciousness about faking it, and then treat of some especially anxiety-provoking settings in which we feel exposed and the risk of exposure is at its highest.

## Faking Sleep

Insomnia is one of those states it is virtually impossible to defeat by direct action, unless the direct action is to admit defeat and take a knock-out pill. Some of us are so self-tormenting that we test the pill once we have taken it by trying to stay awake to see whether we have been duped with a placebo. I nod off all the time reading scholarly articles, but if I read one in order to overcome my insomnia it loses its power to knock me out because I know I am reading not to read, but in order to fall asleep. I see through the trick.[1]

We have seen this problem before: it is not easy to have the left hand act as if it doesn't know what the right hand is doing. Yet people do it all the time. Our vanity makes us gullible; there is no difficulty in seeing ourselves prettier, smarter, and more interesting than in fact we are. Indeed, some of us endure bouts of seeing ourselves as dumber, uglier, and duller than we are. We, however, usually do not think of underevaluation as self-deception, perhaps because we have a hard time accounting for vanity, the usual culprit, driving it, though we have seen that it can. Proud pessimists, proud depressives, and proud humble souls are hardly uncommon. But deceiving ourselves into better or worse images of ourselves is a whole lot easier than deceiving ourselves to sleep. Is it because tricking ourselves to sleep can't piggyback on our vanity as can the self-deceptions we engage in regarding brains and looks? Or does it have more to do with the neuropsychology of falling asleep?[2]

If we find it next to impossible to fake ourselves to sleep, some of our earliest efforts at faking have to do with faking others into believing we were asleep. We fake sleeping long before we learn to fake looking alert and interested. It is not easy to fake being asleep. When we fake politeness, attentiveness, or concern, our eyes are open and we can read from the looks of others how well the act is going over. The problem with faking sleep is that our eyes are closed, and if we crack them open even a teeny bit to check out how the act is being received, we've blown it. Remember too how difficult it is to feign a normal conversation when you know someone is eavesdropping, as in the case of Ophelia and Gertrude. It is not much easier to fake sleep when someone is watching to see whether you are sleeping. You feel the power of his gaze; it cramps your muscles, it makes your heart pound faster and so loudly as to give you away for sure; it screws up your breathing, it makes your eyes squint tighter than they would if closed in sleep.

The demand to fake sleep falls on the child at two key times: (1) when way past bedtime the kid is supposed to be asleep but is either reading or talking to a sibling or sleepover guest, or (2) when way past rising time the kid is trying to play on an adult's pity to let him lie there instead of being roused up to go to church or in my case shul. In adulthood we fake sleep to avoid ***; if you thought sex, you have only yourself to blame. My thought was of avoiding the talkative dullard seated next to me on a transcontinental flight.[3]

The faking of sleep is usually in the service of a bad cause – weaseling out of duty, avoiding contact with a particular person. I wonder whether the mechanism by which we come to acquire a conscience – the process, according to some theories, by which we internalize the Father, the parental No – doesn't rely heavily on the experience of faking sleep as a child: your eyes shut, Father looking on, examining, detecting, you unable to see him but fantasizing and anticipating the worst.

It is actually scarier with Mother looking on, because you know she is better at discerning the fake, even if she is more inclined to let you lie in. Father does not care whether it is a fake, except that if you are faking, it deprives him of the added pleasure of actually waking you up. In either case you feel they see through you. Why are you even putting on the charade? When they let you lie there it is not, you suspect, out of kindness or out of love of your cuteness, but that they wish to torment you for an entire geological age. They are making you squirm on purpose, to let you know that your transgression is allowed by their grace alone and not by the virtue of your deceptiveness, should they decide to allow it. It is only later, during adolescence, that you realize how easy it is to trick parents when, though they pretend otherwise, they are too scared to want to find out what you are really up to anyway.

At night the child is more likely to have his faking excused than in the morning; wanting to read late bodes much better for his character development than wanting to sleep late. At night the torture your parents deliver actually helps you. They will come to your bedside and turn your lamp off and then kiss you as you "sleep." For once you actually welcome their kisses because it allows you to act as if they awakened you.

When it comes time to be rousted out to go to services to pray, there are no kisses; there is nothing cute about you. Still they test to see whether you are sleeping or faking, for there is a moral difference between morning and night. Bad enough that you have to be awakened in the morning when your sense of responsibility should have done it for you, but that you are faking sleep betrays a depraved and willful turning of your back on Responsibility. Let his heart pound a little harder until the kid fears it will surely explode and kill him if he fakes another second; then rip the covers off and indicate how many minutes he has to get ready. Little did they know that I was already conducting my own prayer service, praying they would buy the act, praying God to intervene and make them merciful; He, however, is a jealous God and instead steeled their resolve to crush the whining resistance they had yet to face.

## Facing Those Who Know or You Fear Might Know

Faking sleep is an intense experience because the child knows he is skating on thin ice, knows he is faking, and knows that it is likely he will suffer the humiliation of having such an obvious fake exposed. The whole world can hear the poor kid's heart pounding. Faking sleep is a training ground, training us for higher-stakes fakes, as when we grow up to lecture on property or on self-consciousness and there are philosophers of mind in the crowd.

The fear of exposure is perhaps greatest when we have to perform before people we know to be experts. Experts come in two main varieties: those who are experts on the subject on which you are lecturing, and those who are experts on you, such as your family or friends. Have you ever taught a class with your father or spouse or kid sitting in the class? They see the act, the pose, and the pretenses. They are painfully aware of all your nervous tics, which, until the VCR and camcorder came along to jolt you out of your self-deceptive paradise, you had blithely believed yourself to have been without. You know they must be squirming or barely able to suppress the giggles; or they feel sick with embarrassment for you and for their connection to you, even when you are doing a job that is holding the first category of experts at bay.[4] But you suspect you haven't held that first class of experts – the ones who really know something about the subject matter – at bay for long. You know they will expose your faking it: yes, I always suspected Miller to be a fraud, substituting stories for analysis and apparently having no knowledge of my seminal article that has already said everything on the topic there is to say.

Afterward the subject experts tell you how much they enjoyed it. If you allow yourself to feel relief at their comments you cannot delude yourself that they are sincere, only that they have decided to keep you guessing as to when they will blow your cover. Yet you are grateful that they chose to fake pleasure in the performance rather than expose you by setting off a gong during it, if only for your wife's sake. Prof Z actually left in the middle, though. You are sure it was in disgust, not because he had to go to the bathroom. Or he had to go to the bathroom in disgust; that's how bad it was. Then they kept whispering to each other and nodding, agreeing that you were a complete and total fraud. Worse, your students in the audience were wonderful: they rallied to you; they actually looked engaged, they asked good questions. But of course you read their engagement as a sign that they knew you were in trouble and they were trying to save the situation to alleviate their own painful embarrassment at your plight.

You somehow survive. You seem to be treated no worse than before, leading you to wonder whether the experts of the first type are as smart as their writings and their reputations had you believing they were; maybe they were dim enough to buy the act. Or, if not, they enjoyed the fact that they need not fear your exposing their fraudulence; the whole corrupt enterprise gets to continue, with mutual forbearance triumphing yet again.[5]

Those paranoid thoughts might be held to bespeak low self-esteem, but in fact they exist almost simultaneously or in rapid oscillation with the opposite belief that is equally delusional but on the positive side. You feel you were really something; man, were you good, putting on the show of shows, strong in substance, not somber or grave. And if you are a fraud, then what the hell is everyone else, especially Prof A, who gave the Big Wig Lectures last year, completely vacuous, trite, and pious, in which a good third of the time was spent clearing his throat? If he is the real thing, then you are the real thing plus. Then in the next second you worry that all your judgments are so infected by emotion and interest that you don't have a clue. You have I-beams, logs, a whole redwood forest stuck in your eyes. Upon reflection, days later, you decide that somewhere in the dull middle is the truth regarding yourself, though the truth about Prof A is right where you pegged him. In the words of George Gascoigne, one of our better unread poets,

Yet therewithal I can not but confesse,
That vayne presumption makes my heart to swell,
For this I thinke, not all the worlde (I guesse)
Shootes bet than I, nay some shootes not so well.[6]

You don't know all you should, but you know enough to deliver fair value, with an occasional new small idea ("new" hardly means original; it means no one has said it in your field for about thirty years); you muddle through. You, however, cannot shake the suspicion that you are still flattering yourself, in exactly the way you would have to serve up flattery to get yourself to fall for it. You still fear you might be tricking yourself to believe that you are not a fraud. You admit you fake it all the time but claim that that kind of faking is in the interests of the scholarly enterprise and your merely staying alive in it, not a cynical appropriation of a status you have no business occupying. That would mean you are a total fraud, and today, at least, you choose to believe you are not one.

I do not mean this to be a paranoid account. It is meant only to capture anxieties that intrude occasionally; or more accurately, it is that they threaten to intrude but only rarely do so in full regalia. These anxieties I would guess are part of the substance, and if not the substance then the detritus, of normal middling self-monitoring. A certain amount of worry, which takes the form of feeling we are faking it, has to be part of the psychological package of what it means to have to play so many different roles. There are whole domains in which we are mostly confident of our abilities to perform the roles asked of us in a reasonably competent fashion, in which we feel pretty much at one with the role, but not so uncritically immersed that we lose our sense of whether we are doing OK in the performance. We also know that we have honed our remedial skills of poise and tact to save ourselves at a reasonable cost when we botch it, or to help others save themselves when they do. These are the central moral and social skills demanded of us in the Goffmanian moral order.

Not that Goffman's moral order does not have its paranoid moments, but mostly his description strikes us as apt and the stuff of normal presentations of a normal self. Some of our faking leaves us feeling very vulnerable to exposure. The risks are not evenly distributed across all social domains. They are especially high when we gauge a big hunk of our self-esteem, as in our professional competence or in courtship and sex. Nor is feeling anxiously self-conscious likely to be distributed equally up and down the relevant hierarchy. Those who must please others to survive, low but not so low as to have no hope of advancing, those on the make trying to rise, those who come from pariah or disfavored groups who fear a false move means pogroms, those others who are stigmatized in more personal ways – for these souls the costs of screwing up are greater.[7] The complacently secure can afford a duller inner life, but as I have written elsewhere, once democratic norms become generally accepted, even high-ranking people lose their complacency and come to worry they may be being judged as fools by those beneath them and are disturbed that they are being so judged.[8]

Performing before experts is one way of describing the agonies of courtship. No matter that each person is a miserable wreck before the other. That other is an expert of his or her own tastes as they apply to you. You are judged either to pass muster or to have failed. There is no disputing the expertise of the taste that condemns you. At my age I experience vicariously the miseries of courtship watching my teenagers. Both my wife and I were surprised to find we feel more excruciating pain on behalf of the pathetic boys who call the uninterested Bess for dates than we do for Bess having to figure out how to turn them down. Appallingly, we almost end up siding with the guy so that we can be spared witnessing his humiliation. Bess, this guy has called three times; he wants to come to your play; aren't you going to call him back and tell him when it is? Dad, he is so dumb; I mean do you want to hear the dumb jokes he thinks are funny? She then tells me one, and well, I guess he's got it coming. But the agony.

I would never be a teenager again even if it meant having a full head of hair. You perform and are judged a fool, and the very fact that you are performing means you have judged the other desirable; you have hung yourself out to dry. More pathetic, though, is that our endless vanity never lets up. It is not only rejection by those we find desirable that is painful; it is also no fun to be thought undesirable by people you do not desire. Caring to be desired or approved of never stops; we perform courtship rituals in effigy for those we do not want (within some limits to be sure) and still care that they do not want us. Most of us accept that people are playing in implicit leagues. To be judged a reject by someone who you accept is in a higher league has a certain justice to it; though painful, it can be understood as a proper reprimand for your presumption. To be rejected by someone in a lower league than you fancy you are in, however, is not only a *lese majestie* but also is evidence, very disorienting evidence, that you may be operating under a serious delusion as to the league you are truly in.

What about those small-stakes encounters, though, in which the role is second nature, the risks of exposure low, and if you are exposed, no big deal – things such as having a sneezing fit, bumping into someone when not paying attention? A quick "I'm sorry" or "Pardon me" sets everything to right. Yet even in such trivial matters there is danger. All it takes is one pratfall. Gerald Ford was voted out of office because he tumbled down an airplane gangway, exposed as faking badly the minimal competence of being able to descend a staircase.

And what of the poor woman law student in her serious interview suit who trips on her way into class and splats on the floor? Bad enough had she been in jeans and a sweatshirt. Caught faking it as a young professional, as a competent human who could get dressed up and walk at the same time. It is worse for a woman too, because skirts mean revelations, and the world holds women to a higher standard of bodily monitoring than it does men. Only the poor prof who witnessed the scene matched her: he had hurriedly gone to the bathroom before class and forgotten to zip up. Up to the moment a student in the front row pointed it out to him he had been posing as an authority figure. The professor, scrambling to save himself and the woman, decided to devote the first twenty minutes of the class to the themes of this book, especially given that it was interview season for the students, the season in which their own anxieties about faking it were the centerpiece of their psychic existence.

### Did You Know How Big You Blew It Back Then?

These momentary botchings of performance demand another performance, the one of recovering. It demands, as Goffman says, and I have noted, poise from you and hopefully tact rather than laughter from the others. But their tact is also painful, because you know how hard a time they are having managing your pratfall. You fear you are now in touch with the real you; it is not the you who is running the show, because that is precisely what the real you was not doing. The real you was the guy asleep at the switch who didn't see the patch of ice; it is the real you who must now suffer. The real you feels the shame and knows that in a nanosecond you have to set about trying to salvage the wreckage. A red face, unwilled, and thus the perfect response, shows you shameable. That buys you enough time for the real you to put on a mask again. Quick, set everyone at ease for the burden you have imposed on them not to laugh at you. Make a quick joke. You are back playing a role, but you, yes you, are still feeling humiliated; the real you is the one feeling the panic. And you fear the real them will be revealed when they get the giggles at your expense. Nothing convinces us so much of its authenticity as the giggles at another's expense.

We are at unaccommodated man. Unaccommodated man, however, stripped as he is, remains a social being, whose true self is a self that cannot escape the judging eyes of others who still do not relinquish their demand that he maintain a respectable self, for the shame of it if he does not, and for the pride of it (yes, there is a sunny side too) if he really manages something admirable. The core unaccommodated you is still a creature of vanity. Thinking back then, it must have been the real me, a very embarrassable real me, who drew the line at how much davening I would fake, how loud I would not cheer at a pep rally, or how nothing in the world could get me to say "groovy." My true inner self sets limits and draws the line at certain kinds and amounts of faking, not so much out of fear of looking like a fool – though that too – as the fear of actually feeling like a fool.

I opened this book with those momentary doublings that occur when you stand outside yourself and see yourself as some not so friendly other might see you. But what if instead of spreading ourselves thin over many roles and even expanding into multiple selves and voices, we found our self shrinking down to one part of our body? Sexual desire might reduce us in such a way to our genitals. Compare too the feeling of being taken over by a discrediting failing. When you were a teenager and had an enormous zit prominently exposed on your face, did you not feel as if that zit were *you*? There was only a little of you that remained that wasn't that zit; that was the part of you that felt so ever keenly that all you were to yourself and others was that zit. Whatever desperate attempts you made at disguise, masking, faking only called more attention to it. You were not making it up; people teased you, your brothers and sisters laughed at you; you saw people avert their eyes and be equally unable to prevent their eyes from fixing on it. A stain on your pants or dress can at times take you over too. The problem with these discrediting failings is that they feel as if you have finally been stripped of all poses. You are stripped, naked, authentically a discredited being. Not faking at all.

Not just discrediting bodily blemishes, but discrediting deeds shrink a person to an unwelcome essence too. Do you remember the kid who in third grade wet his pants, or picked his nose and ate it? Sure you do. No matter what he became in later life, be it a big CEO or a famous actor, that is what you remember about him. He, I suppose, gets the benefit of not knowing that you see him that way, but because you see him that way he should, you feel, go into a witness protection program. A mistake or habit at nine years old will never let him make satisfactory amends for the disgusting image rooted in your mind. What if that person were you? Will it be forgotten? Depends what it was. The girl, Robin, will forgive if not forget that you crashed the car into a tree because you forgot to put it in park before you grabbed at her in teeny-bop obligatoriness, not in anything resembling passion. Surely every kid had gaffes like that; they are the stuff of comedy, not soul-destroying in the least. As with the zit, you can live them down; their power to discredit is of short duration. But what about the especially egregious lapses, the ones that were dignity-destroying, perhaps irremediably so? Not just the failures to control your bodily secretions, emissions, and excretions in a nondisgusting way, but the times you got caught up in a lie, got caught faking it, were exposed?

Now you remember. It is all coming back. More than one kid wet his or her pants back then, but the one you remember is the one who made it hard on everyone else by completely collapsing, or because it was the kid you hated already for being a crybaby. The others must have handled it; in fact you think you may have wet your pants too. You must have. You cannot even recall. Not all big deals turn out to be big deals.

# Afterword

THIS JOURNEY THROUGH THE LAND of faking it has been something of an antipilgrimage, it having no earthly or celestial city as its end point. But it is only an antipilgrimage because there is no exit, no real conclusion to the journey.[1] As for worshipfulness, though, there is plenty. The book is an homage to the extraordinary richness and deep interestingness of the most mundane matters in psychic and social life. We did indeed get mired in the Slough of Despond, as when I contemplated the boundlessness of anti-Semitism, but for most of the time we settled in at Vanity Fair, taking day trips into its suburbs and nature preserves (which are testimonies to man getting nature to fake it too). The tour guide obviously is not Bunyan's Christian. He is, instead, a wandering, and occasionally a meandering, Jew. Yet I bet his sensibility is not unfamiliar to most readers.

I have taken "faking it" colloquially. I have tried to let the notion exfoliate as it does in conversation, the style revelatory and expansive rather than strictly logical and restrictive. If the exposition appears at times to proceed by free association, that freeness is, trust me, contrived. I have not so much set out to prove a thesis as to give the reader, as I indicated in the introduction, a feel for the terrain, for the custom of the country. The point of the book is that faking it is no simple point, but many points. Consider, for instance, that the "it" in faking it is variously a role, a disposition, an emotion, a character trait, a commitment, an experience, or an entire identity.

Faking it is like the words "good" or "real," which have engaged philosophers from Aristotle to Austin;[2] it is not easy to get a grip on them. But just because a colloquial expression such as "faking it" has no "single, specifiable, always-the-same meaning"[3] does not mean that anything goes, for it does not have a large number of different meanings either. The range of relevance is constrained. Though I cannot see by their looks how my kids are related to me, to the outsider they look like Millers, even if looking like Millers means they mostly look like my wife, a Koehler. Faking it thus offers a *family* of topics, and though it defies reduction to a unified theory the little fakelets have the resemblance that family members come to have. All these faked "its" in the last sentence of the preceding paragraph are united also at the practical level by fears about our competence in playing both true and false roles truly and, at an airier level, by our anxieties about the ultimate authenticity of any of these "its."

Do not read me as willing to martyr myself for faking it, or as irremediably hostile to the idea of authenticity. But, like it or not, we are stuck with faking it. If we try to avoid it by refusing to don masks or strip our veils we are only playing a role that has a lengthy and complex history, predating the cynics, and ever so susceptible to hypocritical and false forms. Some accommodation with faking it is in order. And though quests for authenticity prompt some raillery from me, not all such quests are silly, and some indeed are necessary or unavoidable. What, in effect, is that niggling self-doubt, that stream of self-consciousness that colors the voice of this book, but constantly to be worrying about, and holding oneself up to, a standard of genuineness? From whence the chronic anxiety if there weren't some deep urge to be whole and true? The urge, though, is often self-defeating, for it is what keeps us doubting the quality of our motives and makes us wonder whether we are really getting there or aren't just faking it. Should that doubting cease, it is no more likely to be a sign we have become one with our true selves than that we are in the throes of seamless self-deception or Paxil.

We seem destined to recapitulate at the individual level various historical movements of authenticity and purification. We thus find ourselves driving the money changers from our temples every now and then, stripping away the costumery of certain roles, junking whole roles that have become too ornate, too in-your-face false. But the attempts to get back to true basics mostly succumb to the vanity of human wishes; they never quite measure up to the hopes we had for them. We do not escape the anxieties of authenticity once we embark on the quest or once we get to the Celestial City. Even there, doubt exists or Satan would not have fallen.

Such movements have brought us Christianity, Protestantism within Christianity, various civil rights and social justice movements on behalf of pariah groups. Still, a gay out of the closet, a Jew out of the ghetto, and Protestants of whatever sect, from the highest Anglican to Shakers and Pentecostals, will hardly have resolved once and for all the problems of faking it and authenticity. At best the doubts are relocated, but I doubt they are any less intense, rather more so in fact because of the pretension of the claim to have attained the pure and the authentic.

Do not read me to be sidling toward the conclusion that the most authentic persona might be a voice similar to this book's narrator's. That voice's anxious self-doubt, self-mockery, constant ironizing, and occasional bitterness need not mean that this voice is meaningfully self-examining or struggling for psychic unity and authenticity. A possessor of such a voice may find the comedy of the process its own reward, or as providing a topic for a book. And not all simple pleasures or simple miseries need elude him.[4]

But do read me as suggesting that faking it partakes in a serious way in the struggle to maintain one's dignity and honor. The self-watching internal eye that prompts the anxieties of faking it and authenticity are very similar to the external eyes of an honor/shame culture. In some deep respects it is all about measuring up, and mostly about not quite measuring up. If the stakes are often not of the seriousness that lead to shame, they are surely the stuff of constant embarrassment.

Some readers might wonder whatever happened to the unconscious in my story. Freudians will be mystified at best, incredulously dismissive at worst, especially considering that the master was given only a cameo appearance as a bad comedian. The neglect is deliberate. The unconscious, the existence of which I am not about to deny, plays a different role in the world of fakery, largely one subsumed under the notion of self-deception. Though some of our motives may indeed be unconscious, there is no reason ever to trust someone who claims that his motivations are unconscious, nor even someone who claims that for another, because he is usually either a therapist or one who cants like one. "Oh, I must have done that because of some bizarre unconscious desire" is an excuse, an avoiding of responsibility, not an explanation, though once in a blue moon the excuse may turn out to have some reasonable probability of being true. I continue to believe more than ever that the diction and substantive categories of moral discourse in the seventeenth and eighteenth centuries – vanity, pride, honor, self-command, passions, interest, and various emotion terms – are so much better at getting at the richness of human social and psychic experience than the diction of twentieth-century depth psychology.

LET ME SITUATE THIS BOOK in a broader perspective. Various political movements and moral theories have tended to divide humankind into two groups. We thus have saved and damned, faithful and infidel, Christian and Jew, left and right, East and West, capitalist and proletarian, black and white, woman and man, gay and straight, and so on. In present academic discourse the favored dichotomies are based on the last four: class, race, and gender (including sexual orientation).[5] These are held by those committed to seeing the world so cabined also to be an issue of left and right, and thus too of being saved or damned. On certain confined terrains these binary theories can indeed cast much light into the murk, but their acolytes are always too ambitious on their behalf. As you have seen by now, none of these favored dichotomies underpins my analyses, at least consciously. Yes, I make some gestures toward the discomforts that class, gender, and racial differences cause us as they relate to faking it in conventional encounters. But I studiously avoid explaining much of anything in light of these pairings; they provide examples, not explanations.

In the kind of moral psychology that I am drawn to, none of these contrasting pairs does so well at capturing human foible as my preferred pair: knave and fool. This pairing lies at the heart of faking it, appearing often as deception (knave) and self-deception (fool). Some might reply that the more seriously intended pairings in the preceding paragraph are not meant to get at something as trivial as foibles or fakery, but at more gravely grounded issues of right, justice, and salvation. Besides, there is a lack of high seriousness in the word "foible." Call it sin or evil, and then make the evil banal, and then high theory can sneak foible, in disguise, into its country club, but not in all its riotous and varied grotesquerie. Human foible undoes much highfalutin theory: mere mortals, dull as we are, are inevitably too complex for pairings as restrictive as man–woman, white–black, gay–straight, capitalist–worker, and the theories such oppositions support.

The knave–fool pairing differs from the others because it gets at human behavior at its most interesting; it is as expansive as its nemesis, the self-interested-rational-actor model of human behavior, is limiting and limited. It forces us to contemplate, sometimes mordantly, sometimes even lovingly, the wondrous complexity of the simplest face-to-face encounters, the comic pretensions of our hopes and dreams, our postures and poses, all our various forms of fakery. Knave–fool does not reduce us to one dimension but keeps all our motives, desires, fears, and hopes, all aspects of us – as workers, friends, sexual beings, parents, children, believers or unbelievers – on the table for discussion and gentle raillery. It is a particularizing dichotomy. It loves stories and details, mostly comic ones, but tragic ones too. Is not *Othello* a fool–knave story no less than the standard comic trickster tale?

The knave–fool distinction, historically and perhaps even necessarily, is wedded to a misanthropic style. Some may thus find the distinction a distasteful one, unworthy of decent-spirited souls. But that misanthropy need not be of a savage Swiftian sort; it is equally suited to the more amiable moral vision of a Fielding. The knave–fool view of human moral possibility desperately seeks human goodness and even recognizes its possibility, but it sees the forces arrayed against goodness as undefeatable. It laments the fragility and vulnerability of human goodness. It fears that the good person will be eaten alive, plundered, not just by knaves but by other fools too, and, worse, by his own foibles.

Foibles, of course, are usually held to be the lot of the fool. But it is not only the good person or the fool who is undone by foible; the knave is undone by them too. As I tried to show in the discussions of being hoist with one's petard and of Chaucer's alchemist, the knave is often his own fool, even outsmarted by fools, just as the genre of the slick urban knave cleaned out by his country cousin would have it. The fool–knave distinction is porous indeed, with any single person playing both roles quite frequently, sometimes shifting from fool to knave and back again within the confines of a single social interaction. Think of the motives, moves, stratagems, defenses, and humiliations of a first date. Think too of poor Wile E. Coyote.

This book is a small effort in an ancient tradition of moral writing. Its primary article of faith is that humankind is vain, inescapably vain, comical and foolish, though nonetheless, both in spite of and because of these traits, capable of extraordinary achievements. If this were not the case, this moral tradition would have no motive. It ridicules us for our boundless vanity because it aspires to more. Still, that is not a reason to turn its back on the small virtue of muddling through, even if it cannot pass up the opportunity to give muddling a heavy dose of comic and satirical treatment. For the most part, this book sides with those who see some virtue to our vanity. We are something more than mere fools for wanting so badly to look good to ourselves and to others, so badly that we actually end up delivering on some of the goods we hope to be esteemed and praised for. The same impulse that sends some to a plastic surgeon for an implant sends others to deeds worthy of an epic hero.

Our vanity, though, is seldom so seamless that it succeeds in suppressing all our doubts about faking it. Now come, like so many Grendels in the night, those niggling anxieties that pierce through the vain veneering. They disorient us in dizzying attempts to figure out who we really are and where we really stand. But that sick feeling in the pit of the stomach, real as it is, is also part of a pose, as I am proving right now as I write this for public consumption. That does not make it fake, however. Not all poses are false in the same way, nor even false at all. Yet we often worry they are; and we, or if you do not wish to be included in that "we" then I, suffer real bouts of wondering when the other shoe is going to fall, the shamming exposed to the light of day. But I am not sure whether the first shoe has even fallen yet or whether both have. I think I may have lost count.

# Notes

## One. Introduction

1. Robert Nozick (*Philosophical Explanations* 257) is willing to confess to much more: "My departmental colleagues are meticulous intellects who instill in students the importance of mastering all the details whereof they speak; while I think it is important for students also to learn how and when to fake things, to glide over topics with a plausible patina."
2. See Miller, *Bloodtaking and Peacemaking*; "Clint Eastwood and Equity"; "Deep Inner Lives."
3. See Kerrigan's superb *Revenge Tragedy*, making the argument for the necessary linking of revenge and drama.
4. One still cannot quite say "woman on the street" without raising improper suggestions.
5. Emerson, "The Comic," 8.157.

## Two. Hypocrisy and Jesus

1. Trollope, *The Claverings* ch. 5.
2. Nietzsche sees us as no less given over to lies and self-deception when sleeping as when awake, rather more so in fact: "Man permits himself to be lied to at night, his life long, when he dreams, and his moral sense never even tries to prevent this – although men have been said to have overcome snoring by sheer will power" ("On Truth and Lie," 43–44).
3. See Shklar, *Ordinary Vices* 58; Trilling, *Sincerity and Authenticity* 16, comes close to making the same observation.
4. See Fingarette's discussion of sincerity (*Self-Deception* 50–52), distinguishing a shallow and a deep sincerity: in the former the person means the promise he makes at the moment he is making it, but he is too thoughtless and free with them and they are unreliably kept; in the latter the person spells things out to others the same as he spells them out to himself and does so in a way that "reflects the engagement correctly and aptly." As usual, good novelists get there first: "That he was sincere, too, no one who knew him well ever doubted, – sincere, that is, as far as his intentions went. When he endeavoured to teach his flock that they should despise money, he thought that he despised it himself" (Trollope, *Rachel Ray* ch. 5).

5. On hypocrisy in general see Shklar, *Ordinary Vices* 45–86; the most astute unraveling of the vice I know of is Melville's in *The Confidence Man*. The classic treatment of the religious hypocrite as con man is Moliere's *Tartuffe*.

6. The judgment of hypocrisy in this case is an external one, about ranking the propriety of certain motives in displays of piety. Jesus' hypocrite is hardly being dishonest in the sense of failing to match words and deeds or words and intentions; he likes giving alms because he wants the glory, which he is noisily open about. What Jesus is complaining about is the hijacking of a pious ritual for such unashamed glorying.

7. See Melville on strategies of maintaining self-respect under the burden of gratitude; *The Confidence Man* chs. 3–4.

8. Jesus is not counseling giving anonymously, for that is not suggested here; the pauper will still know the identity of his benefactors. Anonymous giving does not solve the problem of playing to the glorious applause of one's internal audience. The pride of turning one's back on the more obvious public attempts at approbation is a frequent topic of seventeenth-century moralists; see discussion in Lovejoy, *Reflections* 99–112. Even earlier the friar in Chaucer's *Summoner's Tale* tells about his own "private" self-mortifications lest they go unnoticed.

9. This is the standard conundrum at the core of the philosophical self-deception problem; see ch. 4n6.

10. Many in the self-esteem movement would say that our psychic biasing is more prone to see our own specklike faults as logs.

11. Jesus does not call those who are about to stone the adulteress in John 8 hypocrites. He confines the word "hypocrite" to settings where it can sensibly have its Greek meaning of theatrical actor, which is precisely why the trumpeting almsgiver is to him the hypocrite par excellence.

12. An aside on the mote–beam metaphor: how is one supposed to visualize a log sticking out of an eye unless it be the eye of Polyphemus? I find the image puzzling. How can we not know we have a log in our eye even if we are blinded by it? Consider too the problem with specks in our own eyes; they hurt so much we feel they must be logs. But ask someone to look in there and they see nothing. The log–speck metaphor appears better suited to describing how our own little *pains* seem so much greater than other people's big pains.

13. See Elster's discussion, *Alchemies* 87–88, on the "double perversity of amour-propre." See also La Rochefoucauld, M 31.

14. See Hebb's experimental evidence that we are much better at reading others' emotions than our own ("Emotion in Man and Animal").

15. A similar case for going easy on the hypocrisy of blaming others for faults one has oneself is made by Hazlitt ("On Cant," 360): "We often see that a person condemns in another the very thing he is guilty of himself. Is this hypocrisy? It may, or it may not. If he really feels none of the disgust

and abhorrence he expresses this is quackery and impudence. But if he really expresses what he feels (and he easily may, for it is the abstract idea he contemplates in the case of another, and the immediate temptation to which he yields in his own, so that he probably is not even conscious of the identity or connexion between the two), then this is not hypocrisy, but want of strength and keeping in the moral sense." Hazlitt, in his essay, makes hypocrisy a very narrow category. Much of what many of us would call hypocrisy he claims is canting, the former involving a true inward despising of what he affects outwardly to admire. The canter affects to admire more than he really does, as when people of a certain class and set of pretensions ooh and ah over Merchant–Ivory films or the latest BBC production on *Masterpiece Theater*. Not that Hazlitt is much easier on canters than on hypocrites: "Hypocrisy is the setting up a pretension to a feeling you never had and have no wish for. There are people who are made up of *cant*, that is of mawkish affectation and sensibility; but who have not sincerity enough to be *hypocrites*, that is, have not hearty dislike or contempt enough for anything, to give the lie to their puling professions of admiration and esteem for it" (366). Hazlitt is one of the brighter of the unread jewels in the canon of English literature.

16. Langland, *Piers Plowman* B 1.183–184: "You will no more benefit from your masses and devotions than Malkyn does of her virginity that no man wants to take from her anyway."

17. Shklar (*Ordinary Vices* 49) suggests that Jesus recognized the tension within his own message that leads him to blame the faultfinder for seeing motes in others' eyes while himself finding faults in ostentatious almsgiving and obeying the Sabbath rules, among many others. The rebuker's role is a tricky one.

18. Thus too the invective hurled at the scribes and Pharisees in Matt. 23.23 ff.

19. Jesus also might be suggesting that his healing makes it under the old Sabbath rules because it is no different from feeding a flock, which he understands his healing of the sick to be in his role as Shepherd. The metaphor then would make the sick woman analogous to an animal that is being fed on the Sabbath. Hence no violation of the rules. But such an interpretation would miss the sense that Jesus is out to challenge an entire legal culture, not just the interpretation of one particular law.

20. Jesus has an answer to this: though it is not a good thing to be ostentatious in matters of daily ritual (where I advise small self-deceptions to get the motive right), I am spreading the gospel, and my ostentation in such a cause is necessary, for I am trying to get the word out.

21. See Bierce's very Protestant definition: "*rite*, n. A religious or semi-religious ceremony fixed by law, precept or custom, with the essential oil of sincerity carefully squeezed out of it."

### Three. Antihypocrisy

1. Montaigne, 3.10, "On Restraining Your Will," 1157–1158.
2. Twain, "Capt. Stormfield's Visit to Heaven," 854.
3. Is the person who pretends to vices he does not have a hypocrite? Does culpable false seeming run only in the direction of falsifying upward – pretending to virtue – rather than falsifying downward? What of the clean-cut kid pretending to badness – the drinking, womanizing, drugging that I mentioned earlier – in order to have the tough guys think him not so contemptible? Do we call him a hypocrite because, given the frame of reference, he is pretending upward toward the cool; or do we refuse to "honor" him with the dignity of hypocrisy and instead think him merely pathetic, a wannabe?
4. See Elster, *Alchemies* 93–94.
5. On unostentatious virtue as suspect because of the approbation of one's internal audience, see the discussion in Elster, *Alchemies* 92–94; and Lovejoy, *Reflections* 99–112.
6. One of the most insightful character studies of the pridefulness of humility is Trollope's Rev. Crawley in *Last Chronicle of Barset*.
7. On pus-drinking saints, see Bell, *Holy Anorexia*; also my discussion in *The Anatomy of Disgust* 157–163.
8. Trollope, *Rachel Ray* ch. 5.
9. Franklin, *Autobiography* 90.
10. *Hávámal* st. 76, my trans.
11. Lovejoy, *Reflections* 153–193; see Smith, TMS VI.iii.46: "The great secret of education is to direct vanity to proper objects"; also Hirschman, *The Passions* 20–31.
12. Even La Rochefoucauld appreciates the good things that flow from our vanity; see, for example, M 150, 200, 220.
13. *The Idiot* II.11.
14. Victor Klemperer in one of the many astute asides in his diaries captures the hokum of the pastoral in this way: "When politicians idealize rural labor, they are always being hypocritical" (*I Will Bear Witness* July 19, 1937, I.230).
15. On pastoral cultures and mandatory sheep rustling, see Herzfeld, *Poetics*, and Campbell, *Honour*. Hampshire supposes that "the ideal of natural-ness of feeling, uncorrupted by reflection" is unattainable "once we have built up a sophisticated vocabulary of intentional states, of emotions, sen-timents, attitudes" ("Sincerity," 248–249). I have argued elsewhere that lack of a specific and rich vocabulary of emotions need not prevent implicit emotion talk of substantial subtlety. The feeling, with a description of the context generating it, will do much to make up for a lack of a specific emotion vocabulary. See *Humiliation* ch. 3.
16. See Hawthorne, *The Blithedale Romance*; Packer, *Transcendentalists* 466–470.
17. Raverat, *Period Piece* 214.

18. Aquinas, *Summa* 2.2 Q111, A4.
19. On this tradition, see Hirschman, *Rhetoric* 10–42.
20. Nashe, *Christs Teares* 75v.
21. TMS II.ii.2.1; in Smith's scheme it is not via self-deception that we end up adopting more generous principles but rather by a sympathetic mechanism making us see our own motives and behaviors from the viewpoint of an impartial spectator, whose views we then are moved to adopt as our own. Still, the impartiality of the impartial spectator is often threatened by various self-deceptions.
22. Elster, *Alchemies* 332–342.
23. John Locke was not distressed in the least by adding the heavenly payoff to the scales so that virtue would be more attractive to mere earthly mortals. The heathens that argued that virtue was its own reward "satisfied not many with such airy commendations." One must open the eyes of men "upon the endless, unspeakable joys of another life" to "find something solid and powerful to move them" to virtue; see Locke, *Reasonableness* c. 245, and the discussion in Herzog, *Without Foundations* 104–105.
24. See Tocqueville (429; discussed in Elster, *Alchemies* 359), who doubts that a Christian who alleges as the motive of his good deeds his quest for salvation is really properly describing his true motivation: "I respect them too much to believe them." But maybe Tocqueville is holding God and God fearers to motives that may offend Tocqueville's sensibility and ours but not His. Might it not be that the rules of non–self-interested motives just don't apply when the self-interest is pursuit of God's favor? Scripture is full of instances in which the message from God is, "Obey me or I will squash you, and you should praise and obey me precisely because of fear." Fear is an emotion that prompts one kind of very basic self-interested behavior. Maybe there is a double standard. Ostentatious shows of piety directed only toward God, even if intended to get treasure in heaven or avoid annihilation, are OK. If directed toward man, sorry, you are a hypocrite.
25. This is a corollary to the well-known Weberian and Tawnian theses on Calvinist anxieties about salvation.
26. The most famous testimony to Hume's sweetness of character and greatness of soul comes from his friend Adam Smith. See the letter from Smith to William Strahan, Nov. 9, 1776; reproduced in Hume, *Essays, Moral, Political and Literary* xliii–xlix.
27. Hume, "On the Dignity and Meanness of Human Nature," *Essays, Moral, Political and Literary* 86.

### Four. Virtues Naturally Immune to Hypocrisy

1. In *The Mystery of Courage* I argued that ultimately the distinction between physical and moral courage collapses, except on one issue: moral courage must be lonely courage. Now it occurs to me that susceptibility

to hypocrisy might also be a basis for distinguishing them. Shamming moral courage is a frequent vice in the academy. One "speaks out" against racism, imperialism, sexism, and so on. Zero risk is run, though the air is thick with self-congratulation for taking a courageous stand. Such hypocrisy is a vice not only of the PC crowd; I am one of those older people who think some wars need to be fought, but I surely won't be the one fighting them.

2. Some kinds of fakery are not even vaguely virtuous. Thus the malingerer who feigns illness, or Falstaff, who lies about deeds not done or stages fake brave deeds, as when he stabs corpses and then claims to have killed them; *I Henry IV* 5.4.128.

3. See Miller, *Mystery of Courage* 42–45, 84–88.

4. According to one compelling view, for a threat to work as a threat it must induce the behavior it desires in the other; to have to carry out the threat means the threat did not do its job. See Schelling, *Strategy of Conflict* 35–43.

5. You surely want to deceive your enemies about more than your courage; see Sun Tzu, *The Art of War*. Moreover, you may want to deceive them equally about your courage in either direction. You mostly want them to fear your bravery, but the common Scythian tactic was to feign cowardly flight and then turn and hack down their pursuers; see Plato, *Laches* 191a–c.

6. This is the core of the self-deception puzzle in the philosophical literature. The literature is extensive; see, for example, Davidson ("Deception"), Pears (*Motivated Irrationality*), Fingarette (*Self-Deception*), and Mele (*Self-Deception Unmasked*). The issues seem largely to center on how the mind can compartmentalize itself to let the deception work. Lazar, however, would remind us that much belief formation takes place not in a cold, rational environment but under the influence of strong emotions, where our purely rational systems are being pressured ("Deceiving Oneself"). It is now theorized that the brain is made up of various mechanisms, systems, and structures that have a quasi-independent existence and are in incomplete communication with each other, thus allowing for self-deception, internal arguments, and so on; see Pinker, *How the Mind Works* 421–423; also Trivers, *Social Evolution* 416: "The mind must be structured in a very complex fashion, repeatedly split into public and private portions, with complicated interactions between the subsections." The problem remains a puzzle.

7. OED s.v. politeness, 3, from a manners book of 1702: *Eng. Theophrast.* 108.

8. The nineteenth-century novels of manners are masterful at presenting these perfectly polite conversational battles, for which it is hard to improve upon the conversations of Elinor and Lucy in Austen's *Sense and Sensibility*.

9. Proper use of tact and poise is the central moral virtue in what is often thought of as Goffman's amoral universe; Giddens, "Erving Goffman,"

113, makes the case for Goffman's world being a moral order precisely because of the centrality of the virtue of tact.

10. *Mansfield Park* ch. 28.

11. *Sense and Sensibility* ch. 21.

12. Santayana, *Soliloquies* 133–134, quoted in Goffman, *The Presentation of Self* 57.

13. See Lovejoy, *Reflections* 135–136. The seventeenth-century French moralists viewed the chief motive behind vanity to be the desire for praise, not the fear of shame. The two go hand in hand, but the inner lives of persons whose primary motive is fear of shame are miles apart from those of people whose primary motive is to seek praise.

14. Notice that the log in our own eye not only causes us to exaggerate the faults of the other but also can just as easily construe his bad intentions as good if seeing them that way serves the cause of our self-love.

15. Chesterfield, *Letters* March 9, 1748; the last sentence is from Oct. 19, 1748.

16. *Sense and Sensibility* ch. 7.

17. For example, ch. 4, where each plays up to the expectations of her type and each is delighting in playing it up for the other.

18. Elinor states clearly that the demands of propriety, meeting the expectations of others, govern only in small matters. Thus to Marianne: "... but when have I advised you to adopt their sentiments or conform to their judgment in serious matters?" (ch. 17).

## Five. Naked Truth

1. See the discussion in Elster about contrary mechanisms being equally plausible in so many settings; virtually every proverb coexists with another proverb that depends on an opposite view of what the default position of so-called human nature is; *Alchemies* 10–23.

2. On offers you cannot refuse but not in the Mafioso sense, see Austen, *Mansfield Park* ch. 12: "I wish my good aunt would be a little less busy! And to ask me in such a way too! without ceremony, before them all, so as to leave me no possibility of refusing. *That* is what I dislike most particularly. It raises my spleen more than anything, to have the pretence of being asked, of being given a choice, and at the same time addressed in such a way as to oblige one to do the very thing, whatever it be!"

3. See *Jones v. Clinton*, 990 F. Supp. 657 (E. D. Arkansas), 1998.

4. Trollope, *Framley Parsonage* ch. 24; see also Nyberg, *The Varnished Truth*, in praise of varnishing truth.

5. See Goffman, *Presentation of Self* 81n6, who, like Mead, believes that many of the psychological and philosophical puzzles about self-deception may be better understood by starting from the social setting and moving in.

## Six. In Divine Services and Other Ritualized Performances

1. Bergson's theory of the comic puts the pratfall right at its center; *Laughter*. The comic, in his view, depends on rendering humans as puppets or mere lumps of matter.

2. The story never ceases to prompt fear and trembling. In one Jewish tradition Isaac dies of fright and needs resurrecting with divine dew. The tradition derives from a gloss on Gen. 31.42, in which Jacob makes reference to "the God of my father, the God of Abraham, and the *fear* of Isaac"; see *Etz Hayim*, Haftarah for Pesah, Intermediate Shabbat, 1307.

3. I am desperate to locate the citation: about fifteen years ago I heard a paper read at a medieval conference quoting such a text, but I cannot recall who gave it or what year.

4. The first mention comes from Evragius (4th century) as the noonday demon that tempts the hermit from the duties of the ascetic life. *Acedia*, before it was reformulated as sloth, was specifically understood as despair, what we would think of as depression, characterized by boredom, dejection, and disgust with fulfilling religious duty. See Wenzel, *The Sin of Sloth*.

5. See, for example, http://www.project-awareness.org/page_shmooze.htm and http://www.aish.com/spirituality/growth/Soul_Matters_5_Prayer_Made_Practical.asp.

6. Maimonides is stricter. You must concentrate during prayer services on the prayers. "The mind should be freed from all extraneous thoughts... and not regard the service as a burden which he is carrying" (*Book of Adoration* "Laws of Prayer," 2.ii.4.16).

7. Behavior primarily motivated to set an example is often felt to be some sort of faking it, a kind of pious fraud.

8. Catholic mental prayer can still be roughly scripted, as in St. Ignatius' spiritual exercises, but with the particulars left to the worshiper.

9. Though we cannot will spontaneity, we can fake it rather convincingly at times. When we are surprised we script our behavior into the expected way of acting surprised. You, for instance, can be genuinely surprised by a gift or surprise party and still know that you must show off that surprise in a certain way to please the crowd or else be perceived as an ingrate and a bungler of the occasion.

10. See my discussion in *The Mystery of Courage* 215–217.

11. Raverat, *Period Piece* 212.

12. See *Ta'anit* 2.15a in Steinsaltz, *Talmud* XIV, 4.

13. Jewish ritual takes these kinds of oaths to God seriously indeed. It is too dangerous to have them floating around unretracted. The Kol Nidre prayer chanted at the commencement of the Yom Kippur liturgy voids all such casual and not so casual imprecations. See Rawson, *God, Gulliver, and Genocide* 12, on exaggerated murderous invective, "a volatile combination of 'meaning it,' not meaning it, and not not meaning it."

14. See, for example, Psalms 44, 74.
15. For example, the exquisite Psalm 92; see Smith, TMS passim.
16. A person who goes on too long or too often speaking in tongues, I have been informed, will be given a subtle message to wrap it up. When people stop interpreting or refuse to interpret the sounds the ecstatic person is uttering, the point is to be taken to close up shop. The next week the pastor might even focus on the text that says that interpretation is required for a valid revelation; 1 Cor. 14.5ff; 2 Pet. 1.20–21. There are also different practices among Pentecostal churches. Some consider that the longer you run into lunch time the more successful the service; others might prefer mobilizing more social control to give brother X or sister Z the message in order to get home before the football game starts.
17. See Steinsaltz, *Essential Talmud* 102.
18. Maimonides, *Book of Adoration* "Laws of Prayer," 2.ii.9.2–3. For another strategy for passing time during the Amidah see Goldberg, *Bee Season* 50–51.
19. Maimonides, 2.ii.10.1.
20. Maimonides, 2.ii.6.2. Anxiety about finishing the Amidah in a reasonable time plays a role in Chasidic tales; see, for example, the story of Reb Mordecai available in *The Making of Chassidim: A Letter Written by the Previous Lubavitcher Rebbe, Rabbi Yosef Yitzchak Schneersohn* (Brooklyn, NY: Sichos In English) at http://www.sichosinenglish.org/books/making-chassidim/08.htm.
21. Greenblatt, *Renaissance Self-Fashioning* 13–14.
22. Leviticus 22.4. Rabbinic law says it is permissible for a scholar of repute, known for his truthfulness, to lie about the bed he has slept in "lest signs of nocturnal emission be found there" (Maimonides, *Book of Torts* "Laws of Robbery and Lost Property," 11.iii.14.13).
23. "Hineni," in Silverman, *High Holiday Prayer Book* 124; see also Maimonides, *Book of Adoration* "Laws of Prayer," 2.ii.15.6–7 (priestly benediction is effective even if the priest is not a man of integrity. The benediction's force comes from God, not the priest).
24. See Elster, *Alchemies* 336: "Neither philosophy nor social science is of much help in explaining how we may believe partly or weakly in the ideas that we present ourselves to others as believing fully and strongly . . . The constant need to assert one's belief in communism in public probably induced *some kind* of mental assent." This modifies a position, similar to Greenblatt's, that Elster had supposed earlier to govern in pathological cultures of hypocrisy such as obtained in the USSR or Mao's China, in which the claimed hatred of the class enemy was entirely faked. But one can fake only so long before one may become wholly or in part what one is faking.
25. Consider the plight of people in sixteenth-century England forced in the 1550s to profess Protestantism, Catholicism, and then Protestantism as Edward gave way to Mary, who gave way to Elizabeth.

26. There is a large literature on the conversos and Marranos; see, for example, Bodian ("Men of the Nation") and Netanyahu (*The Marranos of Spain* and *Toward the Inquisition*).
27. Vonnegut, *Mother Night* p. v.

## Seven. Say It Like You Mean It

1. La Rochefoucauld, M 559.
2. Hume, *Treatise of Human Nature* 2.1.1.
3. Or else we would have had to generate a different understanding of what constituted an offense.
4. The thrust of much of Ekman's research is to claim differentiable muscle movement for genuine and fake, involuntary and voluntary, emotion display. But even if we concede the physiological point to Ekman we simply are not very good at picking up on the falsity; most of us can't detect lies very well. See Ekman et al., "A Few Can Catch a Liar." Pinker, *How the Mind Works* 421, comes up with what I find an implausible suggestion that emotions evolved because they were hard to fake. His hypothesis cannot survive your last conversation with your next-door neighbor. Remember that the inept faker has the vanity of his interlocutor helping him sell his false positives. See too the discussion in Nyberg, *The Varnished Truth* 115–122.
5. The existence or mere indiscernibility of the blush in dark-skinned people is discussed by Darwin, *Expression of Emotions* 315–320; nineteenth-century racists argued that the blush showed the moral superiority of the Caucasian race; see Jacobson, *Whiteness of a Different Color* 37.
6. Guilt has come to bear Freudian baggage, which remorse is still mercifully free of. Guilt is now often thought to be more a condition of which the emotion remorse is properly one of the features.
7. The psychological mechanism is more complicated. It is, I believe, that at some primitive core we never really believe an accident is an accident. On the surface this looks like strict liability, but it harbors a belief in animism. Thus the doorsill was out to get us. Why else curse it? See also Miller, *The Anatomy of Disgust* 197–204.
8. Thanks to Larry Kramer for sharing this experience.
9. See Tavuchis on apology versus excuse, *Mea Culpa* 17–18; and Goffman on giving accounts in *Relations in Public* 109–113.
10. Austin, "A Plea for Excuses," 177.
11. Tavuchis's helpful treatment of apology does not adequately distinguish regret from remorse, nor does it worry about the fakeability problem. For a recent critique of the dubious role of apology in so-called restorative justice, see Acorn, *Compulsory Compassion*.
12. Smith makes remorse a compound sentiment "made up of shame from the sense of the impropriety of past conduct; of grief for the effects of it; of pity for those who suffer by it; and of the dread and terror of punishment

from the consciousness of the justly provoked resentment of all rational creatures" (TMS II.ii.2.3). The mere dread and terror of punishment are not sufficient for true remorse without the other components.

13. Langland, *Piers Plowman* B.V.126.

14. Johnson, *A General History* 53.

15. Lewis, *Babbitt* 1.4.

16. Aren't we ashamed of our accidents? We blame ourselves for being the kind of klutzes we are. The distinction between shame and guilt loses its force here, because whether we apologize for what we did or for who we are, we still feel we owe reparations.

17. There is a style of sanctity that seeks suffering and welcomes being wronged so as to be able to forgive or ignore the offense; this is not the stoical style because it is too active, but it incorporates aspects of the stoic regimen. The pathological variant is the battered wife syndrome; the saintly variant is Myshkin.

18. All three elements are necessary; no satisfaction, no absolution, and no absolution if satisfaction is not preceded by contrition and confession. Judaism also makes confession necessary; punishment and satisfaction alone are not sufficient; see Maimonides, *Book of Knowledge* "Laws of Repentance," 1.v.1.1.

19. See further Aquinas, Suppl. Q 15, A 3 on suitable forms of satisfaction.

20. Aquinas, Suppl. Q 12, A 2.

21. Maimonides, "Laws of Repentance," 1.v.2.1.

22. Maimonides, *Book of Torts* 11.iv.5.10; see further "Laws of Repentance," 1.v.2.9 on the sin of continued refusal to forgive.

23. I am adapting this from *Reykdæla saga* ch. 23, taking some small but not crucial liberties. See my discussion in *Bloodtaking and Peacemaking* ch. 2.

24. See Miller, *Bloodtaking and Peacemaking* 368n22; remarkably, the ceremony of begging forgiveness mimics a gruesome ceremony in which the avenger is charged to take revenge by someone displaying the head or some other body part of the victim before him; see Miller, "Choosing the Avenger," 202–203.

25. See, for example, *Njáls saga* ch. 123.

26. See Miller, *Bloodtaking and Peacemaking* 61–68, on the very narrow range in which people understood the claim of accident to be acceptable.

27. Even the once meek and weak Isabella Linton comes to understand that forgiveness worth the name is inevitably coupled with the ability to take revenge: "It is utterly impossible I can ever be revenged, and therefore I cannot forgive him" (Bronte, *Wuthering Heights* ch. 17).

28. Suppose that the parents declare themselves satisfied by the groused I'm sorry they have extorted but that the wronged sibling is not satisfied. In the forgiveness God grants the fasting faithful on Yom Kippur, He pardons only His claim against the sinner; the claim of the person the sinner wronged still must be satisfied; see *Mishna Yoma* 8.9 (quoted in Silverman, *High Holiday Prayer Book* 207).

29. Thus Ahab, I Kings 21.17.
30. Boehm, *Blood Revenge* 133–136.
31. Trollope, *Can You Forgive Her?* ch. 39.
32. Hampshire ("Sincerity," 249) refers to this pleasuring in our own negative emotions as a sentimentalization of the emotion. We thus experience not true remorse in this circumstance but sentimental remorse, and Hampshire takes it to be fundamentally insincere. What if the self-satisfaction comes some time after an initially sincere remorse that prompted forgiveness? The forgiveness probably could not be revoked on such grounds, but the forgiver would be justified in feeling a bit snookered and look for some pretext to reopen hostilities.
33. Klemperer, *I Will Bear Witness* 1.411.
34. Eliot, *Adam Bede* ch. 29.
35. Mead, *Mind, Self, and Society* 170; Trollope, *The Way We Live Now* ch. 8; also see ch. 100.
36. The avoidance of embarrassment, or of making a scene, surely explains as much of Milgram's (*Obedience to Authority*) experimental results as does his theory of obedience to those in hierarchically superior positions.
37. Naipaul, *Mimic Men* 70.
38. Bierce is especially good on the insincerity of repentance; see his definitions for *impenitence, pardon, penitent, redress,* and *reparation*.
39. From Quintus Curtius, first century A.D., from a speech of a man giving a reason a band of soldiers in Alexander's army, mutilated by the Persians, should not return home; cited in Konstan, *Pity* 23.
40. Maimonides argues that impenitence is its own punishment because it justifies punishment of a more aggressive sort in the hereafter (*Book of Knowledge* "Laws of Repentance," 1.v.6.3).
41. This is only the tip of the iceberg on the variety of practices that use the apologetic form but that don't engage the theme of faking it as fruitfully. Someone steps on your foot or bumps you hard because he was not monitoring his movements, and *you* apologize to him. For whatever reason, you may have no interest in making this a big deal and just want to terminate the affair by using your I'm sorry to indicate no offense was taken. Such an I'm sorry demands a response, however, and the proper response is not "I accept your apology" or "I forgive you, son." Your I'm sorry is meant as a polite request for the other to make a submissive gesture. It all happens so fast it is almost reflexive, but if the other does not ask to be pardoned, you will have been wronged.

Compare the very different and hostilely intoned "Excuse me!" You know the type: someone who feels he has been slighted in some way not to be forgiven. This is not a request for an apology, but an indication of a refusal to accept one because it was not already proffered.

Then there are those routinized I'm sorry's, excuse me's, and pardon me's that are designed to preempt offenses about to be given. Thus if I cut in front of you I ask you for proto-forgiveness for the offense I would have given you had I not asked you to forgive me in advance, a request that you cannot deny given the rules of polite excusings. So expected is your pardon that I am already pressing my body into the contested space as I am saying my pardon me. Your conceding the space is pretty much a given, or else I wouldn't have presumed upon you in the first place. Yet should I not give my little sorry in a properly pleasant tone, an unignorable offense will have been given.

### Eight. Flattery and Praise

1. See Konstan's discussion of Plutarch's "How to Tell a Flatterer from a Friend" (*Friendship* 98–103). Dante puts flatterers in the eighth circle of hell, where they wallow in excrement that looks as if it came from human privies. They are covered with "merda" (*Inferno*, 18.113–114). There is a rich anticourt, anticourtier tradition that makes flattery the currency of court.
2. Sonnet 114, v. 2; see Montaigne 2.16, "Of Glory," 703. Even the redoubtable twelfth-century Abbot Samson of Bury St. Edmunds was not immune to it, though he flattered himself to be only feigning to go along with his flatterers, claiming that he could see through their designs: "I am forced into many shams and pretences to keep the convent peaceful" (Jocelin of Brakelond, *Chronicle* 38).
3. One commentator concludes, "There's nothing in Plutarch to flush out the flatterer"; Konstan, *Friendship* 101, quoting Graham Little, *Friendship* 19. Without being very cynical or vicious we may want friends that make us feel good by flattering us on occasion. I have my parents, my spouse, my children, my conscience, and the dean to reprove me; why have friends to do the same?
4. Dostoyevsky, *The Idiot* I.7, 74.
5. Even God and the saints are chided as ingrates for not making fit return on the multitude of prayers extolling their greatness. Thus the rituals of humiliating saints, putting their bones on the ground or in dung, or beating their relics, when they refuse to aid the faithful against their enemies; see Geary, "Humiliation of Saints," and Little, *Benedictine Maledictions*. An analogous ritual in Jewish tradition is performed when God has not seen fit to send rain to relieve a drought. A public fast would be decreed and the ark would be taken out of town and ashes placed on it; see *Ta'anit* 2.15a in Steinsaltz, *Talmud* XIV, 3.
6. See Silbermann, *Grovelling* 74.
7. See La Rochefoucauld's related thought: "The mark of extraordinary merit is to see that those who envy it most are forced to praise it" (M 95). Closely linked with this is the form of envy known as emulation. The praise that issues from the emulous person is not as meanly infected as is the reluctant praise of the conventionally envious. The piano student desperately wants to surpass the maestro who teaches her. But she is moved

to tears by his performances – not to flatter him, though there might be competition among the students to see who can get points for being moved the most, but because the master is an embodiment of all the virtues that draws her to the enterprise. On the necessity of nearness in the relevant hierarchy for envy to arise, see variously Aristotle, *Rhetoric* 2.10.1388a5; Hume, *Treatise* 2.2.8.377; Swift, *Poetical Works*, "Verses on the Death of Dr. Swift," vv. 13–14.

8. Hegel's parable of master and slave is not quite accurate as either a sociological or a psychological matter; *Phenomenology of the Spirit* B.IV.A. Lords took great care to make sure the mockery they suffered at the hands of their slaves was limited to fixed forms and fixed occasions; and surely they cared to be deferred to by their inferiors.

9. Trollope, *The Duke's Children* ch. 77.

10. Austen, *Sense and Sensibility* ch. 10.

11. Silbermann mentions "negative flattery," a "so-called gesture of friendship," in which his colleague made criticisms of insignificant passages in his writing and then praised parts of "which, as he well knew, I was particularly proud. Behind this mask of a brave and loyal lover of the truth we find a great many arse-lickers" (*Grovelling* 75).

12. Congreve, *The Way of the World* 1.6.

13. Melville, *The Confidence Man* ch. 12.

14. Chesterfield, *Letters* October 16, O. S. 1747.

15. Boswell, *Life of Johnson* 188; aetat 45. 1754; Johnson never forgave Chesterfield for treating him with contempt when Johnson sought his patronage for the dictionary.

16. Diderot, *Paradox*.

### Nine. Hoist with His Own Petard

1. The anxiety of talking to Hamlet is given delightful treatment by Stoppard, *Rosencrantz and Guildenstern*.

2. Except perhaps for Dostoyevsky's Underground Man, it seems that obsessive self-observation can only approach but never surpass in any interesting way Montaigne, Hamlet, and, in a different but equally telling way, Samuel Pepys.

3. *Adam Bede* ch. 17; also on the same general theme from *Romola* (ch. 64): "Our naked feelings make haste to clothe themselves in propositions which lie at hand among our store of opinions, and to give a true account of what passes within us something else is necessary besides sincerity, even when sincerity is unmixed." And for a philosophical treatment of the same issue of how hard it is to name or describe our internal states, especially given that the very effort to do so is part of the mix of what that internal state will in the end be, see Hampshire, "Sincerity," 236–244.

4. "This above all" follows immediately upon "Neither a borrower nor a lender be, / For loan oft loses both itself and friend, / And borrowing dulleth th'edge of husbandry." Can Polonius be talking merely of creditor–debtor

relations? Gauge exactly your financial means – "costly thy habits as thy purse can buy" – and then you will not be false to any creditors? But then "this above all" bursts the restraints of such a narrow reading, and we get instead Delphic wisdom.

5. Hamlet means to delve under them to place an explosive charge to collapse their mine. Countermines could also seek to gain entry to the mine by tunneling above and pouring in lethal substances, or by entering and fighting.

6. See Keen, *Laws of War* 48–50, for examples. In saga Iceland the formal blood-brotherhood ceremony required passing under turf to reemerge as brothers; see my "Ordeal in Iceland."

7. This is the term the rake Willoughby uses in an access of self-castigation in *Sense and Sensibility* ch. 44.

8. Alanis Morrissette, an unremarkable Canadian pop singer, had a 1996 hit called "Ironic" in which most of her examples of irony involved no irony at all. One of the many merits of the Internet is that it prompts people who otherwise would not feel compelled to write about such things to do so. Her mistaken ideas about the meaning of irony have spawned numerous hostile and amusing commentaries.

9. Following Trilling, *Sincerity and Authenticity* 120: "Irony is one of those words, like love, which are best not talked about if they are to retain any force of meaning."

10. *Grettir's saga* ch. 45; *Njáls saga* ch. 92.

11. She has the added problem of being and looking young and having to advise elders. Trollope has a nice treatment of a twenty-three-year-old cleric giving his first sermon to graybeards (*Barchester Towers* vol. 2, ch. 4).

12. The ironist doesn't necessarily improve his ironic talents with practice. One suspects that if you have to practice at it you are without the talent for it in the first place.

## Ten. The Self, the Double, and the Sense of Self

1. Wharton, *The Custom of the Country* ch. 6.

2. Hume, *Treatise* 1.4.6.

3. See Nozick, *Philosophical Explanations* 90–94 (the self synthesizes itself by reflexive self-reference); Dennett, *Consciousness* 414–418 (the self as a narrative spun out like a spider spins a web) and cf. Kenny, *The Self* 4 (the self as a mere grammatical error).

4. The work of Walter Mischel, an experimental psychologist, could be read to support some rough form of the Humean position, though Mischel's attack on trait theory need not necessarily dispose of a core self. In his view, we are what the situation demands; there is no core self with stable traits across all settings, except, it seems, the trait of intelligence. The claims made in this literature get less dramatic when it is recalled that the research arose as an attack on the personality trait tests that were given

regularly in high school to help guidance counselors send students to the right segment of the job market. A large body of evidence in the 1960s began to reveal that these tests were not able to predict behavior and performance. I recall the laughter among my high school friends when the test revealed I would do especially well in sales.

5. See the various positions pro and con in Elster, *The Multiple Self*.

6. Strawson, "The Self," 417, admits the insistent anxiety that there may be multiple selves but argues that that experience "is necessarily experience from a single point of view." But that single point of view may be in a state of panic for fear that it cannot locate itself.

7. See Miller, "Sheep, Joking, Cloning and the Uncanny."

8. Hogg's *Memoirs and Confessions of a Justified Sinner*, Dostoyevsky's *The Double*, Freud, "The Uncanny," and Stevenson, *Jekyll and Hyde*, among many other instances, such as Bronte, *Wuthering Heights* (Cathy: "Nelly, I *am* Heathcliff"). Notions of doubling also figure in scapegoating, whipping boys, good angels/bad angels; the nearly universal fascination also continues apace with the rise or invention of so-called multiple personality disorder and the rational choice literature on multiple selves. Twinning is also an aspect of the comic.

9. Maimonides admits that "sometimes one will waver in his mind concerning the Unity of God, as to whether He is One or He is not One" (*Book of Knowledge* "Laws Concerning Idolatry," I.iv.2.3).

10. Mead finds it helpful to distinguish an "I," that present point of consciousness, from the "me" that bears personality and character and has origins external to the individual: "Our view of the self is the individual as we conceive him to exist in the minds of other members of the group. This is the 'me.' The 'I' is the speaker over against the one spoken to, but the attention is given to the other." *The Individual and the Social Self* 92; also, 71; and *Mind, Self, and Society* 178, 225. Mead also speaks of a "primary self." Its job, if I read him correctly, is to give some kind of coherence to all the roles, especially to resolve conflicts among them. We can only account for its presence after the fact; it is not experienced in the present; *The Individual* 74–75.

11. Hume, *Treatise* 2.2.5; Smith, TMS III.i.5.

12. See Pinch (*Strange Fits* 21–44) on Hume's view of the dubious ownership of our own emotions; and her able treatment of personification in relation to the passions (44–50); see also Donald Davie, "Personification," on the centrality of personification to language and thought. For the suggestion that personification does more than just enliven us with passion, but actually is a way of bringing life to the dead, see the allusive tour de force by Cunningham, *In the Reading Gaol* 391–396.

13. On the origins of the feel + emotion term construction in English, see Miller, *Humiliation* 176; see also Austin ("Pretending," 257) who notes that being angry is not the same as feeling angry, because "angry" is considerably more than just the name of a feeling.

14. For the average person it is very hard to separate body types from character and the propriety of and eligibility for certain roles, though philosophers might show we need not feel that way; see the discussion in Parfit *Reasons and Persons* §89.
15. Strawson, "The Self," 407.
16. Mead, *The Individual* 53–54.
17. *The Individual* 46.
18. Ford, *Parade's End* 55; Small, *Road to Richmond* 185. Even a dualist would admit that the body can distract the mind from its thoughts, but I am inclined to claim more for the body's necessary participation in thinking for reasons I suggest in the text because thinking as a conversation implies certain organs of sense, and the language we think in would hardly have a metaphor available to it without recourse to images implicit in being embodied. Notions that assume our embodiment pervade language at every level; see generally Lakoff and Johnson, *Metaphors We Live By*.
19. These kinds of congratulations or cursings of oneself do not carry quite the same meaning when uttered audibly as they do when said only internally; at least this is the case if there are people present who are meant to overhear you. Thus, when I damn myself for missing an easy shot in basketball I do it out loud as a gesture of apology and placation to my teammates.
20. Even respectable scholars end up sounding like self-help books – for example, Charles Taylor, *The Ethics of Authenticity*. His ambitious *Sources of the Self* has some of the same failing as Whig history in that it assumes the excellence of the development that leads to his book. Works such as Taylor's set up the man of honor with a shallow inner life as a strawman that the West has managed to overcome. I defend the depth of the inner life of people of honor in "Deep Inner Lives," and I suggest there that for real shallowness one need only look to the discourse of self that congratulates us on being deep, ending in self-esteem movements and new age sentimentalism.
21. See Parfit (*Reasons and Persons* 277) for an image of persons as "nations, clubs, or political parties."
22. Cf. Giddens, "Erving Goffman," 118.
23. Goffman, *Presentation of Self* 235.
24. Outside tropical zones clothing is surely more "natural" than nakedness. Thus Dennett, *Consciousness* 416: "Clothes . . . are part of the extended phenotype of *Homo sapiens* in almost every niche inhabited by that species. An illustrated encyclopedia of zoology should no more picture *Homo sapiens* naked than it should picture *Ursus arctus* – the black bear – wearing a clown suit and riding a bicycle."

### Eleven. At the Core at Last

1. Freud, *Jokes* 8.81.
2. Cuddihy, *Ordeal of Civility* 24; Freud, *Jokes* 80–81.

3. The days of the prophets officially ended with the death of the last of Jesus' disciples. From then on God spoke through the translators and interpreters of His church. You can speak to God in your tongue, but He would no longer speak directly to you in His. The Protestant sects that accepted contemporary prophecy had to develop means of crediting revelations as authentic. One might see in the practice of speaking in tongues an attempt to prove the authenticity of the revelation by putting it in a kind of incomprehensible tongue that could pass for God's own Hebrew. For an especially good account of the anxieties of authenticity that faced self-styled Anglo-American prophets in the eighteenth century, see Juster, *Doomsayers*.

4. For a brief but suggestive treatment of the theme of Moses' veil and the veil over the Holy of Holies as taken up in the Christian exegetical tradition, see Cunningham, *In the Reading Gaol* 398.

5. Cuddihy (*Ordeal of Civility* 24) reads this joke in a slightly different way, but his central claim strikes me as having much merit, or at least as being very rich in its suggestive possibilities. Cuddihy jokes that for Freud the id is Yid, the Yid, id.

6. For the Son as co-eternal with the Father see Heb. 1.2, where through the Son God made the world; and so, too, John 1.1. See Milton's rendition of the role of the Son in the wars in Heaven: "Son of my bosom, Son who are alone / My world. My wisdom and effectual might" (*Paradise Lost* 3.169–170).

7. Rozin and Fallon, "A Perspective on Disgust," 32.

8. See the discussion in Shapiro, *Shakespeare and the Jews* ch. 1.

9. The online edition of the *Catholic Encyclopedia*, published in 1912, in a hagiography of Torquemada, testifies to the endurance of a view that ended in the destruction of European Jewish culture within three decades: "At that time the purity of the Catholic Faith in Spain was in great danger from the numerous Marranos and Moriscos, who, for material considerations, became sham converts from Judaism and Mohammedanism to Christianity. The Marranos committed serious outrages against Christianity and endeavoured to judaize the whole of Spain."

10. Goffman, *Relations in Public* ch. 6.

11. A similar problem arose in America with regard to black blood; but the courts were inclined to let sleeping dogs lie. By encouraging slander suits for loss of white racial reputation they discouraged zealous efforts to investigate people's racial backgrounds, something many astute racists knew would risk their own claims to purity of blood; see Sharfstein, "Secret History of Race."

12. Eliot, *Complete Poems* "Burbank with a Baedeker: Bleistein with a Cigar," sts. 4–6.

13. Shylock is not mentioned directly, but his presence in the poem is suggested by the allusions to *The Merchant of Venice* ("on the Rialto").

14. See Nietzsche, *Genealogy of Morals* Essay I.

15. *Ressentiment* is not sour grapes: in the sour grapes mechanism you still value sweetness, it is just that you see the particular grapes that are beyond your grasp as not being sweet because you cannot have them; in *ressentiment* you decide that sweetness itself is bad and that those who enjoy it are inferior, evil, or damned.

16. As an aside I note that it is often the case that the charge of *ressentiment* leveled at others is itself a form of *ressentiment*, hurled by losers at winners, or if not quite by losers, by fearful dominators who see their grip slipping. Max Scheler's treatment of *ressentiment*, for instance, strikes me less as an analysis than as an exemplar of it. Scheler, a Jew, was a convert to Catholicism when he sought to defend Christianity against Nietzsche's charges of its being a religion of *ressentiment*.

17. See Miller, *The Anatomy of Disgust* chs. 9–10.

### Twelve. Passing and Wishing You Were What You Are Not

1. That same person can be praised for attempting to "improve" himself by rejecting his tainted people. It is part of the morality of authenticity to welcome or at least to accept certain aspects of ourselves, and to self-realize and self-improve as part of the proper development of our authentic self. But which aspects are to be welcomed and which rejected or improved beyond recognition is part of the flux of political, social, and moral clashes.

2. See Gilman (*Self-Hatred* 6–9) regarding the Jew as black in the European context of the late nineteenth and early twentieth centuries. The most provocative study is still Cuddihy's *Ordeal of Civility*, though in a perverse way I find von Rezzori's *Memoirs of an Anti-Semite* stunningly insightful from the other side.

3. It is also necessary to distinguish a self-hatred deriving from a generalized misanthropy and melancholia, as in the case of Hamlet or Pascal, from those arising from more *ressentiment*-like settings, as is the case of Underground Man, to Jewish self-hatred, which is only partly susceptible to being understood as *ressentiment*. Groucho Marx – "I don't want to belong to any club that would accept me as a member" – hardly means to transform the values of the dominant order. He has internalized their view of his powers of contamination; so his presence ruins the attractiveness of the desired object. He wishes desperately that it were otherwise. See Scheler, *Ressentiment* 52, on self-hatred and *ressentiment*.

4. See Walzer, "Can There Be a Decent Left?"

5. Trollope, *The Way We Live Now* ch. 91.

6. The image of the intrepid middle- or upper-class traveler of the late nineteenth or early twentieth century springs to mind – Edith Durham, Margaret Hasluck – and Margaret Thatcher for a recent exemplar.

7. The English would tell a different story: that their whole style is cultivated because they are the most embarrassable of people, and they contrast

themselves proudly on precisely this trait from the French, whom they see as profoundly unembarrassable; see Ricks, *Keats* 5–6.

8. Compare the ready coupling of leftist politics and patriotism in England (Orwell, E. P. Thompson, et al.) with the smug and embarrassed disapproval of patriotism on the American left; see Walzer, "Can There Be a Decent Left?"

9. Goffman, *Stigma* 73–91.

10. See Yoshino, who discusses the burden of "covering" a stigma such as homosexuality so that an individual "modulates her conduct to make her difference easy for those around her to disattend her known stigmatized trait" ("Covering," 837). Yoshino would prefer a world in which such accommodations are unnecessary. I am not sure I concur if it means abandoning reticence with regard to aspects of one's identity that are not relevant to the moment. Surely the Jewish kid who sings "Hatikvah" in Hebrew, or the Protestant who sings "Onward Christian Soldiers" during their auditions for the junior high play can be reasonably expected to do a better job of "covering" aspects of their identity.

11. See I. J. Singer's work, which is quite good on these matters: *The Family Carnovsky*, also to a lesser degree *The Brothers Ashkenazi*.

12. See Herzog's account (*Poisoning* 321–323) of Coleridge and the stinking Jew.

13. Hilaire Belloc, "The Garden Party," vv. 1–4, *Complete Verse* 219; on this issue see also Smith, TMS I.iii.2.5: "Politeness is so much the virtue of the great, that it will do little honor to any body but themselves. The coxcomb, who imitates their manner, and affects to be eminent by the superior propriety of his ordinary behavior, is rewarded with a double share of contempt for his folly and presumption."

14. The literature on passing, black and Jewish, is enormous. Some of it is of value, but much of it is tainted with the complacent assumptions of a naïve social constructionism that holds that because something is socially constructed it becomes less durable, less real, for that reason. Social constructions, on the contrary, might well be more durable than certain basic aspects of our biology. We will be able to engineer our genes to our liking long before we will rid ourselves of social constructions such as racism. I have found these works of interest: Jacobson, *Whiteness*; Hale, *Making Whiteness*; Gilman, *Self-Hatred* and *Smart Jews*; and Sharfstein, "Secret History." None strike me as being as consistently perspicacious as Goffman's *Stigma*.

15. Not that he will be tossed out on his ear if he is discovered. Goffman notes that when someone's false identity is seen through in a forbidden, out-of-bounds place, where exposure means expulsion, the people seeing through him may choose to avoid making a scene by kicking him out, "an eventuality often so unpleasant to all parties that a tacit cooperation will sometimes forestall it, the interloper providing a thin disguise and the rightfully present accepting it, even though both know the other knows

of the interloping." The understanding is this: don't ever let this happen again, buddy, or I can't promise you such a tactful response; *Stigma* 81. See also Larsen, *Passing* 16: "It wasn't that she was ashamed of being a Negro, or even of having it declared. It was the idea of being ejected from any place, even in the polite and tactful way in which the Drayton would probably do it, that disturbed her."

16. Larsen, *Passing* 55: "White people were so stupid about such things for all that they usually asserted they were able to tell...They always took her for an Italian, a Spaniard, a Mexican, or a gipsy."

17. Gilman, *Smart Jews* 183, cites Terry Abrahamson as claiming to have been an anomaly in his high school locker room in Amundsen, Illinois, in the mid 1960s, but unless the three or four uncircumcised penises loomed very large in his imagination it is hard for me to believe that Amundsen's practices were more retarded than Green Bay's on this issue.

18. See Gollaher's tendentious anticircumcision account, which nonetheless tells the American medical historical tale (*Circumcision* ch. 4). One of the burdens of living in a university town is to find flyers such as the following at your friendly Whole Foods store: "Beautiful music for alternative Jewish Baby Naming Ceremonies. Contact Brandy Sinco, Member of MUSIC (Musicians United to Stop Involuntary Circumcision)." And then Brandy gives a sample verse from a song:

> When we welcome our baby,
> The only tears will be of joy, not pain.
> Our child's body was formed well at birth.
> Let's leave all parts as the creator made.

19. Gollaher, *Circumcision* 94; and J. Levenson, "New Enemies."

### Thirteen. Authentic Moments with the Beautiful and Sublime?

1. Middle Eastern trees to be sure, but still one would think the shade would be tempting; see Maimonides, *Book of Acquisition* "Laws Concerning Neighbors," 12.iii.10.1.

2. Burke, *The Sublime and Beautiful* II.2; Sterne, *Tristam Shandy* 7.42. The terror of having nothing to write about is not the kind of terror that engenders the sublime, even though sublimity may leave us without words.

3. Kant, *Critique of Judgement* 262.

4. For example, Burke, I.7.

5. The special aesthetic emotion engendered by horror films is not really fear either, though it is strongly felt, and perhaps all the more strongly for benefiting from the knowledge that nothing is really at stake.

6. On the compulsion experienced by many to discern the best moment of a sunset or day of fall foliage, see my "Of Optimal Views."

7. *Mansfield Park* ch. 9.

8. The theme of pictures or paintings of a scene displacing the memory of it has been often noted. Stendhal advises not purchasing pictures or engravings on our travels because they will then take over our memory; see W. G. Sebald, *Vertigo* 8. Sebald's works can be seen in part as a wonderful and wistful application of this theme.

9. For the kitsch of ruins, see the recent humorous treatment of this well-studied issue by Dekkers, *Way of All Flesh* ch. 2.

10. For similar sentiments see Huysmans's description (*Against Nature* ch. 11) of des Esseintes' virtual trip to London in the latter decades of the nineteenth century.

### Fourteen. The Alchemist

1. For some illuminating experiments on interest effecting articulation of moral positions, see Batson, "Moral Hypocrisy." The results would bring a knowing smirk to La Rochefoucauld.

2. Elster, *Alchemies* 335.

3. Orwell, "Shooting an Elephant," 152.

4. Experimental evidence suggests it may be too easy to immerse ourselves fully into roles, even ones that require us to abandon or set aside previous moral commitments. This is one of the lessons to be drawn from Milgram's famous experiments. A now infamous psychology experiment at Stanford in the 1970s asked students to assume the roles of prisoners and guards; it had to be halted because the subjects got too immersed in their roles; see Zimbardo, "The Pathology of Imprisonment."

5. Pessimism can be a hypocritical position. See Melville, *The Confidence Man* ch. 9, who notes that feigning pessimism presents opportunities for gain. The ironies of the passage are complex because the words are those of a "confidence man" speaking of Wall Street "bears": "Why the most monstrous of all hypocrites are these bears: hypocrites by inversion; hypocrites in the simulation of things dark instead of bright; souls that thrive, less upon depression, than the fiction of depression."

6. Of the mechanisms available to account for these transformations, Elster (rightly I think) rejects Freudian defense mechanisms as incoherent and does not see mere dissonance reduction, at least in its classic formulation, to be a sufficient explanation either; see *Alchemies* 363–366.

7. Kroeber, *Nature of Culture* 311, cited in Goffman, *Presentation of Self* 21. The point was made earlier by Melville, *The Confidence Man* ch. 16:

> "You talked of confidence. How comes it that when brought low himself, the herb-doctor, who was most confident to prescribe in other cases, proves least confident to prescribe in his own; having small confidence in himself for himself?"
>
> "But he has confidence in the brother he calls in . . . Yes, in this hour the herb-doctor does distrust himself, but not his art."

8. This is the view offered by evolutionary biologists as to why self-deception is adaptive. It helps us be better deceivers of others; see Trivers, *Social Evolution* 415–420. Within limits perhaps, but then why that self-deceiver gains an evolutionary advantage is still not explained, for he is losing to other convincing self-deceiving dupers as much as winning. I think we need to look elsewhere for the evolutionary story of the selective advantages of self-deception. Perhaps it is that it keeps us from killing ourselves in despair by convincing us of our merit in the face of countervailing evidence. Or that it provides the necessary underpinnings for manifest virtues like perseverance; see Flanagan, *Varieties of Moral Personality* 329–332.

9. See *Laxdœla saga* ch. 18; see Miller, "Ordeal in Iceland," 200–203.

10. After he found the Elixir, the successful alchemist would have to make sure he kept gold reasonably scarce or else gold would be cheaper than the lead used to make it, though Elixir itself would still have substantial value.

11. Pound, *ABC of Reading* 99.

12. See primarily Ainslie, *Breakdown of Will*.

13. Austen, *Sense and Sensibility* ch. 4.

14. "The Greeks likewise differed from us in their evaluation of hope: they felt it to be blind and deceitful; Hesiod gave the strongest expression to this attitude in a fable whose sense is so strange no more recent commentator has understood it – for it runs counter to the modern spirit, which has learned from Christianity to believe in hope as a virtue," Nietzsche, *Daybreak* 38; also *Human, All Too Human* 71. See, too, how the Athenian negotiators in the Melian dialogue ridicule hope as the refuge of the weak; Thucydides, *Peloponnesian War* 5.103.

15. There is also a punning reference to good in the sense of assets, for it is the hope of that kind of good that is in part responsible for his misery.

16. Compare Chaucer's Pardoner, who confesses with pride how he cons the ignorant faithful by selling indulgences and then tries to perpetrate the con on the pilgrims he has just confessed to as a joke, but the joke is not taken as one. The canon's yeoman does seem to be genuinely expressing his present beliefs, not as a setup for a future con, though clearly he and his master joined the pilgrimage with a swindle on their agenda.

### Fifteen. "I Love You"

1. Trite as it is, I do recognize that sexual desire can also end transmuted into love, just as the euphemism "making love" would have it.

### Sixteen. Boys Crying and Girls Playing Dumb

1. Goffman, *Presentation of Self* 236–237, citing Komarovsky, "Cultural Contradictions," 188.

2. Would she prefer that he see through her and excuse her? What if he believes the dumb act but then finds her unappealing because he doesn't like dumb girls? In that case would she be even more chagrined for not playing dumb with enough leakage so the smart guy would see through the pose?

### Seventeen. Acting our Roles

1. See Roach's excellent treatment of this period of acting history (*The Player's Passion*).
2. William James, "What is an Emotion?" See Ellsworth, "William James and Emotion," on the common misreadings of James's position.
3. Diderot (*Paradox* 120) does not directly speak to the issue of acquiring the actual feeling by acting as if you have it. He cites a routine Garrick did in a Parisian salon in which within seconds Garrick mimicked a whole array of passions in a tour de force of mimicry. The point Diderot makes is that there was no way possible, given the rapidity, that Garrick could have first engendered the emotion in order to express it; nor was there, by implication, enough time for the display to generate the feelings.
4. One can read LeDoux (*The Emotional Brain*), for example, as James brought up-to-date; instead of looking to gross action tendencies or somatic changes as causing the feeling, LeDoux substitutes the behavior of the amygdala in the brain.
5. See Ekman and Keltner, "Universal Facial Expressions"; Duclos et al., "Emotion-Specific Effects"; Levenson et al., "Voluntary Facial Action"; and Strack et al., "Inhibiting and Facilitating." The latter details an experiment in which people gripped a pen either with their teeth (to engage smile muscles) or with their lips (to engage frown muscles) and then judged cartoons. Those gripping the pen with their teeth found the cartoons funnier.
6. The mechanism that works to accord gesture and sentiment is mysterious indeed. Does, as per James, the psyche observe the actions of the body that houses it and magically take its cue as how to feel, or is a kind of dissonance reduction at work that seeks to get rid of the disharmony of thinking one thing and doing or saying another?
7. See Miller, *The Anatomy of Disgust* 116–117.
8. Regarding anger, Maimonides believes that "one should train oneself not to be angry even for something that would justify anger." But he then advises it might well be wise to fake anger, especially when one is trying to correct children or members of the household (*Book of Knowledge* "Laws Relating to Moral Dispositions and Ethical Conduct," 1.ii.2.3).
9. From Judith VanHoose, UM Law class of 2004.
10. Diderot, *Paradox* 108.
11. Roach, *The Player's Passion* 137, discussing Diderot.

12. Diderot, *Paradox*, French edition, 145, my translation; Penguin edition, 135.
13. Austin ("Pretending," 268) notes that pretending has limits as to how long it can go on before it simply becomes a role, or you become the pretense.
14. For sheer disgustingness nothing matches Swift's "The Progress of Beauty," *Poetical Works* 172; see also Webster, *The Duchess of Malfi* 2.1. The genre is ancient and follows the example of Ovid; see his "On Painting the Face," "The Art of Love," and "The Remedies of Love" in *Art of Love*.
15. See Hughes, "Sumptuary Law."
16. *Grágás* K, c. 155.
17. See, for example, John Chrysostom writing in the fourth century. From *Homilia XIV, De mulieribus et pulchritudine*, quoted by Gerald of Wales writing in the late twelfth century (Hagen trans, at 140).
18. There is surprisingly little social science research on faking orgasm; see Wiederman, "Pretending Orgasm." Literature professors are less shy; see Garber, "Insincerity of Women."
19. See Alloy and Abramson, "Judgment of Contingency"; Taylor and Brown, "Illusion and Well-Being"; also Kruger and Dunning, "Unskilled and Unaware of It"; but see Flanagan's critique placing the truth somewhere in a fuzzy middle, *Varieties of Moral Personality* 315–332. For George Eliot it is a "piteous stamp of sanity" to have a "clear consciousness of shattered faculties," to be able to measure accurately our "own feebleness" (*Romola* ch. 30).
20. Swift, *A Tale of a Tub* sect. 9. The quote, as usual with Swift, is filtered through several layers of ambiguating ironies, but the sentiment is still enough in accord with his general pessimism that I see no reason not to attribute it to him rather than to the fictional author of the tract that makes up the bulk of the tale.
21. See Parfit on the justifiability of the transferability of love among replicas and facsimiles of persons (*Reasons and Persons* §§99, 295).
22. Goffman, *Presentation of Self* 235. One of the burdens of a male's masking in this way is that even a wig to cover hair loss due to chemotherapy would not be excused as a matter of course, as it would be for a woman.
23. "Man is least himself when he talks in his own person. Give him a mask, and he will tell you the truth"; Wilde, *The Critic as Artist* 1045. Diderot's theory of acting can be assimilated to this view. See also Nietzsche's somewhat different twist in *Beyond Good and Evil* §40: "Every profound spirit needs a mask: even more, around every profound spirit a mask is growing continually, owing to the constantly false, namely *shallow*, interpretation of every word, every step, every sign of life he gives."
24. Gide, *L'immoraliste* 420: "On ne peut à la fois être sincère et le paraître"; see also Sartre's attempt to turn sincerity into a form of bad faith, *Being and Nothingness* 2.2.105–112.
25. See Shapiro, *Shakespeare and the Jews* 129.

### Eighteen. False (Im)modesty

1. Chaucer, *Summoner's Tale*.
2. Many of the features of the style we associate with unbearable pomposity Aristotle admired as attributes of the magnanimous man: a contrived measured gait, deep voice, and slow speech; see *Ethics* 4.3.1125a13–15.
3. See Hillaire Belloc, *Complete Verse*: "The Garden Party..."
4. Sometimes, given the horrors of the subject matter, pomposity may work as a form of discretion and decorum, as when, say, a law professor must teach pornography regulation. See Coughlin, "Representing the Forbidden," for a witty tour de force on the fakeries, duplicity, and complicity of anti-pornography scholarship.
5. See Shklar's discussion of snobbery, *Ordinary Vices* 87–137, which is relevant to the point made here.
6. A small qualification. Some forms of self-mockery can be quiet, because they take place as gestures. One rolls one's eyes at oneself. But these gestures are still meant to amuse and get attention, not just to stage, but to upstage, for they are usually exaggerated and broadly comic.
7. The French has *sincérité*; the Penguin translator renders it as *candor*; the idea, as the context suggests, is probably halfway between; see also Eliot, *Adam Bede* ch. 12: "Candour was one of his favorite virtues; and how can a man's candour be seen in all its luster unless he has a few failings to talk of? But he had an agreeable confidence that his faults were all of a generous kind..."
8. *Middlemarch* ch. 17.
9. See Goffman, "Embarrassment," 108n6: "When an individual, receiving a compliment blushes from modesty, he may lose his reputation for poise but confirm a more important one, that of being modest."

### Nineteen. Caught in the Act

1. On states that are very difficult or impossible to will and can be achieved only as byproducts, see Elster, *Sour Grapes* 44–52, who discusses insomnia. *Sour Grapes* deals, from the perspective of rational choice, with more than a few of the themes of this book in a consistently penetrating manner.
2. Tricking yourself to sleep is a harder task than the frequent self-trickings that go on as part of the routine self-deceptions of wishful thinking. The desire to be attractive often leads us to think we are doing better in that department than we are without our having to do anything actually to make us better-looking; the desire to sleep makes us have to do things in preparation. We do not get to the state merely by wishing it.
3. There is no better literary treatment of feigning sleep than *Sir Gawain and the Green Knight* (vv. 1195–1197), where the seductress toys with Gawain's faking, making him feel totally embarrassed not only for how embarrassing the situation is but also for how transparent are his attempts to escape it by feigning sleep; see Miller, *Humiliation* 186. Faking sleep

is not an infrequent theme in literature as people employ the strategy to avoid sex, or to avoid letting late-arriving spouses see that their lateness was a ground for suspicion; see, for example, Wharton, *The Reef* ch. 8.

4. Failures of what Goffman calls audience segregation cause all kinds of embarrassment, blowings of cover, and so on. Ann Arbor is a fairly small town, and my students often see me out with my kids. It is very awkward, especially if they stumble upon me while I am screaming at one of them, or worse, while one of them is screaming at me. On audience segregation see Goffman, *Presentation of Self* 49.

5. There may be a kinder mechanism at work. Sometimes an able person, no fraud at all, gets a good idea that is triggered by the imbecilities of a dullard, and in turn the able person, generously and sincerely, attributes his own good idea to the dullard, because the dullard triggered it in him.

6. "Gascoigne's Woodmanship," vv. 97–100 (1573), in Gascoigne, I.348–352.

7. See generally Goffman, *Stigma*.

8. Miller, *The Anatomy of Disgust* ch. 9–10.

### Afterword

1. I have been taken to task on my reluctance or inability to write conclusions to my books; see Stark, "Courage."

2. Austin, *Sense and Sensibilia*, especially ch. 7, on dimension words and trouser words.

3. Austin, 64.

4. Moments of naturalness are available even to such a type, as they were to Dostoyevsky's Underground Man. Thus Underground Man, that most self-conscious and self-torturing of souls, can report that he made a gesture in "a surprisingly disengaged manner" though he immediately loses his naturalness by being so taken with his having actually succeeded in making an unstudied gesture II.3. He cannot help being surprised by his own naturally engaged manner, thereby managing ex post facto to turn his naturalness into a fake.

5. East–West is also one way of repeating, if not white–black, then white–dark.

# Works Cited

Acorn, Annalise. *Compulsory Compassion: Restorative Justice and the Commandment to Love.* Forthcoming.

Ainslie, George. *Breakdown of Will.* Cambridge: Cambridge University Press, 2001.

Alloy, Lauren B., and Lyn Y. Abramson. "Judgment of Contingency in Depressed and Nondepressed Students: Sadder but Wiser?" *Journal of Experimental Psychology* 108 (1979), 441–485.

Aquinas, St. Thomas. *Summa Theologiæ.* Blackfriars edition. New York: McGraw-Hill, 1964.

Aristotle. *The Ethics of Aristotle: The Nicomachean Ethics.* Translated by J. A. K. Thomson. Rev. ed. Harmondsworth: Penguin, 1976.

Aristotle. *Rhetoric.* Translated by W. Rhys Roberts. In *The Complete Works of Aristotle.* Edited by Jonathan Barnes. Princeton, N.J.: Princeton University Press, 1984. Vol. 2: 2152–2269.

Austen, Jane. *Emma.* 1816. Harmondsworth: Penguin, 1966.

Austen, Jane. *Mansfield Park.* 1814. Harmondsworth: Penguin, 1996.

Austen, Jane. *Sense and Sensibility.* 1811. Harmondsworth: Penguin, 1995.

Austin, J. L. "A Plea for Excuses." In *Philosophical Papers* 3rd ed. Edited by J. O. Urmson and G. J. Warnock. Oxford: Oxford University Press, 1979. 175–204.

Austin, J. L. "Pretending." In *Philosophical Papers* 3rd ed. 253–271.

Austin, J. L. *Sense and Sensibilia.* Oxford: Clarendon, 1962.

Batson, C. Daniel, et al. "Moral Hypocrisy: Appearing Moral to Oneself Without Being So." *Journal of Personality and Social Psychology* 77 (1999), 525–537.

de Beauvoir, Simone. *The Second Sex.* Translated by H. M. Parshley. 1949. New York: Vintage, 1989.

Bell, Rudolf M. *Holy Anorexia.* Chicago: University of Chicago Press, 1985.

Belloc, Hilaire. *Complete Verse.* London: Pimlico, 1991.

Bergson, Henri. *Laughter.* In Wylie Sypher, *Comedy.* Garden City, N.Y.: Doubleday, 1956. 59–190.

Bierce, Ambrose. *The Devil's Dictionary.* 1911. New York: Dover, 1993.

Bodian, Miriam. " 'Men of the Nation': The Shaping of Converso Identity in Early Modern Europe." *Past and Present* 143 (1994), 48–76.

Boehm, Christopher. *Blood Revenge: The Anthropology of Feuding in Montenegro*. Lawrence: University Press of Kansas, 1984.

Boswell, James. *Life of Johnson*. Edited by R. W. Chapman, revised by J. D. Fleeman. Oxford: Oxford University Press, 1970.

Bronte, Emily. *Wuthering Heights*. 1847. Oxford: Oxford University Press, 1998.

Burke, Edmund. *A Philosophical Enquiry into the Origin of our Ideas of the Sublime and Beautiful*. 1757. London: Routledge and Paul, 1958.

Campbell, J. K. *Honour, Family, and Patronage*. Oxford: Oxford University Press, 1964.

Chamfort, Sébastien. *Maximes and Anecdotes*. Monaco, 1944.

Chaucer, Geoffrey. *The Works of Geoffrey Chaucer*. 2nd ed. Edited by F. N. Robinson. Boston: Houghton Mifflin, 1957.

Chesterfield. *Lord Chesterfield: Letters*. Edited by David Roberts. Oxford: Oxford University Press, 1992.

Congreve, William. *The Way of the World*. 1700. Edited by Brian Gibbons. New York: Norton, 1994.

Coughlin, Anne. "Representing the Forbidden." *California Law Review* 90 (2002), 2143–2183.

Cuddihy, John Murray. *The Ordeal of Civility: Freud, Marx, Lévi Strauss, and the Jewish Struggle with Modernity*. New York: Basic Books, 1974.

Cunningham, Valentine. *In the Reading Gaol: Postmodernity, Texts, and History*. Oxford: Blackwells, 1994.

Darwin, Charles. *The Expression of the Emotions in Man and Animals*. 1872. Chicago: University of Chicago Press, 1965.

Davidson, Donald. "Deception and Division." In Elster, *The Multiple Self*. 1985. 79–92.

Davie, Donald. "Personification." *Essays in Criticism* 31 (1981), 91–104.

Dekkers, Midas. *The Way of All Flesh: The Romance of Ruins*. Translated by Sherry Marx-Macdonald. New York: Farrar, Straus and Giroux, 2000.

Dennett, Daniel C. *Consciousness Explained*. Boston: Little Brown, 1991.

Diderot, Denis. *The Paradox of the Actor*. In *Denis Diderot: Selected Writings on Art and Literature*. Translated by Geoffrey Bremner. Harmondsworth: Penguin, 1994; *Paradoxe sur le Comédien*. Edited by Ernest Dupuy. 1902. Rpt. Geneva: Slatkine, 1968.

Dostoyevsky, Fyodor. *The Double*. 1846. Translated by Jessie Coulson. Harmondsworth: Penguin, 1972. 125–287.

Dostoyevsky, Fyodor. *The Idiot*. 1869. Translated by David Magarshack. Harmondsworth: Penguin, 1955.

Dostoyevsky, Fyodor. *Notes from the Underground*. 1864. Translated by Jessie Coulson. Harmondsworth: Penguin, 1972. 13–123.

Duclos, Sandra E., James D. Laird, Eric Schneider, and Melissa Sexter. "Emotion-Specific Effects of Facial Expressions and Postures on Emotional Experience." *Journal of Personality and Social Psychology* 57 (1989), 100–108.

Ekman, Paul, and Dacher Keltner. "Universal Facial Expressions of Emotion: An Old Controversy and New Findings." In *Nonverbal Communication: Where Nature Meets Culture*. Edited by Ullica Christina Segerstrale. Hillsdale, N.J.: Lawrence Erlbaum, 1997. 27–46.

Ekman, Paul, Maureen O'Sullivan, and Mark G. Frank. "A Few Can Catch a Liar." *Psychological Science* 10 (1999), 263–266.

Elias, Norbert. *The History of Manners*. Translated by Edmund Jephcott, vol. 1 of *The Civilizing Process*. 1939. New York: Urizen, 1978.

Elias, Norbert. *Power and Civility*. Translated by Edmund Jephcott, vol. 2 of *The Civilizing Process*. 1939. New York: Pantheon, 1982.

Eliot, George. *Adam Bede*. 1859. Harmondsworth: Penguin, 1985.

Eliot, George. *Middlemarch*. 1872. Harmondsworth: Penguin, 1994.

Eliot, George. *Romola*. 1863. Oxford: Oxford University Press, 1994.

Eliot, T. S. *Complete Poems and Plays, 1909–1950*. New York: Harcourt, Brace, 1952.

Ellsworth, Phoebe C. "William James and Emotion: Is a Century of Fame Worth a Century of Misunderstanding?" *Psychological Review* 101 (1994), 222–229.

Elster, Jon. *Alchemies of the Mind: Rationality and the Emotions*. Cambridge: Cambridge University Press, 1999.

Elster, Jon, ed. *The Multiple Self*. Cambridge: Cambridge University Press, 1985.

Elster, Jon. *Sour Grapes: Studies in the Subversion of Rationality*. Cambridge: Cambridge University Press, 1983.

Emerson, Ralph Waldo. *Letters and Social Aims*: "The Comic" (1876). In *The Complete Works of Ralph Waldo Emerson*, 12 vols. Edited by Edward Waldo Emerson. Boston and New York: Houghton Mifflin and Company, 1903–1904. 8.155–174.

*Etz Hayim: Torah and Commentary*. Edited by David Lieber. New York: Jewish Publication Society, 2001.

Fingarette, Herbert. *Self-Deception*. Berkeley: University of California Press, 2000.

Flanagan, Owen. *Varieties of Moral Personality: Ethics and Psychological Realism*. Cambridge, Mass.: Harvard University Press, 1991.

Ford, Ford Madox. *Parade's End*. A tetralogy: *Some Do Not . . .* (1924); *No More Parades* (1925); *A Man Could Stand Up* (1926); and *The Last Post* (1928). Harmondsworth: Penguin, 1982.

Franklin, Benjamin. *The Autobiography*. New York: Library of America, 1990.

Freud, Sigmund. *Jokes and their Relation to the Unconscious*. 1905. In *The Standard Edition of the Complete Psychological Works of Sigmund Freud*, 24vols. Vol. 8. Edited by James Strachey. London: Hogarth Press, 1953–1974.

Freud, Sigmund. "The Uncanny." 1919. London: Hogarth Press, 1963. SE, 17.218–256.

Garber, Marjorie. "The Insincerity of Women." In *Desire in the Renaissance: Psychoanalysis and Literature*. Edited by Valeria Finucci and Regina Schwartz. Princeton, N.J.: Princeton University Press, 1994. 19–38.

Gascoigne, George. *The Complete Works of George Gascoigne*. Edited by John W. Cunliffe. 2 vols. Cambridge: Cambridge University Press, 1907–1910.

Geary, Patrick. "Humiliation of Saints." *Saints and Their Cults: Studies in Religious Sociology, Folklore and History*. Edited by Stephen Wilson. Cambridge: Cambridge University Press, 1983. 123–140.

Gerald of Wales (Geraldus Cambrensis). *Gemma Ecclesiastica*. Edited by J. S. Brewer. Opera 2. *Rerum Britannicarum Medii Aevi Scriptores* (Rolls Series), vol. 21. London, 1862. (Translation by John J. Hagen, *Gemma Ecclesiastica*. Davis Medieval Texts and Studies, vol. 2. Leiden: Brill, 1979).

Giddens, Anthony. "Erving Goffman as a Systematic Social Theorist." In Giddens, *Social Theory and Modern Sociology*. Stanford, Calif.: Stanford University Press, 1987. 109–139.

Gide, André. *L'immoraliste*. In *Romans, Recits et Soties*. Paris: Gaillimard, 1958. 365–472.

Gilman, Sander L. *Jewish Self-hatred: Anti-Semitism and the Hidden Language of the Jews*. Baltimore: Johns Hopkins University Press, 1986.

Gilman, Sander L. *Smart Jews: The Construction of the Image of Jewish Superior Intelligence*. Lincoln: University of Nebraska Press, 1996.

Goffman, Erving. "Embarrassment and Social Organization." In *Interaction Ritual: Essays in Face-to-face Behavior*. Chicago: Aldine, 1967. 97–112.

Goffman, Erving. *The Presentation of Self in Everyday Life*. New York: Anchor, 1959.

Goffman, Erving. *Relations in Public*. New York: Basic Books, 1971.

Goffman, Erving. *Stigma: Notes on the Management of Spoiled Identity*. New York: Simon and Schuster, 1963.

Goldberg, Myla. *Bee Season*. New York: Doubleday, 2000.

Gollaher, David. *Circumcision: A History of the World's Most Controversial Surgery*. New York: Basic Books, 2001.

*Grágás. Laws of Early Iceland: Grágás II. The Codex Regius of Grágás*. Translated and edited by Andrew Dennis, Peter Foote, and Richard Perkins. Winnipeg: University of Manitoba Press, 2000.

Greenblatt, Stephen. *Renaissance Self-Fashioning*. Chicago: University of Chicago Press, 1980.

*Grettir's saga*. Translated by Denton Fox and Hermann Pálsson. Toronto: University of Toronto Press, 1974.

Hale, Grace Elizabeth. *Making Whiteness: The Culture of Segregation in the South, 1890–1940*. New York: Pantheon, 1998.

Hampshire, Stuart. "Sincerity and Single-Mindedness." In *Freedom of Mind and other essays*. Princeton, N.J.: Princeton University Press, 1971. 232–256.

*Hávámal*. In *Edda: die Lieder des Codex Regius*. 3rd edition by Hans Kuhn. Heidelberg: Carl Winter, 1962. 17–44.

Hawthorne, Nathaniel. *The Blithedale Romance.* 1852. New York: Library of America, 1983. 629–848.

Hazlitt, William. "On Cant and Hypocrisy." Dec. 1828. In *Selected Essays.* Edited by Geoffrey Keynes. New York: Random House, 1930. 353–366.

Hebb, Donald O. "Emotion in Man and Animal: An Analysis of the Intuitive Processes of Recognition." *Psychological Review* 53 (1946), 88–106.

Hegel, G. W. F. *Hegel's Phenomenology of Spirit.* Translated by A. V. Miller. Oxford: Oxford University Press, 1977.

Herzfeld, Michael. *The Poetics of Manhood: Contest and Identity in a Cretan Mountain Village.* Princeton, N.J.: Princeton University Press, 1985.

Herzog, Don. *Poisoning the Minds of the Lower Orders.* Princeton, N.J.: Princeton University Press, 1998.

Herzog, Don. *Without Foundations: Justification in Political Theory.* Ithaca, N.Y.: Cornell University Press, 1985.

Hirschman, Albert O. *The Passions and the Interests: Political Arguments for Capitalism before its Triumph.* Princeton, N.J.: Princeton University Press, 1977.

Hirschman, Albert O. *The Rhetoric of Reaction: Perversity, Futility, Jeopardy.* Cambridge, Mass.: Harvard University Press, 1991.

Hogg, James. *Memoirs and Confessions of a Justified Sinner.* 1824. Edinburgh: Canongate, 1991.

Hughes, Diane Owen. "Sumptuary Law and Social Relations in Renaissance Italy." In *Disputes and Settlements: Law and Human Relations in the West.* Edited by John Bossy. Cambridge: Cambridge University Press, 1983. 69–99.

Hume, David. "On the Dignity and Meanness of Human Nature." In *Essays, Moral, Political, and Literary,* based on the 1777 edition. Edited by Eugene F. Miller. Indianapolis: Liberty Classics, 1987. 80–86.

Hume, David. *A Treatise of Human Nature.* 1739–1740. Edited by L. A. Selby-Bigge. 2nd ed. by P. H. Nidditch. Oxford: Clarendon, 1975.

Huysmans, J-K. *Against Nature.* Translated by Robert Baldick. Harmondsworth: Penguin, 1959.

Jacobson, Matthew Frye. *Whiteness of a Different Color: European Immigrants and the Alchemy of Race.* Cambridge, Mass.: Harvard University Press, 1998.

James, William. "What is an Emotion?" 1884. In *William James: Collected Essays and Reviews.* London: Longmans, 1920. 244–275.

Jocelin of Brakelond. *Chronicle of the Abbey of Bury St. Edmunds.* Translated by Diana Greenway and Jane Sayers. Oxford: Oxford University Press, 1989.

Johnson, Captain Charles. *A General History of the Robberies and Murders of the Most Notorious Pyrates and also Their Policies, Discipline, and Government.* London, 1724. Rpr. New York: Garland, 1972.

Juster, Susan. *Doomsayers: Anglo-American Prophecy in the Age of Revolution.* Philadelphia: University of Pennsylvania Press, 2003.

Kant, Immanuel. *The Critique of Judgement.* 1790. Oxford: Clarendon, 1952.

Keen, M. H. *The Laws of War in the Late Middle Ages*. London: Routledge and Kegan Paul, 1965.

Kenny, Anthony. *The Self*. Milwaukee, Wis.: Marquette University Press, 1988.

Kerrigan, John. *Revenge Tragedy: Aeschylus to Armageddon*. Oxford: Clarendon Press, 1996.

Klemperer, Victor. *I Will Bear Witness*. Translated by Martin Chalmers. 2 vols. New York: Random House, 1998–1999.

Komarovsky, Mirra. "Cultural Contradictions and Sex Roles." *American Journal of Sociology* 52 (1946), 184–189.

Konstan, David. *Friendship in the Classical World*. Cambridge: Cambridge University Press, 1997.

Konstan, David. *Pity Transformed*. London: Duckworth, 2001.

Kroeber, A. L. *The Nature of Culture*. Chicago: University of Chicago Press, 1952.

Kruger, Justin, and David Dunning. "Unskilled and Unaware of It: How Difficulties in Recognizing One's Own Incompetence Lead to Inflated Self-Assessments." *Journal of Personality and Social Psychology* 77 (1999), 1121–1134.

Lakoff, George, and Mark Johnson. *Metaphors We Live By*. Chicago: University of Chicago Press, 1980.

Langland, William. *The Vision of Piers Plowman*. Edited by A. V. C. Schmidt. New York: E. P. Dutton, 1978.

La Rochefoucauld, François, duc de. *Maxims*. 1665. Translated by Leonard Tancock. Harmondsworth: Penguin, 1959.

Larsen, Nella. *Passing*. 1929. Harmondsworth: Penguin, 1997.

*Laxdæla Saga*. Translated by Magnus Magnusson and Hermann Pálsson. Harmondsworth: Penguin, 1969.

Lazar, Ariela. "Deceiving Oneself or Self-Deceived? On the Formation of Beliefs 'Under the Influence.'" *Mind* 108 (1999), 265–290.

LeDoux, Joseph. *The Emotional Brain: The Mysterious Underpinnings of Emotional Life*. New York: Touchstone, 1996.

Levenson, Jon D. "The New Enemies of Circumcision." *Commentary* 109 (March 2000), 29–36.

Levenson, Robert W., Paul Ekman, and Wallace V. Friesen. "Voluntary Facial Action Generates Emotion-specific Autonomic Nervous System Activity." *Psychophysiology* 27 (1990), 363–384.

Lewis, Sinclair. *Babbitt*. 1922. New York: Library of America, 1992. 487–844.

Little, Graham. *Friendship, Being Ourselves with Others*. Melbourne: Melbourne Text Publishing, 1993.

Little, Lester K. *Benedictine Maledictions: Liturgical Cursing in Romanesque France*. Ithaca, N.Y.: Cornell University Press, 1993.

Locke, John. *The Reasonableness of Christianity*. 1695. Edited by George W. Ewing. Washington, D.C.: Regnery, 1997.

Lovejoy, Arthur O. *Reflections on Human Nature*. Baltimore: Johns Hopkins Press, 1961.

Maimonides, Moses. *Mishneh Torah: The Book of Knowledge*. Vol 1. Translated by Moses Hyamson. New York: Feldheim Publishers, 1981.

Maimonides, Moses. *Mishneh Torah: The Book of Adoration*. Vol. 2. Translated by Moses Hyamson. New York: Feldheim Publishers, 1981.

Maimonides, Moses. *Mishneh Torah. The Code of Maimonides: The Book of Torts*. Vol. 11. Translated by Hyman Klein. New Haven, Conn.: Yale University Press, 1954.

Maimonides, Moses. *Mishneh Torah. The Code of Maimonides: The Book of Acquisition*. Vol. 12. Translated by Isaac Klein. New Haven, Conn.: Yale University Press, 1951.

Mandeville, Bernard. *The Fable of the Bees or Private Vices, Publick Benefits*. 1732. 6th ed. Edited by F. B. Kaye. 2 vols. Oxford: Clarendon Press, 1924. Rpr. Indianapolis: Liberty Press, 1988.

Mead, George Herbert. *The Individual and the Social Self: Unpublished Work of George Herbert Mead*. Edited by David L. Miller. Chicago: University of Chicago Press, 1982.

Mead, George Herbert. *Mind, Self, and Society from the Standpoint of a Social Behaviorist*. Edited by Charles W. Norris. Chicago: University of Chicago Press, 1934.

Mele, Alfred R. *Self-Deception Unmasked*. Princeton, N.J.: Princeton University Press, 2001.

Melville, Herman. *The Confidence Man*. 1857. Harmondsworth: Penguin, 1991.

Milgram, Stanley. *Obedience to Authority*. New York: Harper and Row, 1974.

Miller, William Ian. *The Anatomy of Disgust*. Cambridge, Mass.: Harvard University Press, 1997.

Miller, William Ian. *Bloodtaking and Peacemaking: Feud, Law, and Society in Saga Iceland*. Chicago: University of Chicago Press, 1990.

Miller, William Ian. "Choosing the Avenger: Some Aspects of the Bloodfeud in Medieval Iceland and England." *Law and History Review* 1 (1983), 159–204.

Miller, William Ian. "Clint Eastwood and Equity: The Virtues of Revenge and the Shortcomings of Law in Popular Culture." In *Law in the Domains of Culture*. Edited by Austin Sarat and Thomas Kearns. Ann Arbor: University of Michigan Press, 1998. 161–202.

Miller, William Ian. "Deep Inner Lives, Individualism, and People of Honour." *History of Political Thought* 16 (1995), 190–207.

Miller, William Ian. *Humiliation: And Other Essays on Honor, Social Discomfort, and Violence*. Ithaca, N.Y.: Cornell University Press, 1993.

Miller, William Ian. *The Mystery of Courage*. Cambridge, Mass.: Harvard University Press, 2000.

Miller, William Ian. "Of Optimal Views and Other Anxieties of Attending to the Beautiful and Sublime." *Journal of Visual Culture* 1 (2002), 71–85.

Miller, William Ian. "Ordeal in Iceland." *Scandinavian Studies* 60 (1988), 189–218.

Miller, William Ian. "Sheep, Joking, Cloning and the Uncanny." In *Clones and Clones: Facts and Fantasies about Human Cloning*. Edited by Martha C. Nussbaum and Cass R. Sunstein. New York: W. W. Norton, 1998. 78–87.

Milton, John. *John Milton: Complete Poems and Major Prose*. Edited by Merritt Y. Hughes. New York: Odyssey Press, 1957.

Mischel, Walter. "Personality Dispositions Revisited and Revised." In *Handbook of Personality: Theory and Research*. Edited by Lawrence A. Pervin. New York: Guildford Press, 1990. 111–134.

Molière, Jean Baptiste Poquelin de. *Le Tartuffe*. 1669. Edited by Jean Serroy. Paris: Gallimard, 1997. English translation: Richard Wilbur. *Tartuffe*. New York: Harcourt, Brace, 1992.

Montaigne. *Michel de Montaigne: The Complete Essays*. Translated by M. A. Screech. Harmondsworth: Penguin, 1991.

Naipaul, V. S. *The Mimic Men*. 1967. New York: Vintage, 2001.

Nashe, Thomas. *Christs Teares over Jerusalem*. London: Printed by James Roberts, 1593.

Netanyahu, Benzion. *The Marranos of Spain: From the Late 14th to the Early 16th Century According to Contemporary Hebrew Sources*. 3rd ed. Ithaca, N.Y.: Cornell University Press, 1999.

Netanyahu, Benzion. *Toward the Inquisition: Essays on Jewish and Converso History in Late Medieval Spain*. Ithaca, N.Y.: Cornell University Press, 1997.

Nietzsche, Friedrich. *Beyond Good and Evil*. 1886. Translated by Walter Kaufmann. New York: Vintage, 1966.

Nietzsche, Friedrich. *Daybreak: Thoughts on the Prejudices of Morality*. 1881. Translated by R. J. Hollingdale. Cambridge: Cambridge University Press, 1982.

Nietzsche, Friedrich. *Human, All Too Human*. 1886. Translated by R. J. Hollingdale. Cambridge: Cambridge University Press, 1996.

Nietzsche, Friedrich. *On the Genealogy of Morals*. 1887. Translated by Walter Kaufmann and R. J. Hollingdale. New York: Vintage, 1967.

Nietzsche, Friedrich. "On Truth and Lie in an Extra-Moral Sense." 1873. Translated by Walter Kaufmann. In *The Portable Nietzsche*. New York: Viking, 1954. 42–47.

*Njáls saga*. Translated by Magnus Magnusson and Hermann Pálsson. Baltimore: Penguin Books, 1960.

Nozick, Robert. *Philosophical Explanations*. Cambridge, Mass.: Harvard University Press, 1981.

Nyberg, David. *The Varnished Truth: Truth Telling and Deceiving in Ordinary Life*. Chicago: University of Chicago Press, 1993.

Orwell, George. "Shooting an Elephant." In *The Collected Essays, Journalism and Letters of George Orwell*. Edited by Sonia Orwell and Ian Angus. Vol. 1. *An Age Like This: 1920–1940*. New York: Harcourt Brace, 1968. 235–242.

Ovid. *The Art of Love and Other Poems*. Translated by J. H. Mozley. Cambridge, Mass.: Harvard University Press, 1929.

Packer, Barbara L. *The Transcendentalists*. In *The Cambridge History of American Literature*, vol. 2, 1820–1865. Edited by Sacvan Bercovitch. Cambridge: Cambridge University Press, 1995. 329–604.

Parfit, Derek. *Reasons and Persons*. Oxford: Clarendon, 1984.

Pears, David. *Motivated Irrationality*. Oxford: Oxford University Press, 1984.

Pinch, Adela. *Strange Fits of Passion: Epistemologies of Emotion, Hume to Austen*. Stanford, Calif.: Stanford University Press, 1996.

Pinker, Steven. *How the Mind Works*. New York: W. W. Norton, 1997.

Plato. *Laches*. Translated by Benjamin Jowett. In the *Collected Dialogues of Plato*. Edited by Edith Hamilton and Huntington Cairns. Bollingen Series LXXI. New York: Pantheon, 1961. 123–144.

Pound, Ezra. *ABC of Reading*. 1934. New York: New Directions, 1960.

Raverat, Gwen. *Period Piece*. 1953. Ann Arbor: University of Michigan Press, 1991.

Rawson, Claude Julien. *God, Gulliver, and Genocide: Barbarism and the European Imagination, 1492–1945*. New York: Oxford University Press, 2001.

*Reykdœla saga*. In *The Complete Sagas of the Icelanders*. Edited by Viðar Hreinsson. Reykjavík: Leifur Eiríksson, 1997. 4.257–302.

Rezzori, Gregor von. *Memoirs of an Anti-Semite*. Translated in part by the author and in part by Joachim Neugroschel. New York: Vintage, 1991.

Ricks, Christopher. *Keats and Embarrassment*. Oxford: Clarendon, 1974.

Roach, Joseph R. *The Player's Passion: Studies in the Science of Acting*. Newark: University of Delaware Press, 1985.

Roth, Philip. *The Human Stain*. New York: Vintage, 2000.

Rozin, Paul, and April E. Fallon. "A Perspective on Disgust." *Psychological Review* 94 (1987), 23–41.

Santayana, George. *Soliloquies in England and Later Soliloquies*. New York: Scribner's, 1922.

Sartre, Jean-Paul. *Being and Nothingness*. Translated by Hazel E. Barnes. New York: Washington Square Press, 1992.

Scheler, Max. *Ressentiment*. Translated by Lewis B. Coser and William W. Holdheim. Milwaukee, Wis.: Marquette University Press, 1994.

Schelling, Thomas C. *The Strategy of Conflict*. Cambridge, Mass.: Harvard University Press, 1960.

Sebald, W. G. *Vertigo*. Translated by Michael Hulse. New York: New Directions, 1999.

Shakespeare. *The Complete Works*. Edited by Alfred Harbage et al. Baltimore: Penguin, 1969.

Shapiro, James S. *Shakespeare and the Jews*. New York: Columbia University Press, 1996.

Sharfstein, Daniel J. "The Secret History of Race in the United States." *Yale Law Journal*. In press.

Shklar, Judith. *Ordinary Vices*. Cambridge, Mass.: Harvard University Press, 1984.

Silbermann, Alphons. *Grovelling and Other Vices: The Sociology of Sycophancy*. Translated by Ladislaus Löb. London: Athlone Press, 2000.

Silverman, Morris, ed. *High Holiday Prayer Book*. New York: Prayer Book Press, 1951.

Singer, I. J. *The Brothers Ashkenazi*. 1937. Translated by Joseph Singer. Harmondsworth: Penguin, 1993.

Singer, I. J. *The Family Carnovsky*. 1943. Translated by Joseph Singer. New York: Vanguard, 1969.

*Sir Gawain and the Green Knight*. Edited by J. R. R. Tolkien and E. V. Gordon. 2nd edition edited by Norman Davis. Oxford: Clarendon Press, 1967.

Small, Abner. *The Road to Richmond*. Edited by Harold Adams Small. Berkeley: University of California Press, 1939.

Smith, Adam. "Letter from Adam Smith, L.L.D. to William Strahan, Esq. Nov. 9. 1776." Reproduced in Hume, *Essays, Moral, Political and Literary* xliii–xlix.

Smith, Adam. *The Theory of Moral Sentiments*. Edited by D. D. Raphael and A. L. Macfie. 1st ed. 1759. Oxford: Clarendon Press, 1976.

Stark, Andrew. "Courage: A Mystery or Not?" *The Antioch Review* 60 (2002), 244–249.

Steinsaltz, Adin. *The Essential Talmud*. Translated by Chaya Galai. New York: Basic Books, 1976.

Steinsaltz, Adin. *The Talmud: The Steinsaltz Edition*. Vol. 14. Translated by Israel V. Berman. New York, Random House, 1995.

Sterne, Laurence. *Tristram Shandy*. 1759–1767. Edited by James A. Work. Indianapolis: Odyssey Press, 1940.

Stevenson, Robert Louis. *The Strange Case of Dr. Jekyll and Mr. Hyde*. 1886. Harmondsworth: Penguin, 2002.

Stoppard, Tom. *Rosencrantz and Guildenstern Are Dead*. London: Faber and Faber, 1967.

Strack, Fritz, Leonard L. Martin, and Sabine Stepper. "Inhibiting and Facilitating Conditions of the Human Smile: A Non Obtrusive Test of the Facial Feedback Hypothesis." *Journal of Personality and Social Psychology* 54 (1988), 768–777.

Strawson, Galen. "The Self." *Journal of Consciousness Studies* 4 (1997), 405–428.

Sun Tzu. *The Art of War*. Translated by Samuel B. Griffith. Oxford: Oxford University Press, 1963.

Swift, Jonathan. *Poetical Works*. Edited by Herbert Davis. London: Oxford University Press, 1967.

Swift, Jonathan. *A Tale of a Tub*. 1704. Edited by Angus Ross and David Woolley. Oxford: Oxford University Press, 1986.

Tavuchis, Nicholas. *Mea Culpa: A Sociology of Apology and Reconciliation*. Stanford, Calif.: Stanford University Press, 1991.

Taylor, Charles. *The Ethics of Authenticity.* Cambridge, Mass.: Harvard University Press, 1991.

Taylor, Charles. *Sources of the Self: The Making of the Modern Identity.* Cambridge, Mass.: Harvard University Press, 1989.

Taylor, Shelley E., and Jonathan Brown. "Illusion and Well-Being: A Social Psychological Perspective on Mental Health." *Psychological Bulletin* 103 (1988), 193–210.

Thucydides. *History of the Peloponnesian War.* Translated by Rex Warner. Rev. ed. Harmondsworth: Penguin, 1972.

Tocqueville, Alexis de. *Democracy in America.* Translated by George Lawrence; edited by J. P. Mayer. Garden City, N.Y.: Anchor, 1969.

Trilling, Lionel. *Sincerity and Authenticity.* Cambridge, Mass.: Harvard University Press, 1971.

Trivers, Robert. *Social Evolution.* Menlo Park, Calif.: Benjamin/Cummings, 1985.

Trollope, Anthony. *Barchester Towers.* 1857. Harmondsworth: Penguin, 1983.

Trollope, Anthony. *Can You Forgive Her?* 1865. Harmondsworth: Penguin, 1972.

Trollope, Anthony. *The Claverings.* 1867. Oxford: Oxford University Press, 1986.

Trollope, Anthony. *The Duke's Children.* 1880. Harmondsworth: Penguin, 1995.

Trollope, Anthony. *Framley Parsonage.* 1861. Harmondsworth: Penguin, 1984.

Trollope, Anthony. *Last Chronicle of Barset.* 1867. Harmondsworth: Penguin, 1986.

Trollope, Anthony. *Rachel Ray.* 1863. Oxford: Oxford University Press, 1998.

Trollope, Anthony. *The Way We Live Now.* 1875. Harmondsworth: Penguin, 1994.

Twain, Mark. "Extract from Captain Stormfield's Visit to Heaven." 1907. In *Collected Tales, Sketches, Speeches, and Essays, 1891–1910.* New York: Library of America, 1992. 826–863.

Vonnegut, Kurt. *Mother Night.* 1961. New York: Delta, 1999.

Walzer, Michael. "Can There Be a Decent Left?" *Dissent* (Spring 2002), 19–23.

Webster, John. "The Duchess of Malfi." In *John Webster and Cyril Tourneur.* New York: Hill and Wang, 1956.

Wenzel, Siegfried. *The Sin of Sloth: Acedia in Medieval Thought and Literature.* Chapel Hill: University of North Carolina Press, 1967.

Wharton, Edith. *The Custom of the Country.* 1913. New York: Library of America, 1985. 621–1014.

Wharton, Edith. *The Reef.* 1912. New York: Library of America, 1985. 349–620.

Wiederman, Michael W. "Pretending Orgasm during Sexual Intercourse: Correlates in a Sample of Young Adult Women." *Journal of Sex & Marital Therapy* 23 (1997), 131–139.

Wilde, Oscar. *The Critic as Artist.* 1891. In *Complete Works of Oscar Wilde.*
London: Collins, 1948. 1009–1059.

Yoshino, Kenji. "Covering." *Yale Law Journal* 111 (2002), 769–939.

Zimbardo, Philip G. "The Pathology of Imprisonment." In *Down to Earth
Sociology: Introductory Readings.* 11th ed. Edited by James M. Henslin.
New York: Free Press, 2002. 272–277.

# Index

abnegation, 65–66. *See also* prayer

absolution. *See* penance

accents, 203; academic, 145; American vs. English, 144–145; Katherine Hepburn's, 145; lapsing into a southern, 39; self-consciousness about, 39–40

accidents, 249. *See also* apologies; remorse

*acedia*, sloth, 62

acting: Diderot's theory of, 195–196; *Mansfield Park* and, 199; teaching children emotion display and, 196–197; Walter Shandy's theory of, 195, 196

actors: characterlessness of, 198–200; as doer and as fake doer, 7; making up, 202; vs. thin-lipped moralists, 199–200; waitresses as, 200

addiction: alchemist's theory of, 173–177; gambling and, 174; hope and, 174–177

aesthetics: vs. moral, 208–209, 210; posing and, 154; religious conversion and, 68. *See also* anxiety; art; sublime

affectations: of hipness, 49; of prissiness, 48

airs: giving none, 215; putting on, 43

alchemy: deception and self-deception and, 170–176; as metaphor for mechanisms of transmuting motives, 167–168;

pride and avarice as vices of, 169. *See also* Chaucer; Elster; Nashe; transmutation

alchemists: curiosity of, 171; reputation of, 170

alcohol, 48; as bootstrapping aid, 34

allegory, 123

almsgiving, hypocrisy and, 11–12, 28

Americans: craven self-hatred of, 144; modest self-hatred of, 143–144, 147–148; patriotic pride of, 146–147, 148. *See also* English; self-hatred

Amidah, 68–72; on Rosh Hashanah, 69

anger: fake, 262; self-command and, 44

anti-depressants, 205–206; compared to yoga, 205

anti-essentialism. *See* relativism

antihypocrisy: looking bad in order to be good, 20–23. *See also* Becket; hypocrisy; More; Twain

anti-Semite, -ism, 134, 139, 232; fears of pollution of, 136; *limpieza de sangre* and, 136; misogyny and, 138; *1912 Catholic Encyclopedia* and, 256; uncanny lunacy of, 150; visions of Shylock and, 137

anxiety, 4–7; passim; appreciating art and beauty and, 155–156, 158–161; doubling and, 126; experts failing and, 158–160